D1430936

WHITE INNOCENCE

Colfax Public Library
613 Main St. P.O. Box 525
Colfax, WI 54730
715-962-4334

WHITE INNOCENCE

Paradoxes of Colonialism and Race

Gloria Wekker

Duke University Press
Durham and London
2016

© 2016 Duke University Press
All rights reserved
Printed in the United States of America
on acid-free paper ∞
Designed by Amy Ruth Buchanan
Typeset in Quadraat by Copperline

Library of Congress Cataloging-in-Publication Data
Names: Wekker, Gloria, author.
Title: White innocence : paradoxes of colonialism
and race / Gloria Wekker.
Description: Durham : Duke University Press, 2016. |
Includes bibliographical references and index.
Identifiers: LCCN 2015042542 |
ISBN 9780822360599 (hardcover : alk. paper) |
ISBN 9780822360759 (pbk. : alk. paper) |
ISBN 9780822374565 (e-book) |
Subjects: LCSH: Racism—Netherlands. |
Netherlands—Race relations. | Sexual
minorities—Netherlands.
Classification: LCC DJ92.B53 W455 2016 |
DDC 305.8009492—dc23
LC record available at http://lccn.loc.gov/2015042542

Cover art: Hand-painted Delft blue plate,
Holland (details). © Christine Osborne
Pictures / Alamy Stock Photo.

To future generations of antiracist activists
To Robin, Rosa, Minne, Finn, Milan, Ceriel, Ravi, Josephine, and Lucy
To my brother Paul (1959–2011)

CONTENTS

ACKNOWLEDGMENTS

. . . and on the other side, the bright
look of innocence, the white dove
of peace, magical heavenly light

Frantz Fanon, *Black Skin, White Masks*

□————————————————□

This book has been a long time in the making and thinking through. In the course of the past two decades, after coming back to the Netherlands from Los Angeles in 1992, where I had done my PhD, looking at the Netherlands with fresh eyes regularly sent frissons of discomfort and alienation up my spine. My anthropological eyes, making the familiar world strange, received strong, new impulses to make sense of the Netherlands, where I had grown up after I was one year old. After my return, I often had the feeling that I was involuntarily seeing the emperor, the Netherlands, without his clothes on, in his most detestable nakedness. It now often struck me that interracial situations, conversations, and phenomena that would be totally unacceptable in a U.S. context would pass without any frowns or critical comments in the Netherlands. Starting from the 1990s and into the first decade of the twentieth century, this process was intensified by an unprecedented turn toward a neorealist discourse (Prins 2002), when the murders of populist politician Pim Fortuyn in 2002 and filmmaker Theo van Gogh in 2004 gave rise to an exceptional bluntness in the interracial domain. The evasive attitude around race that had been customary in civilized circles—somewhat like our impulse, as Toni Morrison (1992a) remarked about the United States, "not to talk with the hunchback about his hump"—virtually disappeared. Many Dutch people, never shy in voicing their opinions, now felt justified in uttering statements, especially toward Muslims, one more offensive and willfully humiliating than another. It is worth recollecting that in the 1970s and 1980s, it was Moluccan and Afro-Surinamese Dutch people who were thought to be the unassimilable Other. Meanwhile, what remained the same was that in the avalanche of publications attempting to understand society and the resentment afflicting the white Dutch population, there was an avoidance of race as a fundamental social and symbolic grammar orchestrating affect and understandings, a glaring omission that induced me to write this book. It is also one of the ways in which I am realizing the program I had in mind when I formally accepted the chair in gender and ethnicity, Faculty of the Humanities, at Utrecht University in 2002, to study whiteness (Wekker 2002a).

We are living in hopeful times: a second wave of antiracist activism is taking off. It is very heartening to see that a new generation of brave antiracist activists has stood up in the past years both outside and inside the academy. I dedicate this book to them, and to a generation after them, my grandnieces and grandnephews: Rosa, Robin, Minne, Finn, Milan, Ceriel, Ravi, Josephine, and Lucy, a rainbow-colored tribe. May they all live in a world that recognizes them for who they are and that will let them live in active solidarity or without having to carry the burden of their skin color, thus without "white innocence."

I want to thank my colleagues at the Department of Women's Studies, at Utrecht University, with whom I worked so hard for so many years: Rosemarie Buikema, Rosi Braidotti, Berteke Waaldijk, Sandra Ponzanesi, Iris van der Tuin, Marta Zarzycka, Babs Boter, Eva Midden, and Kathrin Thiele. We would not have gotten anywhere without the steady support of Trude Oorschot. I think with fondness of the many talented students in the one-year master of arts program, of which I was the coordinator until 2012, and whom I have had the pleasure to teach and see grow. I am always amazed to get news from them and find out where they have wound up and what each of them is doing to make a difference in the world. Especially dear to me are the students I have supervised through their PhDs, Cassandra Ellerbe-Dueck, Sabrina Marchetti, Lena Eckert, and Shu-yi Huang; and the students that I am still supervising, Heather Hermant, Phoebe Kisubi Mbasalaki, and Yvette Kopijn, from whom I learn so much and who keep me on my toes. I also thank Shu-yi and Heather for inviting me to their home universities, Shin Hsin University in Taipei, Taiwan, and York University in Toronto, Canada, where a tribute to Audre Lorde, "The Contemporary Urgencies of Audre Lorde's Legacy," jointly organized with the University of Toronto, took place in March 2013. I received much-welcomed responses from Jin Hariwatorn, Enakshi Dua, Anna Aganthangelou, and Honor Ford Smith on an early version of chapter 4. I thank Maayke Botman for the many conversations about the way that race works in the Netherlands that we have had in the course of the years. My student assistants have been very helpful. I especially want to thank Erin van de Weijer, who helped me out on numerous occasions with making PowerPoint presentations, and most recently I have depended on Mirna Sodre de Oliveira. Mark Hazeleger has been indispensable to solve my "computer blues" at a moment's notice, and I thank Gon Buurman for her fine photography.

I want to acknowledge my colleague Philomena Essed for her courage in putting "everyday racism" on the agenda in the Netherlands at an early stage. I also thank her and Isabel Hoving for their initiative to bring out the edited volume Dutch Racism in 2014, after three decades of silence on racism. I also wish to thank professors Nina Lykke, Cecilia Åsberg, Berit Starkman, and my fellow scholars at GEXcel International Collegium for Advanced Transdisciplinary Gender Studies at Linköping University, Sweden, where I spent a two-month sabbatical in November and December 2009. In addition, this book was also made possible by a year's sabbatical at NIAS, the Netherlands Institute for Advanced Studies, in Wassenaar, in 2011–2012. I have given many talks in the Netherlands and abroad in the past years, too many to mention here, but I would like to collectively thank the people who invited me and my audiences for their feedback and allowing me to put my ear to the ground in so many different places, from Paramaribo to Tallinn to Cape Town.

Thanks to historians Rosemarijn Hoefte and Alex van Stipriaan for commenting on the introduction. An earlier version of chapter 1 appeared as "Diving into the Wreck: Exploring Intersections of Sexuality, Race, Gender, and Class in the Dutch Cultural Archive," in P. Essed and I. Hoving, eds., Dutch Racism (2014) and is reprinted here with permission of Editions Rodopi, b.v. A special thank you goes to Frances Gouda and to the excellent editing work done by Isabel Hoving. I want to thank the organizers of the George Mosse lecture series at the University of Amsterdam, especially Gert Hekma, where I presented a very first version of chapter 4 in September

2009. Furthermore, I thank Mari Hermans for our productive collaboration in writing the chapter "Aisha Is Cool" in *Lesbo-Encyclopedie* (Hermans and Wekker 2009), Juul van Hoof and Hanneke Felten of Movisie in Utrecht, Glenn Helberg of OCAN, and Stefan Dudink for his insightful comments. A very early version of chapter 5 was delivered as a presentation at Feministisch Verzet (Feminist resistance) in Utrecht, on November 15, 2013. Thanks to research MA students at the time, Annette Krauss, Gianmaria Colpani, and Katrien Smiet for inviting me. Thanks to Dineke Stam for her comments on the coda.

I also want to thank the Amsterdam branch of SIT, the School for International Training, under the directorship of Yvette Kopijn and her team, including Nancy Jouwe, who gave me the opportunity to present work in progress on chapter 3 to the students. I want to thank my (imagined) community of black American, British, German, Swedish, and Caribbean feminists (f/m) with whom I stand shoulder to shoulder, among whom I want to mention some by name: Audre Lorde and Claudia Mitchell-Kernan, the chair of my dissertation committee at UCLA and first black female teacher. I want to thank my friends and colleagues M. Jacqui Alexander, Gail Lewis, and Ann Phoenix, who although they are objectively farther and far away, never feel that way. I feel fortunate in knowing all three of you, by the sustenance of your work and for making me feel less lonely during the process of writing. Phone and Skype conversations with Jacqui, often past my midnight, always bring up new angles and insights. I am happy to be a small part of the launching of the Tobago Center for the Study and Practice of Indigenous Spirituality. May Yemanyá and Oshun continue to bless us.

Several people have discussed chapters or ideas in the book with me and I want to thank Saskia Wieringa, Halleh Ghorashi, Nancy Jouwe, Fenneke Wekker, Rosemarijn Hoefte, Alex van Stipriaan, Christien Brinkgreve, Dineke Stam, Toke Hoppenbrouwers, Alexandra Miller, Patricia Schor, Geertje Mak, Annette Krauss, Mikki Stelder, Polly Wagenaar, Ama Koranteng-Kumi, Stefan Dudink, Michael Haman, Rodney Wekker, and Lindsey Louis. A special thank you to Alex Miller for editing a chapter. Of course, I remain responsible for any judgments in error, despite their incisive comments. Furthermore, there are people who would never let me forget the book and urged me to finish it: Jennifer Tosch, Dienke Hondius, Guno Jones, and Nancy Jouwe. Fellow members of the Scientific Council of NiNsee—the National Institute for the Study of Dutch Slavery and Its Legacy—Alex van Stipriaan, Guno Jones,

Dienke Hondius, Kwame Nimako, and Francio Guadeloupe have jointly created an atmosphere in which the urgency of this study always remained crystal-clear. A special mention is due to the Collective of Transcultural Therapists in Amsterdam, Anna de Voogt, Glenn Helberg, Urmy MacNack, Kitlyn Tjin-a-Djie, Hermine Klok, Dirck van Bekkum, Fariba Rhmaty, and Pui Fan Yip, thanking them for the important work that they do and for collectively brainstorming with me over chapter 3.

I want to thank my family and my in-laws in the Netherlands, Suriname, and the Dominican Republic for their support and their warmth. Last but not least, my friends Diny Zanders, Twie Tjoa, Claudette van Trikt, Andrée Douglas, Thea Doelwijt, Marijke van Geest, Rachelle Tjin-a-Djie, Anita van den Berg, Sheila Arthur, Tieneke Sumter, and Marjan Sax, whom I saw less often than I wanted to, for their insights and patience.

Finally, I want to thank my loves Maggy Carrot and Altagracia Ramirez Felíz, who light up my life with laughter, lightness, and adventure and who help me to realize the best and most generous self that I can be, in this unorthodox but exciting life that we have chosen, in which the personal cannot help but be political.

All the energies poured into critical theory, into novel
and demystifying theoretical praxes—have avoided the
major, I would say the determining political horizon
of modern Western culture, namely imperialism.

Edward Said, "Secular Interpretation"

"A Particular Knowledge . . . "

This book is dedicated to an exploration of a strong paradox that is operative in the Netherlands and that, as I argue, is at the heart of the nation: the
passion, forcefulness, and even aggression that race, in its intersections
with gender, sexuality, and class, elicits among the white population, while
at the same time the reactions of denial, disavowal, and elusiveness reign
supreme. I am intrigued by the way that race pops up in unexpected places
and moments, literally as the return of the repressed, while a dominant
discourse stubbornly maintains that the Netherlands is and always has
been color-blind and antiracist, a place of extraordinary hospitality and
tolerance toward the racialized/ethnicized other, whether this quintessen-
tial other is perceived as black in some eras or as Muslim in others. One of
the key sites where this paradox is operative, I submit, is the white Dutch
sense of self, which takes center stage in this book. I strongly suspect that
with national variations, a similar configuration is operative in other international settings that have an imperial history. It is my—admittedly ambitious and iconoclastic—aim to write an ethnography of dominant white

presentation. In a Dutch context this is iconoclastic because
ıot acknowledged as a racialized/ethnicized positioning at all.
generally seen as so ordinary, so lacking in characteristics,
ɔ devoid of meaning, that a project like this runs a real risk
sidered emptiness incarnate. My main thesis is that an un-
:d reservoir of knowledge and affects based on four hundred
:h imperial rule plays a vital but unacknowledged part in dom-
ıg-making processes, including the making of the self, taking
:h society.

ploration, I am guided by the concept of the cultural archive
which foregrounds the centrality of imperialism to Western
: cultural archive has influenced historical cultural configura-
ırrent dominant and cherished self-representations and cul-
ıneral nineteenth-century European framework, Edward Said
ıe cultural archive as a storehouse of "a particular knowledge
res of attitude and reference . . . [and,] in Raymond Williams'
rase, 'structures of feeling.' . . . There was virtual unanimity
: races should be ruled, that there *are* subject races, that one race
ıd has consistently earned the right to be considered the race
ı mission is to expand beyond its own domain" (1993, 52, 53).
ıntly, what Said is referring to here is that a racial grammar, a
ture of inequality in thought and affect based on race, was in-
ıineteenth-century European imperial populations and that it is
leep reservoir, the cultural archive, that, among other things, a
:lf has been formed and fabricated. With the title White Innocence,
:ing an important and apparently satisfying way of being in the
ıncapsulates a dominant way in which the Dutch think of them-
being a small, but just, ethical nation; color-blind, thus free of
; being inherently on the moral and ethical high ground, thus a
ght to other folks and nations. During the colonial era, the match
:herlands with the Dutch East Indies, its jewel in the crown, was
ıngratulatory fashion thought of like a match made in heaven:
:test people of Europe brought together with the quietest people
Meijer Raneft, cited in Breman 1993). I attempt a postcolonial, or
lecolonial,[1] intersectional reading of the Dutch cultural archive,
:ial attention for the ways in which an imperial racial economy,
gendered, sexualized, and classed intersections, continues to

ıction

underwrite dominant ways of knowing, interpreting, and feeling. I argue that in an "ethnography of dominant white Dutch self-representation" (cf. Doane 1991), sexual racism turns out to play a prominent role. I offer an exploration of the ways in which race, which by dominant consensus has been declared missing in action in the Netherlands, became cemented and sedimented in the Dutch cultural archive, and how race acquired gendered, sexualized, and classed meanings during more than four hundred years of "colonialism of the exterior" (Brah 1996).

In a U.S. context, where decidedly more work has been done on the cultural archive than in Europe, Toni Morrison has insightfully addressed what slavery did to the white psyche.[2] In an interview with Paul Gilroy, Morrison states, "Slavery broke the world in half, it broke it in every way. It broke Europe. It made them into something else, it made them slave masters, it made them crazy. You can't do that for hundreds of years and it not take a toll. They had to dehumanize, not just the slaves but themselves. They have had to reconstruct everything in order to make that system appear true" (Gilroy 1993, 178).

I, too, am interested in "the dreamer of the dream" (Morrison 1992a, 17), what the system of oppression did to the subject of the racialized discourses constructing blacks as inferior, intellectually backward, lazy, sexually insatiable, and always available; that is, I am oriented toward the construction of the white self as superior and full of entitlement. I offer my reading of the consequences of slavery in the western part of the empire, Suriname and the Antilles, on white Dutch self-representation. The bulk of the book is dedicated to an investigation of how these complex configurations have become intertwined with current dominant regimes of truth, with an emphasis on cultural productions in the past two decades.

The book's main thesis is thus that an unacknowledged reservoir of knowledge and feelings based on four hundred years of imperial rule have played a vital but unacknowledged part in the dominant meaning-making processes taking place in Dutch society, until now. This insight has already been ominously and forcefully formulated by one of the forefathers of postcolonial studies, Martiniquan Aimé Césaire (1972) in his much-overlooked *Discourse on Colonialism*. Césaire, writing immediately after World War II, courageously chastised Europe: "What am I driving at? At this idea: that no one colonizes innocently, that no one colonizes with impunity either; that a nation which colonizes, that a civilization which justifies colonization—

and therefore force—is already a sick civilization, a civilization that is morally diseased, that irresistibly, progressing from one consequence to another, one repudiation to another, calls for its Hitler, I mean its punishment" (1972, 39).

Césaire drew intimate connections between the racist methods used in the colonies to discipline the "natives"—the Arabs in Algeria, the coolies of India, and the blacks of Africa—and the Nazi methods later used and perfected against the Jews and other others in Europe. The memory of the Holocaust as the epitome and model of racist transgression in Europe erases the crimes that were perpetrated against the colonized for four centuries. This excision coincides with the representation that the history and reality of Europe are located on the continent and that what happened in the colonies is no constitutive part of it. This frame of mind—splitting, displacement, in psychoanalytical terms—is still operative to this day, for instance, in the way that the memory of World War II is conceptualized. It is the memory of what happened in the metropole and of the many Jews who were abducted and killed, not about what happened in the colonies at the time (Van der Horst 2004). Trying to insert those memories into the general memory often meets with hostility and rejection.[3]

At the same time, this regime of truth has enabled Europe to indulge in the myth of racial purity, as homogeneously white. The statement "no one colonizes innocently; no one colonizes with impunity either" points to the deeply layered and stacked consequences colonization has had for the European metropoles and their sense of self, which also forms my point of departure. It is noteworthy that while the concept of race finds its origin in Europe and has been one of its main export products, still it is generally the case that race is declared an alien body of thought to Europe, coming to this continent from the United States or elsewhere. In *European Others*, Fatima El-Tayeb powerfully states, "To reference race as native to contemporary European thought, however, violates the powerful narrative of Europe as a colorblind continent, largely untouched by the devastating ideology it exported all over the world. This narrative, framing the continent as a space free of 'race' (and, by implication, racism), is not only central to the way Europeans perceive themselves, but also has gained near-global acceptance" (2011, xv).

Discussions in different disciplinary areas, including gender studies, about the appropriateness of race as an analytic in Europe often reach untenable conclusions that other categories like class are more pertinent to the European reality or that the supposed black-white binary of U.S. race relations makes it unfit as a model for studying European societies (Bourdieu and Wacquant 1999; Griffin with Braidotti 2002; Lutz, Vivar, and Supik 2011). In this introductory chapter, I first sketch three long-standing paradoxical features in dominant Dutch self-representation, which collectively point to white innocence (Wekker 2001). Next, I outline the three central concepts I use in this study—innocence, the cultural archive, and dominant white Dutch self-representation—and subsequently I lay out the theoretical and methodological stakes of the project; finally, I map the chapters.

Paradoxes in White Dutch Self-Representation

In trying to capture some significant features of white Dutch self-representation, a good place to start is three paradoxes that immediately present themselves to the eye of the outsider (within).[4] The dominant and cherished Dutch self-image is characterized by a series of paradoxes that can be summed up by a general sense of being a small but ethically just nation that has something special to offer to the world. Current exceptionalism finds expression in aspirations to global worth, which are realized in The Hague being the seat of several international courts of justice, such as the Rwanda and Srebrenica tribunals. Just as during the imperial era, Our Indies, that vast archipelago of Indonesian islands known as "the emerald belt," were what set the small kingdom of the Netherlands apart and made it a world player, now the Netherlands prides itself on its role as an adjudicator of international conflicts. Thus, the mid-twentieth-century trauma of losing Our Indies,[5] which fought for their independence from the Netherlands during two wars, finds a late twentieth-century parallel in the fall of Srebrenica (1995), in former Yugoslavia, when at least six thousand Muslim men and boys under the protection of a Dutch UN battalion were killed by Serbians under the command of General Ratko Mladić. Together with his superior, Radovan Karadzic, a Bosnian-Serbian leader, Mladić has been on trial in The Hague since 2012, with various postponements and reopenings of the tribunal. The two events, thoroughly different as they are, have significantly shaken the cherished Dutch self-representation.

A first paradox is that the majority of the Dutch do not want to be identified with migrants, although at least one in every six Dutch people has migrant ancestry. Whether it is Spanish and Portuguese Jews, Huguenots, Belgians, Hungarians, people from Indonesia, Suriname, Antilleans, or Turks and Moroccans, the Netherlands is a nation of (descendants of) migrants. Of course there are different ways to identify for elite migrants—Huguenots, Sephardic Jews (among others, Spinoza), Flemings, English, and Scottish—who came with capital and know-how and who helped launch Dutch prosperity, and for other, lumpen migrants, especially Germans and Scandinavians. But my point is exactly that the class positionings of one's migrant ancestors are less significant than their places of origin, specifically whether their heritage in terms of visible difference in skin color could be shed as fast as possible. While several migratory movements, mainly from surrounding or nearby countries, such as Germany, France, Portugal, Spain, and Italy, occurred from the sixteenth century on, the country remained overwhelmingly white until the middle of the twentieth century. Postwar migration to the Netherlands consisted of three major groups: postcolonial migrants from the (former) empire,[6] labor migrants from the circum-Mediterranean area and recently from Eastern Europe,[7] and refugees from a variety of countries in Africa, Asia, Latin America, and the Middle East. All in all, of a total population of 16.8 million people, 3.6 million (21.4 percent) are allochthonous (i.e., coming from elsewhere), 2 million of which are "non-Western" (12 percent) and 1.6 million (9.4 percent) Western (CBS 2014, 26). If one goes back further in history than three generations, probably the percentage of migrants would be even higher. The specific use of the term "migrant" is problematical in a Dutch context, because, depending on the country of birth, interpellating especially the four largest migrant groups—Turks, Moroccans, Surinamese, and Antilleans—the children and grandchildren of migrants remain migrants until the fourth generation. I return to this and related terminology in the section on theory and methodology.

The ubiquitousness of migrant pasts is, however, not the dominant self-image that circulates in dominant Dutch self-representation. Whereas in the private sphere stories may be woven about a great-grandmother who came from Poland, Italy, or Germany, in the public sphere such stories do not add to one's public persona; they are rather a curiosity. There is a popular TV program *Verborgen Verleden* (Hidden past), in which well-known Dutch people go in search of their ancestry. Almost invariably, foreign ancestors show up, as well as the other way around, ancestors who went to Our Indies or Suriname. Invariably, this comes as a great surprise to the protagonists. I read this phenomenon as saying something significant about Dutch self-representation, for instance, in comparison with North American self-representation, where everyone knows and seemingly takes pride in their ancestry: in the Netherlands there is minimal interest in those elements that deviate from Ur Dutchness, which might mark one as foreign, or worse, *allochtoon*, that is, racially marked.

Belonging to the Dutch nation demands that those features that the collective imaginary considers non-Dutch—such as language, an exotic appearance, *een kleurtje hebben*, "having a tinge of color" (the diminutive way in which being of color is popularly indicated), outlandish dress and convictions, non-Christian religions, the memory of oppression—are shed as fast as possible and that one tries to assimilate. For new immigrants, for instance, the test for entrance into the Netherlands, the so-called integration exam, turns "the right of citizenship into a demand for cultural loyalty" (De Leeuw and van Wichelen 2014, 339), whereby cultural values, such as gender and gay equality, which are at least contested in Dutch circles, are presented as normative and nonnegotiable to newcomers. In the public sphere the assimilation model of monoethnicism and monoculturalism is so thorough that all signs of being from elsewhere should be erased. Of course, those who can phenotypically pass for Dutch, that is, those who are white, are in an advantageous position. It is migrants with dark or olive skin who do not succeed in enforcing their claim on Dutchness or have it accepted as legitimate. The main model for dealing with ethnic/racial difference is assimilation and those who cannot or will not be assimilated are segregated (Essed 1994). Thus, notwithstanding the thoroughly mixed makeup of the Dutch population in terms of racial or ethnic origins, the dominant representation is one of Dutchness as whiteness and being Christian. This image of Dutchness dates from the end of the nineteenth century, with the centralization and standardization of Dutch language and culture (Lucassen and Penninx 1993).[8]

My own family migrated to the Netherlands in December 1951, when my father, who was a police inspector in the Surinamese force (Klinkers 2011), qualified to go on leave for six months to the "motherland," where we eventually stayed permanently. I admire my parents for having made the decision to migrate, both of them twenty-nine years old, with five children under eight years of age, because migration at the time, given the price of passage by boat, meant that they would most likely never see their families and country of birth again. The regulation for leave in the motherland was of course meant for white Dutch civil servants only, who should not "go native," losing their sense and status of being Dutch, but my father had risen to a rank where he qualified for that perk. He had already started to learn Latin on his own in Paramaribo, wanting to study law in Amsterdam, which was not possible in Suriname. The highest secondary educational level in Suriname at the time was MULO or more extended lower education (Gobardhan-Rambocus 2001), and he had to pass an exam in Latin, *colloquium doctum*, to be admitted to the University of Amsterdam. In one of our family albums, there is a photo of the five Wekker siblings in Artis, the wonderful zoo that we lived practically next door to (figure I.1). It was only decades later that I realized that the reason why we found our first house in the old Jewish neighborhood of Amsterdam was that 70 percent of Jews in the Netherlands were abducted during World War II.

On a sunny day in the summer of 1952, the Wekker siblings, of which I was the youngest at the time,[9] were sitting on and standing by a donkey in Artis. At the edges of the photo are postwar white, Dutch people, in simple summer clothes, looking at us, enamored because we were such an unusual sight: "just like dolls." My mother, in later years, would often speak of the uncomfortable sensation that wherever we went, we were the main attraction. She drew the line at curious strangers touching our skin and hair. My mother was deeply disillusioned about the fact that, having come to the motherland, we did not have an indoor shower and had to bathe in a tub in the kitchen, as was usual at the time. We had had an indoor shower in Suriname and now had to go to the communal bathhouse every Saturday (Wekker 1995). We were one of the first Afro-Surinamese families to migrate to the Netherlands, where previously mostly single men and women had come to seek opportunity in the motherland. My family became subject to the same postwar disciplining regime that was meant for

Figure I.1 The Wekker siblings in 1952.
Photo from the collection of the author.

"weakly adjusted," white lower-class people and orientalized Indonesians (Indos) coming from Indonesia in the same period (Rath 1991). Indos are the descendants of white men and indigenous women, who formed an intermediate stratum between whites and indigenous people in the colony, and for whom it was no longer safe, after World War II, to stay in Indonesia, which was fighting for its independence from the Netherlands. The postwar uplifting regime consisted of regular unexpected visits from social workers, who came to inspect whether we were duly assimilating, that is, whether my mother cooked potatoes instead of rice, that the laundry was done on Monday, that we ate minced meatballs on Wednesday, and that the house was cleaned properly. I imagine that if we had not measured up, we would have fallen under the strict socialization regime meant for those postwar, working-class families, who failed the standards and were sent to resocialization camps. Clearly, a gendered regime was operative, where, as in all families at the time, men were supposed to work outside the home and women were good housewives. What has remained firmly in our family lore of those early years is that the Dutch were curious but helpful; an atmosphere of benevolent curiosity toward us reigned (Oostindie and Maduro 1985).

Let's briefly fast-forward and juxtapose this situation to an event five decades later in May 2006, the fateful night when Minister Rita Verdonk of Foreigners' Affairs and Integration, white and a former prison director, representing the VVD (the conservative People's Party for Freedom and Democracy), repeatedly told Ayaan Hirsi Ali, a black female member of parliament for the same party and a former refugee from Somalia, that since she had lied about her exact name and her date of birth in order to obtain Dutch citizenship, the minister was now forced to revoke it.[10] Playing on the time-honored expression *gelijke monniken, gelijke kappen* (equality for all),[11] this could also mean that Hirsi Ali would lose her seat in parliament. This night has etched itself into my consciousness and that of many others, as a traumatic wake-up call to our precarious existence as people of color in the Dutch ecumene. For many white Dutch people, the event was shocking and deeply unsettling, too, because it brought the German occupation back to mind, of being witness to a frightening display of authoritarian rule that brought back the *Befehl ist Befehl* ethos of the war years, that is, rules exist to be obeyed (Pessers 2006). Thus, the differing cultural imaginaries—World War II for the white majority versus an existential feeling of being unsafe for people of color as eternal foreigners—that different parts of the population experienced were brought home forcefully that night. Although race was not mentioned at all, Verdonk was frightening in her lack of imagination and lack of intellectual agility in presenting her arguments for the decision to revoke Hirsi Ali's citizenship.[12] She just read out loud, over and over, what her civil servants had written down for her. A deeply existential fear overtook many of us, sitting mesmerized through the televised spectacle, which went on all night: For if this could happen to Hirsi Ali, who was then seemingly at the top of her game, having injected the debate on multicultural society with her radical anti-Islam positions, seeing Islam as basically incompatible with a modern society and with women's and gay emancipation (Ghorashi 2003), then what about the rest of us? Who among us, black, migrants, and refugees, would ever be able to feel safe again in the Netherlands? She was at the height of her popularity among a circle of some influential white feminists, but especially among middle- and upper-class white men, and she basked for a while in their enamoration; they called themselves "friends of Ayaan" and dubbed her "the new Voltaire." Her popularity was, in my reading, to a large extent due to a toxic combination of the exoticization of a noble, enlightened black African princess and the fact that Hirsi Ali's teachings—it is not "we" who have to change, but "them," the Muslim barbarians, who do not fit into the modern Dutch nation—gave license to many of her followers to say things out loud about Muslims that had been unspeakable before. The element of sexual racism was abundantly present. Her figuration acted, on an emotional and sexual plane, as the catalyst for releasing the pent-up feelings brewing in the cultural archive; an intelligent black woman, beautiful, attractive, with a mysterious, wounded sexuality that would supposedly be healed by white male intervention. Apart from the well-known white male rescuer fantasy, the entire configuration is consonant with an often-invoked white man's dream to be with an intelligent black woman, who always already has the sexual capital of wildness and abandon at her disposal that has traditionally been associated with black women (Bijnaar 2007). This is the dream that the male protagonist of Robert Vuijsje's (2008) best-selling novel *Alleen maar nette mensen* (Only decent people) entertains. The spectacle staged on and around Ayaan Hirsi Ali also brings to mind the hypothesis of Jan Nederveen Pieterse (1990) that Europe is more fascinated by black women, while the United States is obsessed with black men. These fantasies were intimately connected to the Dutch cultural archive, and they were reduced to ashes and smoke once Hirsi Ali found her bearings at the American Enterprise Institute in Washington, DC. She found herself a new lover, a couple of academic notches above the old one, and generally had little use for the Netherlands and her old admirers anymore, who were left by the wayside like jilted lovers. In the spring of 2013, she obtained U.S. citizenship.

From the benevolence embedded in a 1952 snapshot to the public abjection of a powerful black woman, I am interested in the self that constructs these hysterical, excessive, repressed projections. Throughout the text, I use such thickly descriptive and analytical vignettes to make sense of the Netherlands, having lived through such widely diverging attitudes, climates, and discourses toward the black, migrant, and refugee other.

SECOND PARADOX:
INNOCENT VICTIM OF GERMAN OCCUPATION

A second marked paradox in dominant Dutch self-representation involves the recent past. The dominant self-image is that of innocent victim of German occupation during World War II. This representation has for a long time overlooked other populations that were intimately involved in the horrors of the time and who are more correctly conceptualized as (co)victims of the Dutch, and the gradual realization of this omission has thrown a less favorable light on the preparedness of the Dutch to protect and defend their fellow citizens, the Jews, than had earlier been imagined. Although a fourteen-volume standard work was published, The Kingdom of the Netherlands during World War II (De Jong, 1969–1991), it is only in the past three decades that the fate of the majority of Dutch Jews, who were transported to and killed in German concentration camps, has taken a more central place in the historiography of and the literature about World War II (Leydesdorff 1998; Withuis 2002; Hondius 2003; Gans 2014). Whether it was because of the excellent administrative system that kept track of the particulars of the citizenry, and that served the Germans well in their deadly mission, or because of lack of empathy with the Jews, from no other Western country, with the exception of Poland, were as many Jews abducted and murdered in German concentration camps as from the Netherlands. As in other nations, unidirectional memory has focused on the Holocaust (Rothberg 2009), seemingly erasing all other traumas.[13]

The second overlooked aspect, which lasted until the end of the 1960s and still regularly rears its head and is then conveniently forgotten again, is that the Netherlands perpetrated excessive violence against Indonesia, which was fighting for its independence in roughly the same period and which had been fully expected to return to the imperial fold after its occupation by the Japanese. This violence hardly forms part of the Dutch self-image, much less the more than 100,000 victims of "pacification" outside of Java, at the turn of the twentieth century (Schulte Nordholt 2000). It is only in periodical, temporary flares that the historical connections between the Netherlands and Indonesia are lit up, the latest episode of which is the widows of Rawagede, West Java, who have sued the Dutch state for compensation for the massacre of their 431 husbands, fathers, and children in 1947. The euphemistic term "police actions" for two wars speaks volumes about a self-image that embraces innocence, being a small but just and ethical guiding nation, internationally. The title *White Innocence* bespeaks this feature of Dutch self-representation.

THIRD PARADOX:
THE DUTCH IMPERIAL PRESENCE IN THE WORLD

The third, overriding paradox involves the more distant past: There was, until the last decade of the twentieth century, a stark juxtaposition between the Dutch imperial presence in the world, since the sixteenth century, and its almost total absence in the Dutch educational curriculum, in self-image and self-representations such as monuments,[14] literature, and debates about Dutch identity, including the infamous debates about multicultural society in the past two decades, which have resulted in the almost unanimous conclusion that multiculturalism has failed. Judging by curricula at various educational levels, from grade school to university level, it is the best-kept secret that the Netherlands has been a formidable imperial nation. Students in my classes are always surprised and appalled when they hear about the Dutch role in the slave trade and colonialism, often for the first time. In the last decades some change in consciousness of the Dutch imperial past has come about. In 2006, a national committee composed a national historical canon with fifty windows, or separate items, that covered the aspects of Dutch national history that students were supposed to know about: "those valuable elements of our culture and history that we would like through education to transmit to new generations" (Van Oostrom et al. 2006, 4). Six of these fifty windows have something to do with colonialism, slavery, and the slave trade. Although slavery has been a part of the compulsory core goals of history education since 1993, it is up to the individual teacher to decide how much time to devote to the topic. Research on sixteen secondary schools in Amsterdam showed that the number of hours varied from less than one school hour to more than twelve hours, depending on the racial positioning of the teacher and the composition of the school population (Mok 2011).

An earlier noteworthy event in the breaking of silence around the Dutch imperial past was the establishment of a monument to commemorate slavery in Amsterdam in 2002, which was initiated by the Afro-European women's organization Sophiedela and a briefly favorable political climate, with a national government including the Labor Party and D66 (Democrats 66). These parties were favorably inclined to honor the requests of Sophiedela and other black organizations for a monument. Subsequently a counterpart was established: NiNsee, the National Institute of Dutch Slavery and Heritage past and present, also founded in 2002.[15] This institute, subsidized by the government and the city of Amsterdam, sadly did not live to celebrate its tenth birthday, because it was, like other memorials to the past such as the library of the Royal Tropical Institute and other institutions in the cultural field, abolished by the government Rutte-I, 2010–2012, in which the Conservative Democrats, VVD, in coalition with the Christian Democrats, were supported by Geert Wilders's xenophobic and populist Party for Freedom, PVV. This unholy trinity managed, despite the protected status of NiNsee and guarantees for its continued existence and growth, to end its subsidized status as of January 1, 2013. In an ethno-nationalist frenzy and on the attack against cultural "leftist hobbies," fueled by PVV, against "everything that is of value,"[16] the infrastructure to produce and disseminate knowledge about Dutch slavery past and present was almost annihilated. That anything, the barest shell, is left standing of NiNsee is due to the city of Amsterdam, traditionally led by the Labor Party and other leftist parties, which continues to subsidize the offices and a minimal staff. Professor of sociology Abram de Swaan raised a rare voice when he spoke at the 150-year Commemoration of the Abolition of Slavery on July 1, 2013:

> NiNsee was a gesture of contrition, an institutional way to apologize for past crimes of the Netherlands towards its Afro-Caribbean population. That is no small matter. It is about restoring one's own honour by honouring the humanity of the other. It is about a debt of honour. You cannot just withdraw that gesture when it happens to be a convenient way to cut costs. To retract that gesture is dishonourable. It was and is a mortal insult to all Africans they once enslaved. (2013, 6)

He lucidly remarked that the fate of NiNsee mirrors how the Netherlands looks at its postcolonial citizens: "still not taken seriously, not their past of slavery, nor their present presence in this country" (De Swaan 2013, 6). And I would add: disposable, with nothing meaningful to contribute in terms of knowledge production, nothing that "we" would want or need to know about, who should assimilate and quit moaning about the past. Thus, what we see in the fate of NiNsee is not merely a cutting of costs in dire economic times, but, in light of the cultural archive, an active excision of a fledgling knowledge infrastructure that might have produced valuable knowledge about "us."

———□————————□———

We are still a long way away from understanding the complex relationships between the Dutch global, imperial role, on the one hand, and the internal erasure of this role and the current revulsion against multiculturality, on the other. The past forms a massive blind spot, which barely hides a structure of superiority toward people of color. As long as the Dutch imperial past does not form part of the common, general store of knowledge, which coming generations should have at their disposal, as long as general knowledge about the exclusionary processes involved in producing the Dutch nation does not circulate more widely, multiculturalism now cannot be realized, either. People of color will forever remain allochtonen, the official and supposedly innocuous term meaning "those who came from elsewhere," racializing people of color for endless generations, never getting to belong to the Dutch nation. The counterpart of "allochtonen" is autochtonen, meaning "those who are from here," which, as everyone knows, refers to white people. Thus, the supposedly most innocent terms for different sections of the population are racializing, without having to utter distasteful racial terms (Wekker and Lutz 2001). I return to this terminology in the section on theory and methodology.

Forgetting, glossing over, supposed color blindness, an inherent and natural superiority vis-à-vis people of color, assimilating: those are, broadly speaking, the main Dutch models that are in operation where interaction with racialized/ethnicized others is concerned. Persistently, an innocent, fragile, emancipated white Dutch self is constructed versus a guilty, uncivilized, barbaric other, which in the past decades has been symbolized mostly by the Islamic other, but at different times in the recent past blacks (i.e., Afro-Surinamese, Antilleans, and Moluccans) have occupied that position. It is within this dominant context that black, migrant, and refugee communities have had to come to self-actualization in the past seventy years. Black Dutch people (and other racialized/ethnicized others) are confronted with an enormous paradox. The implicit and infernal message, the double bind we get presented with all the time is: "If you want to be equal to us, then don't talk about differences; but if you are different from us, then you are not equal" (Prins 2002). This basic but deep-seated knowledge and affect, stemming from an imperial cultural archive, will have purchase too in other former imperial nations, where a now near other has to be dealt with in proximity.

Three Central Concepts

INNOCENCE

It is heartening to see, with a number of recent publications, the first sign in three decades (Balkenhol 2014; Essed and Hoving 2014; Hondius 2014a and b) that older and younger scholars are—against all odds and certainly not making it easy on themselves, in terms of a propitious mainstream academic career—engaging with the history and the present of Dutch race relations.[17] It seems—to use an apt watery metaphor—as if a long-blocked-off stream has suddenly found the proverbial hole in the dyke and is now rushing forth. In this section, I want to lay out how I understand and use the three central concepts in this book, that is, innocence, the cultural archive, and white Dutch self-representation. Let's first consider innocence. Amid the complexity and the manifold understandings of Dutch racism that are unfolding, I am foregrounding the notion of white innocence, although I certainly do not contest nor erase the other approaches that have been put forward, and I invoke them whenever appropriate. Innocence, in my understanding, has particular resonance in the Dutch landscape, not only because it is such a cherished self-descriptor, but also because it fits with a chain of other associations that are strongly identified with: First, there is innocence as the desired state of being that is invoked in the Christian religion. While since the end of the 1960s Christian churches as institutions have crumbled, the underlying worldview has not. Jesus is the iconic innocent man. He does not betray others; he shares what little he possesses; he does not use violence nor commit sins; he lives in poverty; he cures the sick, turns the other cheek, and is goodness incarnate—yet he is sentenced to death.[18] He undergoes this treatment for the good of humanity, selflessly putting others' interests before his own. Unquestionably, there is a nobility in Jesus that is to be emulated and that many people, notwithstanding widespread secularism, subscribe to. Second, there is the association of innocence with being small: a small nation, a small child. Being small, one might easily and metaphorically be looked upon as a child, not able to play with the big guys, either on the block or in the world, but we have taken care of the latter predicament by being a trustworthy and overeager U.S. ally.[19] An undisputed corollary of being a small child is, in our located, cultural understanding, its undiluted innocence and goodness. Being small, we need to be protected and to protect ourselves against all kinds of evil, inside and outside the nation. Third, in a traditional worldview, innocence also carries feminine connotations, as that which needs to be protected, that which is less strong and aggressive but more affectionate and relational. Fourth, innocence, furthermore, enables the safe position of having license to utter the most racist statements, while in the next sentence saying that it was a joke or was not meant as racist.[20] The utterer may proclaim to be in such an intimate, privileged relationship to the black person addressed, that he or she is entitled to make such a statement. I pay attention to this preferential mode of bringing across racist content by means of humor and irony in chapter 1. Fifth, the claim of innocence is also strong in other European, former imperial nations, such as Sweden. It is striking that we still lack studies of whiteness, within a European context, that would also enable intra-European comparisons (but see Griffin with Braidotti 2002). The case of Sweden is interesting, because characteristics comparable to the Dutch case come to the fore, that is, the widespread and foundational claim to innocence, Swedish exceptionalism, and "white laughter" (Sawyer 2006; Habel 2012). This commonality might point to innocence, not knowing, being one of the few viable stances that presents itself when the loss of empire is not worked through, but simply forgotten. The anger and violence accompanying innocence may be understood as a strand within the postcolonial melancholia syndrome (Gilroy 2005), and I return to it in chapter 5.

Innocence, in other words, thickly describes part of a dominant Dutch way of being in the world. The claim of innocence, however, is a double-edged sword: it contains not-knowing, but also not wanting to know, capturing what philosopher Charles W. Mills (1997, 2007) has described as the epistemology of ignorance. Succinctly stated, "the epistemology of ignorance is part of a white supremacist state in which the human race is racially divided into full persons and subpersons. Even though—or, more accurately, precisely because—they tend not to understand the racist world in which they live, white people are able to fully benefit from its racial hierarchies, ontologies and economies" (Sullivan and Tuana, 2007, 2). This not-understanding, which can afflict white and nonwhite people alike, is connected to practices of knowing and not-knowing, which are forcefully defended. Essed and Hoving also point to "the anxious Dutch *claim of innocence* and how disavowal and denial of racism may merge into what we have called *smug ignorance*: (aggressively) rejecting the possibility to know" (2014b, 24). Using the r-word in a Dutch context is like entering a minefield; the full force of anger and violence, including death threats, is unleashed, as the case of Zwarte Piet or Black Pete shows so clearly (chapter 5).[21] The behavior and speech acts of his defenders do not speak of innocence but rather of "*an ignorance militant, aggressive, not to be intimidated, an ignorance that is active, dynamic, that refuses to go quietly—not at all confined to the illiterate and uneducated but propagated at the highest levels of the land, indeed presenting itself unblushingly as* knowledge" (Mills 2007, 13, emphasis in original).

I expressly mean innocence to have this layered and contradictory content, this tongue-in-cheek quality: notwithstanding the many, daily protestations in a Dutch context that "we" are innocent, racially speaking; that racism is a feature found in the United States and South Africa, not in the Netherlands; that, by definition, racism is located in working-class circles, not among "our kind of middle-class people"; much remains hidden under the univocality and the pure strength of will defending innocence. I am led to suspect bad faith; innocence is not as innocent as it appears to be, which becomes all the more clear, again as the case of Zwarte Piet/Black Pete illuminates.

In sum, innocence speaks not only of soft, harmless, childlike qualities, although those are the characteristics that most Dutch people would wholeheartedly subscribe to; it is strongly connected to privilege, entitlement, and violence that are deeply disavowed. Loss of innocence, that is, knowing and acknowledging the work of race, does not automatically entail guilt, repentance, restitution, recognition, responsibility, and solidarity but can call up racist violence, and often results in the continued cover-up of structural racism.[22] Innocence also includes the field that has become the center of my explorations: sexual racism. There is denial and disavowal of the continuities between colonial sexuality and contemporary sexual modalities. Since innocence is not monolithic, nor fixed or immutable, and since it involves psychic and cultural work, in all the chapters I am concerned with the question of how innocence is accomplished and maintained.

Often when I have given presentations in the Netherlands on the topics in this book, people have asked me where this cultural archive is located: is it in Amsterdam or in Middelburg, the capital of the province of Zeeland, the site from which slavers left for Africa, their first stop on the triangle trade route? My answer is that the cultural archive is located in many things, in the way we think, do things, and look at the world, in what we find (sexually) attractive, in how our affective and rational economies are organized and intertwined. Most important, it is between our ears and in our hearts and souls. The question is prompted by a conception of an archive as a set of documents or the institution in which those documents are housed.[23] My use of the term refers to neither of those two meanings, but to "a repository of memory" (Stoler 2009, 49), in the heads and hearts of people in the metropole, but its content is also silently cemented in policies, in organizational rules, in popular and sexual cultures, and in commonsense everyday knowledge, and all of this is based on four hundred years of imperial rule. I read all of these contemporary domains for their colonial content, for their racialized common sense. The content of the cultural archive may overlap with that of the colonial archive, in which the documents, classifications, and "principles and practices of governance" (Stoler 2009, 20) pertaining to the colonies are stored. Knowledges in different domains have travelled between colonies and metropoles and vice versa, but with the cultural archive I expressly wish to foreground the memories, the knowledge, and affect with regard to race that were deposited within metropolitan populations, and the power relations embedded within them.

I stay close to the spirit in which Edward Said used the concept of cultural archive, as outlined above, although he does not give many clues as to how to operationalize it, outside the domain of culture, taken as poetry and fiction, that is, the body of novels metropolitan authors produced during imperialism. Said convincingly shows how those novels were not insulated from "the prolonged and sordid cruelty of such practices as slavery, colonialist and racial oppression and imperial subjection" (1993, xiv), but helped fuel imperial expansion and subjecthood in the metropole. My objects of study pertain to dominant white self-representation, to policies, principles, and practices, and to feelings. In my reading, the transmitting of racialized knowledge and affect between the colonial and the metropolitan parts of empire took place within what can be conceptualized as one prolonged and intense contact zone (Pratt 1992). It helps to conceptualize the cultural archive along similar lines as Bourdieu (1977) does for habitus, that is, "that presence of the past in the present," a way of acting that people have been socialized into, that becomes natural, escaping consciousness. The habitus of an individual springs forth from experiences in early childhood, within a particular social setting, often a family, and Bourdieu understands such processes in terms of class. Habitus is "history turned into nature" (Bourdieu 1977, 78), structured and structuring dispositions, that can be systematically observed in social practices. In a comparable fashion, racial notions must also have been transmitted to following generations, sometimes above, often below the level of consciousness. I am not implying that the cultural archive or its racialized common sense has remained the same in content over four hundred years, nor that it has been uncontested, but those historical questions, important as they are, are not, cannot be my main concern. Standing at the end of a line, in the twenty-first century, I read imperial continuities back into a variety of current popular cultural and organizational phenomena.

WHITE DUTCH SELF-REPRESENTATION

What does it mean to think in terms of dominant white Dutch self-representation? I understand the Dutch metropolitan self, in its various historical incarnations, as a racialized self, with race as an organizing grammar of an imperial order in which modernity was framed (Stoler 1995; McClintock 1995). Racial imaginations are part and parcel of the Dutch psychological and cultural makeup; these imaginations are intertwined with our deepest desires and anxieties, with who we are.[24] Although the project does not aim to be predominantly historical, it cannot escape addressing certain historical questions, because it offers such a different reading of Dutch history than dominant versions of that history rehearse. "To account for racism is to offer a different account of the world," as Sara Ahmed (2012, 3) aptly remarked. Amid the grand narratives that mediate Dutch self-understanding—the perennial struggle against the water, the eighty-year armed resistance against being part of the Spanish Empire, the Golden Age, the struggle for religious freedom and pillarization—i.e. living within a Catholic, a Protestant, a socialist or a Humanist pillar as a way for people of different religious convictions to live peacefully together, the centrality of a way of negotiating to solve disputes, called *polderen*[25]—none evokes race (e.g., Schama 1987; Israel 1998; Shorto 2013). Most often, religious, class and regional differences have been foregrounded as the primary differences that need to be taken into account when examining our culture. It is intriguing that imperial cultural figurations have stayed impervious to scrutiny for so long, in spite of rare voices to the contrary. I am operating on the assumption that race has been sorely missing from dominant accounts of the Netherlands and that this racial reign began with the Dutch expansion into the world in the sixteenth century. The construction of the European self and its others took place in the force fields of "conquest, colonisation, empire formation, permanent settlement by Europeans of other parts of the globe, nationalist struggles by the colonised, and selective decolonisation" (Brah 1996, 152). Contemporary constructions of "us," those constructed as belonging to Europe, and "them," those constructed as not belonging, though the specific groups targeted vary over time, still keep following that basic Manichean logic. This entails the fundamental impossibility of being both European, constructed to mean being white and Christian, and being black-Muslim-migrant-refugee.

Theoretical and Methodological Stakes of the Project

The kind of analysis that I undertake here, postcolonial and intersectional, builds on insights that unfortunately have not found much fertile ground yet in a Dutch context. My approach has three innovative aspects, which together will show the purchase of the model that I propose.

RACE, GENDER, AND SEXUALITY

First, I am simultaneously bringing together the central analytical concepts of race, gender, and sexuality, that is, intersectionality, in approaching white self-representation. Intersectionality is a theory and a methodology, importantly and initially based on black feminist thought, which not only addresses identitarian issues, as is commonly thought, but also a host of other social and psychological phenomena. It is a way of looking at the world that takes as a principled stance that it is not enough merely to take gender as the main analytical tool of a particular phenomenon, but that gender as an important social and symbolical axis of difference is simultaneously operative with others like race, class, sexuality, and religion (Crenshaw 1989; Wekker and Lutz 2001; Botman, Jouwe, and Wekker eds.

2001; Phoenix and Pattynama eds. 2006; Davis 2008; Lutz, Vivar, and Supik eds. 2011; Lykke 2010 and 2011; Lewis 2013; Cho, Crenshaw and McCall 2013). In fact, these grammars of difference coconstruct each other. The concepts of race, gender, and sexuality are lodged in different disciplinary academic fields, pointing to the alienness of thinking intersectionally in the traditional academic organization. Let's start with the more straightforward concepts: gender is located within the interdisciplinary field of gender studies. The school of thought called intersectionality finds a home in the interdiscipline of gender studies, although it has increasingly been taken up in other disciplines in the social sciences and the humanities as well. Sexuality, as another important axis of signification, finds a home in sexuality studies, where first gay and lesbian studies were initiated, later to be followed by queer studies, which takes distance from a fixed, immutable, inner sexual identification. It bears noting at this point that both of these (inter)disciplines behave as if their central objects of study—gender and sexuality—can be studied most intensely if other axes of signification are firmly kept out of sight. For both gender studies and sexuality studies or queer studies, this means that, a commitment to intersectionality notwithstanding, race is mostly evacuated.

Race presents a more complicated case in a Dutch context. It is a term that is not commonly utilized, since World War II, except to indicate varieties of animals and potatoes (Nimako and Willemsen 1993). Ethnicity is the term more often used, and it indicates the social system that gives meaning to ethnic differences between people—to differences based on origin, appearance, history, culture, language, and religion. Ethnicity, culture, and culturalization, supposedly softer entities, which, again supposedly, operate on cultural rather than on biological terrain, have been used in such hardened ways that biology and culture have become interchangeable in the stability that is ascribed to the cultures of others. In Dutch commonsense thought, but also in many academic discourses, the remarkable thing is that when ethnicity is invoked, it is "they," the other, allochthones, who are referenced, not autochthones. Just as within gender it is most often women and femininity that are called up, not men or masculinity, so within the realm of ethnicity being white is passed off as such a natural, invisible category that its significance has not been a research theme. As in many other places, such as the United States, "ethnic," as in ethnic cuisine, ethnic music, is everything except white. There is thus a systematic asymmetry in the way we understand these dimensions, where the more powerful member of a binary pair—masculinity, whiteness—is consistently bracketed and is thereby invisibilized and installed as the norm (Wekker and Lutz 2001).

In the move to ethnicity and subsequently to culture and culturalization (Ghorashi 2006), the work that race used to do, ordering reality on the basis of supposed biological difference (although the term was banished), is still being accomplished. There is a fundamental unwillingness to critically consider the applicability of a racialized grammar of difference to the Netherlands. However, in the main terms that are still circulating to indicate whites and others, the binary pair autochtoon-allochtoon/autochthones-allochthones, race is firmly present, as well as in the further official distinction in the category of allochtoon: Western and non-Western. Both concepts, allochtoon and autochtoon, are constructed realities, which make it appear as if they are transparent, clearly distinguishable categories, while the cultural mixing and matching that has been going on cannot be acknowledged. Within the category of autochtoon there are many, as we have seen, whose ancestors came from elsewhere, but who manage, through a white appearance, to make a successful claim to Dutchness. Allochtonen are the ones who do not manage this, through their skin color or their deviant religion or culture. The binary thus sets racializing processes in motion; everyone knows that they reference whites and people of color respectively. The categories are not set in stone, however: In the past decades, some groups have been able to move out of the construction allochtoon. For example, Indos have firmly moved out and Surinamese people are on their way out, and it is now Islamic people, constructed as the ultimate other, who seem firmly lodged within it.

However much it is disavowed and denied in a Dutch context, I take race to be a fundamental organizing grammar in Dutch society, as it is in societies structured by racial dominance. I view race as a "socially constructed rather than inherently meaningful category, one linked to relations of power and processes of struggle, and one whose meaning changes over time. Race, like gender, is 'real' in the sense that it has real, though changing, effects in the world and real, tangible, and complex impacts on individuals' sense of self and life chances" (Frankenberg 1993, 11). I use the term "race" in this book, sometimes merely as race or racialization, sometimes in the combination race/ethnicity. That is, following Stuart Hall

(2000), I use race and ethnicity as two sides of the same coin, subsuming and merging a more natural, biological understanding of race with a more cultural view.

Finally, let me say something about the terms "black" and "white." I use them not as biological categories but as political and cultural concepts. As Stuart Hall remarks about "black": "The moment the signifier 'black' is torn from its historical, cultural and political embedding and lodged in a biologically constituted racial category, we valorize, by inversion, the very ground of racism we are trying to deconstruct. In addition, as always happens when we naturalize historical categories (think about gender and sexuality), we fix that signifier outside of history, outside of change, outside of political intervention" (1992, 29, 30). I follow Frankenberg's conceptualization of whiteness, in that whiteness refers to "a set of locations that are historically, socially, politically, and culturally produced, and, moreover are intrinsically linked to unfolding relations of domination. Naming 'whiteness' displaces it from the unmarked, unnamed status that is itself an effect of its dominance" (Hall 1992, 6).

When we finally, then, look at the location of the study of race in the academy, we have to conclude that race is not studied in the Netherlands, while ethnicity is, but only in the limited sense that it pertains to the other, as I lay out in more detail in chapter 2. The study of whiteness is strongly underilluminated. Thus, multitudes of studies on Surinamese, Antillean, Moroccan, and Turkish Dutch people, their positionings in the labor market, in education, and in housing are being done in academic institutes for ethnic studies. Popular, recently, are studies on ethnic profiling by the police, especially on men of color, which, as can be expected, is vehemently denied by academic institutes. Equally the recent deaths of young Antillean and Surinamese Dutch men at the hands of the police are downplayed. Other axes of signification, such as gender and sexuality, are in a familiar manner bracketed, put at a distance. In this book, I am breaking with the persistent tradition of foregrounding a single axis, in that I bring race, gender, and sexuality into conversation with each other, on the understanding that they all are part of each other's histories and representations and are refracted through each other (Somerville 2000; Alexander 2005).

The second innovative aspect is that I bring the history of the metropole and of the colonies into conversation with each other. Knowledge about Dutch overseas expansion is, not incidentally, in quarantine in a separate specialization of the discipline of history; it is not an element of Dutch national history. General common and academic sense is the idea that colonialism-of-the-exterior (Brah 1996) has created a sufficiently convenient distance to the former Dutch colonies to make it possible to never have to take persistent imperial patterns of thought and affect into account when studying the Netherlands. It is noteworthy that it was Ann Laura Stoler, an American historical anthropologist who specializes in the Dutch East Indies (Indonesia until 1945), who first made the important observation in *Race and the Education of Desire* (Stoler 1995) that, compared to other European colonial nations like France and Great Britain, it is remarkable that in the Dutch academy, historical research and general ways of knowing have been set up in a way that the history of the metropole is structurally set apart from the history of the colonies. This was evident in the Dutch academy through the fact that within departments of history, the discipline was centrally structured such that there was a preponderance of majors, courses, and specializations that dealt with national history, while a small, separate minority of curricular materials was devoted to the Dutch expansion in the world, meaning colonial history. While this is still the case in Leiden, other history departments have taken different routes in the past decades,[26] but that is not to say that there is an automatic engagement between historical developments that took place in the metropole, say policies on care for the elderly, the destitute, and orphans, and what repercussions these had in the East and the West, or the other way around. The metropolitan and colonial parts of Dutch colonial empire are still overwhelmingly treated, both inside and outside the academy, as separate worlds, the metropolitan and the colonial, that did not impinge upon each other. Stoler's challenge has, with a few exceptions (Waaldijk and Grever 2004; Van Stipriaan et al. 2007; Stuurman 2009; Legêne 2010) not been taken up by Dutch historians. Indeed, Caribbeanist and historian Gert Oostindie (2010, 260–65) is not alone when he argues that postcolonial studies have, with good justification, not found an eager reception nor many practitioners in the Netherlands, and he deems that not much is lost by that fact.

Third and finally, another breach with tradition is that in this book, I confront the very different reception and memories that the eastern and western parts of empire evoke in the Netherlands and how this difference still plays a part in current configurations. Comparison between the eastern part, Our Indies, and the western part of the Dutch empire, Suriname and the Dutch Antilles, is seldom undertaken. Almost by default, when the colonies are invoked, it is the Indies that are meant and foregrounded, usually without giving much attention to the active disappearance of the West. There is not much interaction between scholars specializing in the study of the Indies, on the one hand, and of Suriname and the Antilles, on the other.

Methodologically, I use what Judith Halberstam (1998) calls a scavenger methodology, making use of insights from gender and sexuality studies, discourse and narrative analysis, post- and decolonial theory, and psychoanalysis. I work with interviews, watching TV and reading novels, analyzing e-mail correspondence, my own and others' experiences and organizational structures, rereading historical texts, and doing close readings of various kinds, to eventually and jointly be able to sketch a picture of the cultural archive, the dominant white Dutch self and its representation.

Content of the Book

The first chapter, "Suppose She Brings a Big Negro Home," is devoted to a series of case studies of everyday racist events, taking its inspiration from popular culture, including everyday TV content, experiential accounts, and a novel. One case study deals with racial difference, featuring among others Martin Bril, a popular journalist who uttered a racist statement. Three experiential vignettes collectively point to characteristic, commonly occurring patterns in racism when dealing with black (men and) women in everyday encounters and discourses in the Netherlands: sexualization, relegation to the category of domestic servant/nanny, general inferiorization, and criminalization. To the average Dutch person, there is nothing wrong with any of these events; they are often seen as merely funny. One of the characteristic ways to bring racist content across is by using humor and irony. I will do close readings—Freudian, Fanonian, Du Boisian, and postcolonial—of these meaningful moments and reflect on possible connections with the cultural archive.

Chapter 2, "The House That Race Built," addresses how race does its work in Dutch public policy and in the academy, pertaining to women's issues. More fundamentally, I explore the nature of the fear and aggression that is called up in many white people when they (have to) deal with racial or ethnic issues. I argue that at the root of the attention to the emancipation of women in the sphere of policy is a widespread and deep-seated, racialized conception that suffuses the object of policy making and seemingly naturally and self-evidently divides women into white, allochthonous, and Third World women. Race is at the basis of the division (Wekker 1994), and the same silent racialized ordering is also operative in the academy, in the division of labor within and between disciplines. I am taking up the discipline that I know best and where I was located for almost twenty years: the discipline of women's/gender studies is my special object of exploration, in trying to uncover what the fear of engaging with race/ethnicity consists of, among both students and faculty. Here we are in allied territory, mostly white women who are deeply driven by feelings of social justice, yet, notwithstanding the public claim to be doing intersectionality, they are deeply reluctant to truly grapple with race/ethnicity.

Chapter 3, "The Coded Language of Hottentot Nymphae," analyzes a psychoanalytical case study from 1917, in which three apparently white middle- or upper-class women in analysis in The Hague tell their psychoanalyst that they are suffering from "Hottentot nymphae," the contemporary term for enlarged labia minora, which are commonly associated with black women. Two features are intriguing about this case study: first, while the women use a racialized grammar to understand themselves, the psychoanalyst Dr. J. W. H. van Ophuijsen dismisses their claim and understands them as suffering from Freud's "masculinity complex," thus in terms of gender. I want to explore the meaning of this substitution of gender for race, which sites in society would provide these women with knowledge about race, and, finally, what the stakes are for the women and for the psychoanalyst. A second feature of this case study is that it shows that, contrary to what is commonly assumed, race was firmly present as a discourse in upper-class circles of the metropole, without black people being present in significant numbers. The fact that these women use a racialized discourse to make sense of themselves runs counter to the commonly held view that race was absent in the Netherlands until the late 1940s, when the first postcolonial migrants started to arrive from the East Indies. I analyze the case study in terms of what it can tell us about the cultural archive.

The next chapter, "Of Homo Nostalgia and (Post)Coloniality," addresses gay politics in the Netherlands in the past decade. Starting from the jolting realization that at the penultimate national elections in 2010, white gay men voted overwhelmingly for PVV—the Party for Freedom, led by Islamo- and xenophobe Geert Wilders—I am interested, first, in tracing the history of the Dutch white gay movement in comparison with the women's liberation movement. This leads me, second, to explore how government policy in the field of gay liberation underwrites and sets up one particular, located conceptualization of homosexuality as universal, and how this thinking has become entwined with Islamophobia and nationalism. The strong Dutch version of homonationalism (Puar 2007) forcefully foregrounds the acceptance of homosexuality as the litmus test for modernity, while rejecting Islam. In this exploration, third, the figuration of Pim Fortuyn with his contradictory desires—rejecting Muslims and at the same time preferring them as his sexual partners in dark rooms—plays a pivotal role. His contradictory desires are straight from the colonial past and connect intimately to colonial sexual practices that were stored in the cultural archive.

Chapter 5 engages with popular culture again. I analyze the voluminous e-mail or hate mail addressed by members of the Dutch public to the Van Abbemuseum in Eindhoven, after a project in 2008 initiated by German and Swedish artists Annette Krauss and Petra Bauer critically interrogated the phenomenon of Zwarte Piet. This figuration, a black man with thick lips and golden earrings, clad in a colorful Moorish costume, and wielding deplorable grammar, is imagined to be a servant of a white bishop, Sinterklaas, who hails from Spain. The pair of them come to visit every year at the end of November, culminating in a merry evening on 5 December, when presents are given to children. Zwarte Piet is considered by many white Dutch people to be at the heart of Dutch culture, an innocent and thoroughly pleasant children's traditional festivity, but its critical reception since the 1970s, mainly by black people, precipitates a strong reaction in the majority of Dutch people. Critique of the phenomenon of Zwarte Piet elicits vehemently aggressive and defensive reactions, as expressed in the e-mail bombardment to the museum. I investigate the precise nature of these reactions, the themes the correspondents brought up and the discourses they used to convey their unhappiness. Connecting this vehement affect to Gilroy's (2005) "postcolonial melancholia," I do a reading of the place of Zwarte Piet in white Dutch self-representation, in which innocence, in manifold senses, turns out to be central. What does all of this tell us about the cultural archive and Dutch self-perception?

Collectively these chapters, visiting different social and cultural domains, attempt a critical, intersectional, and decolonial reading of white Dutch self-representation, with special attention to the ways in which the racial economy, with its gendered, sexualized, and classed intersections, continues to underwrite dominant, racist ways of knowing and feeling. A characteristic of the Netherlands is, for those with eyes to see and some reflective capital, a particularly virulent form of racism, prominently displaying itself as sexualized racism, which is immediately denied and disavowed, all against a general background of national self-flattery and collective benevolent readings of the self.

CHAPTER 1

"Suppose She Brings a Big Negro Home"

Case Studies of Everyday Racism

Psychoanalysis can . . . be seen as a quite
elaborate form of ethnography—as a writing of
the ethnicity of the white Western psyche.

Mary Ann Doane, *Femmes Fatales*

In this chapter, I embark on an oceanic journey that I have postponed for quite some time, daunted by the murkiness and coldness of the water. I am interested in the widespread but un(der)explored ways in which race has nestled itself in the Dutch cultural archive, that storehouse of what Edward Said (1993, 52), in a general European framework, described as "a particular knowledge and structures of attitude and reference . . . [and], in Raymond Williams' seminal phrase, 'structures of feeling'" with regard to the racial ordering of the world. In the introduction, I summarized this notion of the cultural archive as a storehouse of ideas, practices, and affect, that which is in between our ears, in our hearts and minds, regarding race, based on four hundred years of imperial rule.

I want to explore the forcefulness, passion, and even aggression that race elicits in the Netherlands, while at the same time elusiveness, denial, and disavowal reign supreme. The concept of disavowal speaks of deep ambiguity with regard to race: repressed material can make its way into consciousness on the condition that it is immediately denied (Wright 1992, 90). Denial and disavowal, the simultaneous affirmation and denial of a thought or desire, are important modes the majority white population uses to deal with race. I am intrigued by the ways in which race pops up in unexpected places and moments, as the return of the repressed, while the dominant discourse stubbornly maintains that the Netherlands is and always has been color-blind and antiracist.

I focus on the ways in which black people, but especially black women, were and are envisioned in the Dutch cultural archive, by bringing various popular and literary representations of black women to the surface, together with some personal experiences with gendered and sexualized racism. Little research about these volatile concoctions, as part and parcel of the cultural text, has so far been done in the Netherlands, although some work needs to be mentioned: for instance, Nederveen Pieterse's 1990 study of images of blacks in Western popular culture, Allison Blakely's (1993) historical work on the role of race in the modern Dutch nation, and Elmer Kolfin and Esther Schreuder (2008), who traced black figurations in Dutch art. The journey before me is to explore the ways in which race became part of the Dutch cultural archive, how it acquired gendered, sexualized, and classed meanings during more than four hundred years, and how these complex configurations became intertwined with dominant regimes of truth, which keep on manifesting themselves to this day. I understand racial imaginations to be part of the Dutch psychological and cultural makeup; these imaginations are intertwined with the deepest desires and anxieties of many Dutch people. I seek to uncover some of the elements of the dominant discourse constructing black women in the Netherlands. bell hooks (1992a) argues that within U.S. racist discourse, black women are not exclusively depicted as inferior; also, and often simultaneously, jealousy and unspeakable yearning are involved. Is the oscillation between extreme attraction to black women and rejection, inferiorization, and relegation to an abject category—a dominant assemblage constructing black women in the United States—also pertinent in the Netherlands, or do we find a different configuration here?

Systemic and Virulent Psychic Residues of Race

It is necessary to explore the ways in which, in the Dutch context, shared, often unexamined fantasies with regard to race continue to shape the ways in which "we" and "they" are constructed and perceived, while dominant common sense has it that race is thoroughly absent in the Netherlands. By engaging with a few varied case studies, taken from TV, public and everyday life, and the literary imagination, I hope to show that race, given all its disparate manifestations, must have been firmly implanted in the cultural imagination in order to leave such systemic and virulent psychic residues.

Although the above sketch of the problem seems to call for a psycho-analytical approach, I am mainly interested in psychoanalysis as an ethnography of the white psyche—after all, the concepts of self and other that came into being in psychoanalysis were dependent on the politics of colonial relations. As a "scavenger theorist and methodologist" (Halberstam 1998, 13), I prefer to adopt an interdisciplinary framework, actively exploring alternative grand narratives in which race, class, gender, and sexuality are taken into account (Morrison ed. 1992b; Abel, Christian, and Moglen eds. 1997; Lane ed. 1998; Campbell 2000; Khanna 2003). I thus make use of insights from gender and sexuality studies, discourse and narrative analysis, postcolonial theory, and psychoanalysis.[1]

Little research about everyday narratives representing black women has so far been done in the Netherlands (but see Essed 1984, 1990, 2002). In my own work on female black diasporic sexuality, I have started to look at the representation of black women in Dutch discourse (Wekker 2006). It is clear that representational regimes of the sexuality of different groups of women do not come into being independently from each other; they are relational (Wekker 2006, 250). In contemporary Dutch multiethnic society, Islamic women are represented as sexually backward and oppressed, but dominant representational regimes of Islamic women in the West have undergone radical changes, from hypersexuality in the late nineteenth and early twentieth centuries to current asexuality (Lutz 1991). Black, that is to say African diasporic, women are generally seen as "too liberated," with a rampant sexuality, doing it indiscriminately with men and with women, doing it for money, "going where their cunts lead them" (De Wit 1993). Asian sexualities, such as the representations of Indo and Thai women, different as they may be, have in common the construction of submissive and ultrafeminine femininities, with long-hair, and attractive in traditional ways.[2] White female sexuality seems to be the neutral, normative variety.[3] Thus we see not only a relational structuring of these representations but also a hierarchy operative.

All of the disparate sources that I use in this chapter point to what could realistically be designated as submerged knowledge, that is, knowledge that is not part of dominant regimes of truth. Just as Richard Dyer (1997, 1) maintains that race is never not in the picture in modern life, so sexuality is never not in play when it comes to representing black women, although other representations also vie for attention.

In the next section, I show three prevalent manifestations of contemporary racism directed at (mostly) black women in the Netherlands. I read the treatment of these variously classed black women, both fictional and real, in light of the repressed cultural archive. Next, I undertake a historical excursion into the Dutch colonial past and speculate about the ways that not only in the colonies, but also in the metropole, a subjectification took place in which sexualized race was centrally deposited in the collective unconscious. As Helen Moglen says, "To achieve a more adequate and more emancipatory understanding of difference . . . we must insist upon the centrality of history in our analyses" (1997, 204). I subsequently present an analysis of the novel *Negerjood in Moederland* (Negro Jew in Motherland), by Surinamese Dutch author Ellen Ombre (2004). I read this novel as an illustration of the set of associations that, as I argue, frequently adhere to black women, no matter what their class background is.[4]

Everyday Narratives of Race and Black Bodies in the Netherlands

NARRATIVE 1: "SUPPOSE SHE BRINGS A BIG NEGRO HOME"
In November 2008, I am watching a very popular Dutch daily TV show in prime time, *De Wereld Draait Door*.[5] The white, male cohost, journalist Martin Bril, is lovingly talking about his two teenage daughters, expressing his expectation that one of these days the oldest one will bring a boyfriend home. To loud laughter and acclaim, he voices his biggest fear: "Suppose she brings a big negro home. . . . "

While I do a double-take at the statement, there is no sign whatsoever, either among the audience in the studio or from the other host at the table, Mathijs van Nieuwkerk, of any inappropriateness in uttering this.[6] I imagine that if someone made a remark about its racism, the response would have been to ridicule and summarily dismiss it and the claimant. In the first instance, I am struck by the way that humor and irony allow Bril to have his cake and eat it too: the—frankly, remote—possibility that he would be called on his racism is skillfully deflected by his humorous presentation. Irony is usually understood as saying one thing but meaning the opposite. In this case, the good listener would immediately understand that Bril cannot possibly mean what he is saying. He means the opposite: It does not matter to him who his daughter brings home. This is a self-flattering reading, which is in line with dominant self-representation: We are not racist. According to Linda Hutcheon (1994) in *Irony's Edge*, irony exists in a fragile equilibrium between the person who utters a statement, the audience who interprets the statement, and the context in which it takes place. In a context in which there is no consensus that "of course we are not racist" Bril's irony does not work for at least part of the audience.

One way to read the situation in a bit more complicated manner is the following. One could argue that the humor arises out of a paradox: The audience is bound by shared images about blacks, images that develop at a very early age.[7] As we will see in chapter 5, children are exposed to derogatory images of Black Pete, the servant of Sinterklaas, the good-hearted bishop who comes to visit yearly, at very young ages, even before they can talk. At the talk show table, everyone seemingly is caught up in the collective denial of the hurtfulness and the damaging nature of those images, as shown by the collective laughter. The fragility of the cultural edifice—sharing negative images about blacks, but simultaneously denying and disavowing them—is shown up when all of a sudden, there is the cheekiness and audacity of the cohost speaking the unmentionable out loud. The fragment shows, in its simplicity, some important aspects of the everydayness of the gendered and racialized construction of sexuality and the sexual construction of race, with the figure of the mythical "big Negro"—and "big" surely does not pertain only to his height here—still largely intact.

Still other readings of this small event are possible. According to a Fanonian reading, what Bril, probably unconsciously, is playing on is "Negrophobia" on the part of white men and women. The phobia associated with blackness consists of sexual anxiety and fear revolving around the image of the overendowed black male who is envisaged as possessing an enormous penis. The white male's simultaneous fear and desire in relation to a sexual potency he can never achieve is for Fanon, following Freud, the inevitable by-product of cultural development (Fanon [1952] 1967; Doane 1991, 216). For both Freud and Fanon, civilization is achieved by the sublimation of sexuality, and since blacks (according to the nineteenth-century revision of the chain of being, where black people were placed closer to the pole of animality and sexuality) freely indulge in sexuality, they not only do not develop neuroses, but they become the canvas on which the civilized white man projects his fears and fantasies.

The episode, finally, also shows how limited and persistent the stock of images, scenarios, relations, and interpretations is, when it comes to representing black men and women. We need to consider the shared racial and sexual fantasies in the Dutch archive, based on four hundred years of colonial relations, to make sense of everyday, casual chains of signification like these.

NARRATIVE 2: "WHY DON'T YOU CALL HER MOTHER?"
Sandrine, a thirty-five-year-old black playwright and mother of two children in Amsterdam, tells the following story:

> My children do not really look like me; they look like their father and are even lighter than him: white, blond, blue eyes. One day, I went to the playground with my four-year-old daughter. She fell off the swing. She was crying and screaming and I rushed forward. Another, white, mother got to Elleke before I did. While I tried to comfort Elleke, the other woman kept trying to push me out of the way. At first I did not pay attention to her or to what she was saying, but all of a sudden it sank in that she was shooing me away, saying, "Why don't you call her mother? Have her mother come here!" I started screaming at her. I could not believe this was happening to me. I was seen as the nanny of my own child, as the domestic worker.[8]

In a similar scenario occurring in the United States, black professor Rhonda Williams (1998, 136), walking in the park with her white lesbian lover's child, was seen by the other white mothers as a nanny, not as the mother of the child. There are many variations to this tale of color differences in a nuclear family and the ways in which they are interpreted in the North American and Dutch archives, which do not show fundamental differences in this respect. A research project I undertook with colleagues shows that, depending on the age of the family members involved and the circumstances, a white father and his adopted daughter of color, or a white mother and her black adopted son, may be mistakenly seen as interracial lovers with an appreciable age difference, which is, of course, more acceptable in the case of the older white man and his Thai daughter than for the white mother with her Colombian son (Wekker et al. 2007, 50–51). There is a different, gendered, valence to the person of color in these configurations: the Thai daughter might easily be taken to be a call girl, semiprostitute, or import bride, while some agency and desire might be ascribed to the son. White women in this configuration, through their positioning at the intersection of age, gender, race, and sexuality, cannot generally claim much respectability. In any case, this research project suggests that the only person who does not get problematized is the white male.

What these various family narratives show is that the dominant regime of truth is that family members should have the same phenotypes, the same skin color. If they do not and the light-skinned or white child is small, the black mother is transformed into a nanny; when the child is an adult, sexuality inexorably enters the picture, and an interracial sexual relationship is constructed. A white child thus supposedly has a white, middle- or upper-class mother, who is working outside the home, and she has for the time being a black woman to look after her. When it comes to young, black children with white mothers, experiential evidence indicates that the dominant script is that the children are assumed to be adopted. It is noteworthy that the cognitive dissonance caused by these multiracial dyads is solved by assigning a dependent, subordinate role to the blacks, both to the children and to the mother: they are adopted and she is hired as a nanny. Thus, agency is granted to whites. In dyads where the blacks are adults, again agency is given to the whites, who, after all, choose to have an exotic lover.

Curiously, knowledge about the intense interracial mixing on which colonial societies like Suriname and the Indies were built, that is, the underlying sexual privileges that enabled white men to often have parallel white and black families (Wekker 2006), did not become part of the cultural archive of white Dutch people. I would conjecture that the self-flattering, white Dutch self cemented only those bodies of knowledge into the archive that were favorable to its own group and disavowed those facts that were unfavorable, that spoke of violence, of forced sexual contacts, and of injustice. What all these family narratives, finally, have in common is a silent, heteronormative contract.

NARRATIVE 3: "INSULTING AN OFFICER ON DUTY"

In October 2004, I got on the subway in my neighborhood, southeast Amsterdam, to go to a meeting, at noon, with the builders of our soon-to-be-finished new apartment. Still talking on my mobile phone with my office, I walked from my home to the subway station and realized there that I had managed to leave my bag at home. So I did not have my public transport pass, but I also did not have money to buy a ticket for the two stops that I needed to travel. I was not too perturbed by the situation, because I knew that chances were relatively slim that I would be stopped on this short journey. On my way out at the station of destination, Ganzenhoef, however, I was stopped by several controllers of the municipal transport system (Gemeentelijk Vervoer Bedrijf [GVB], Municipal Transport Company), who wanted to record my personal data so that I would eventually pay a fine. This took appreciably more time than I could afford, and I made some irritated remarks about the slowness of the process. The GVB officer in charge called in some police officers, who were waiting just outside the station. When they wanted to forcibly move me into a space under the escalator, I resisted the three police officers who were handling me and meanly pinching the flesh of my upper-arms. When they persisted, I called them "fascists." I was then taken in an armored police van to the nearest police station, Bureau Flierbosdreef.

Upon my arrival at the police station, a gendered scenario unfolded, be-cause two men were removed from a cell and I, apparently the only female detainee, was put into it and given a blanket. I had to hand in my shoes, my watch, and my mobile phone. Pretty soon, a police officer came to ask every-one in the holding cells what we wanted to eat: fried rice or fried noodles. I declined, but the offer of food seemed to signify that I was in there for the long haul. All the time, whenever a police officer showed up in the corridor adjoining the cells, I kept protesting against this treatment, adding that I had urgent matters to attend to, but there was no urgency at all in starting the processing. The police treated everyone as if they were jobless anyway, of no account and with nowhere to go. One officer commented with a smirk on his face that they had the right to hold me for six hours without my hav-ing access to a lawyer.

A good while later, a deputy prosecutor came to process my case and told me that I was being detained for "insulting an officer on duty" and that I would have to pay a fine of 220 euros. It was only at this point that I told the officer that I was a university professor and that I had missed an important appointment.[9] I was immediately released—by then it was past four P.M. In the new circumstances, uplifted by class, an officer called my partner, since we were supposed to meet each other at the new apartment at noon. Fate would have it that upon my leaving the police station, the prosecutor gave me an incorrect form instructing me to pay a much smaller fine: only twenty-two euros, which I did. I never heard anything about it again.

I will make three remarks about this scenario. Noteworthy about this deeply humiliating event is, first, that in southeast Amsterdam, 95 percent of the population is black; thus everyone in the subway and everyone in prison was black, while all the officers featured in this story, of the GVB and of the police, were white and overwhelmingly male. The southeast was at the time one of two neighborhoods in Amsterdam where people could be frisked at random for carrying firearms, which, coupled with the disproportionately gendered and racialized division of public labor, makes for an explosive situation in encounters between authorities and citizens. Second, in this narrative, the main theme is not sexualization of me as a black woman, but criminalization: I evidently was seen as a troublesome black woman, badly needing disciplining. No matter what class position I imagined I occupied, in its intersection with race and gender, I was, in the eyes of the white police officers, by definition lower class, jobless, having no urgent matters to attend to, of no significance at all. In this situation, however differently the coconstructing axes of gender, race, and class might have been measured for the police officers and me, as it played out, my assumed class position was trumped by the unearned privileges of their gendered and racialized positionings. Third, for the longest time, I have been reluctant to talk—outside of my inner circle—or write about this experience, out of a misconceived sense of shame that this event would reflect badly on me. I connect my reluctance to W. E. B. Du Bois's (1903) insights about the survival value of "double consciousness" for blacks in any white-dominated society. In particular, it points to the *couleur locale*, the imbrication of each local double consciousness system with locally dominant ways of (not) dealing with race. In the Dutch situation, where there is virtually no oral transmission of knowledge about racism between or within generations of black people, where more or less sophisticated discourses with regard to race and racism are severely lacking, a prominent reaction among blacks (and whites alike) is to deny the seriousness of the racist event, to belittle it, to hold it up to impossible definitional standards, to analyze it to pieces, so that it evaporates into thin air (Essed 1984, 1990). Among Afro-Surinamese people specifically, there is, in addition, an attitude that one should be above discriminatory treatment, that one should somehow have the power, the strength of mind, not to allow others to discriminate against one. This is a somewhat puzzling attitude, which I can only interpret as part of the Afro-Surinamese cultural archive, a gesture of defiance that would place agency in the hands of the enslaved to determine whether the cruel, demeaning behavior of the planter class was internalized. Ironically, this places the burden of survival, of picking up one's pieces, in the here and now with the aggrieved party. We are, thus, dealing in the Netherlands with a situation in which subjects and objects of racism keep each other in a delicate balance and where, until recently, the same evasive discursive repertoires with regard to race were shared. It is a system where both whites and blacks are overwhelmingly invested in denying and disavowing racism.[10] I connect this syndrome, white innocence, to the strong Dutch attachment to a self-image that stresses being a tolerant, small, and just ethical nation, color-blind and free of racism and that foregrounds being a victim rather than a perpetrator of (inter)national violence.

In this section, I have shown three commonly occurring examples of racism, encountered by black men and women in everyday encounters and discourses in the Netherlands: sexualization; relegation to the category of domestic servant, nanny, prostitute, or import bride; general inferiorization; and criminalization. I make no claims about the frequency and the distribution of these events in the myriad microencounters that Dutch society knows on a daily basis, but they do conform to patterns that have been pointed out in the literature (cf. Essed 1990, 232–236; Lubiano 1998; P. Williams 1998, 29–43; R. Williams 1998, 140; Hondius 2014a, 2014b). The racism that blacks encounter on a daily basis is both quiet and vocal, and whites often are ignorant about both varieties. I read these configurations in light of deep-seated patterns in the cultural archive, in which the images preceding blacks systematically depict them as sexually overendowed, as intellectually underendowed, inferior, and as criminals. In the next section, I explore how particular bodies of knowledge pertaining to sexualized racism, but perhaps more importantly the principles conjugating this racial grammar, were deposited and cemented in the cultural archive.

History and Sexualized Racism

In order to get access to this submerged continent, we need to take cognizance of the Dutch cultural imagination, which is based on an archive characterized by strong reflexes to belittle, deny, and erase four hundred years of colonization of its overseas territories, among which South Africa, Indonesia, Suriname, and the Dutch Antilles were its most noteworthy possessions.[11] There have been several efforts, emanating from different circles and at different levels, to open the debate on the nature and the consequences of Dutch colonial history. Thus, for example, six of the issues in the Dutch historical canon can be interpreted as referring to colonialism, slavery, and multiculturalization, yet this history has not been systematically worked through at a national level. Still less have debates and discussions about current Dutch multicultural society been profitably informed by insights about Dutch empire.[12]

The task at hand, the exploration of sexualized racism in the cultural archive, is complicated by two things: first, although the compartmentalization of the discipline of history in metropolitan and colonial counterparts has been overcome in a number of universities, this separation has for a long time precluded bringing the two into one analytical field (Stoler 1995, xi). This means that Dutch national history and colonial history have long been studied in "splendid isolation" from each other (but for noteworthy exceptions see Blakely 1993; Waaldijk and Grever 2004; Van Stipriaan et al. 2007; Legêne 2010; Stuurman 2011), thus making it very difficult to study the genealogy of a dominant, white self-representation in the context of imperialism. Furthermore, the differential material and symbolic weight given to the possession of the East Indies, the jewel in the Dutch crown, is directly correlated with the size and the scope of the bodies of knowledge that were produced pertaining to the colonies in the western part of the empire. Nevertheless there are some promising trajectories, from different disciplines and genres that can be undertaken to get closer to the set task.

In her award-winning novel *Beloved*, Toni Morrison offers a literary reading of what happened to the white self during slavery. She uses psychoanalytic insights as an approach to an ethnography of the white self, describing it in unforgettable images. In the following passage Stamp Paid, a former slave, is describing the world:

White people believed that whatever the manners, under every dark skin was a jungle. Swift unnavigable waters, swinging screaming baboons, sleeping snakes, red gums ready for their sweet white blood. In a way, he thought, they were right. The more colored people spent their strength trying to convince them how gentle they were, how clever and loving, how human, the more they used themselves up to persuade whites of something Negroes believed could not be questioned, the deeper and more tangled the jungle grew inside. But it wasn't the jungle blacks brought with them to this place from the other (livable) place. It was the jungle whitefolks planted in them. And it grew. It spread . . . until it invaded the whites who had made it. Touched them every one. Changed and altered them. Made them bloody, silly, worse than even they wanted to be, so scared were they of the jungle they had made. The screaming baboon lived under their own white skin; the red gums were their own. (1987, 198–99)

What Stamp Paid is illustrating here is that in fixing the other, one fixes oneself as the other of the other (Moglen 1997, 205). While black men and women are struggling to throw off the images that whites have made of them, white men and women are equally bound to and implicated in these representations that stem from their own irrational anxieties and fears. Their own desubjectification and dehumanization is sealed by these images (Moglen 1997, 208). Thus, what I remarked upon earlier in Narrative 3, that is, the balancing act between perpetrators and victims inherent in acts and processes of racism, keeps both parties—when racism remains submerged, not spoken, with either or both parties in denial—fixed. Along similar lines, I illustrated earlier in this chapter how the representations of the sexuality of different groups of women are relational (and hierarchical); they do not stand on their own. Others have addressed what these processes of white self-making under imperialism entailed. Thus, Fanon notes, "In the remotest depth of the European unconscious an inordinately black hollow has been made in which the most immoral impulses, the most shameful desires lie dormant. And as every man [sic!] climbs up towards whiteness and light, the European has tried to repudiate this uncivilized self, which has attempted to defend itself. When European civilization came into contact with the black world, with those savages, everyone agreed: Those Negroes were the principle of evil" ([1952] 1967, 190).

Internalization and splitting, which allows Europeans to maintain an idealized image of themselves (cf. Flax 2010), are the psychoanalytical mechanisms that Fanon refers to. Orlando Patterson has defined slavery as "the permanent, violent domination of natally alienated and generally dishonored persons" (1982, 13). The qualities that define the enslaved are permanence, violence, natal alienation, and dishonor, while the qualities of the master are enshrined in the ultimate godlike power over life and death. It is especially African American female theorists who have taken on gender within this toxic configuration. White masculine domination can only acquire meaning vis-à-vis other men, that is, enslaved men, who as nonpersons before the law cannot defend themselves, nor their wives, children, sisters, or mothers. Enslaved and free black women are the territory over which sexual gratification is reached as well as the further dishonoring of black men (Davis 1981; Carby 1987; Morisson 1992b; Hill Collins 2004).

Zooming in more closely on sexualized racism within the sphere of the Dutch empire, historian and sociologist Rudolf van Lier ([1949] 1977) in his study on the colony of Suriname, *Samenleving in een Grensgebied* (Frontier Society), repeatedly draws attention to the psychological content and the consequences of the system of slavery, with its oppression and dehumanization of the enslaved. He is especially interested, in Toni Morrison's words, in "the dreamer of the dream" (1992, 17), what the system of oppression did to the subject of the racialized discourses constructing blacks as inferior, intellectually backward, lazy, sexually insatiable, and always available, and the white self as superior and full of entitlement. Generally, as in other plantation colonies, van Lier describes colonizers in Suriname as characterized by having "a very tenuous connection to the country, an animus revertendi, a weak tradition, weak social control by law or mores, the secular character of the group, originating from a Christian motherland, the quick social mobility of a few persons, while simultaneously a strong hierarchy was maintained, shadowing the class society overseas" ([1949] 1977, 37).[13]

Characteristics of the Dutch slavery system in Suriname, in comparison with the U.S. system, were, first, colonialism of the exterior versus an internal system; second, the inverted ratio of whites to blacks, with during the eighteenth century in Suriname fifteen blacks to one white, while in the plantation districts this ratio could be as high as sixty-five to one; and third, a Dutch cultural policy that removed the enslaved from whites in physical (except sexual) and linguistic terms: the enslaved in Suriname were not allowed to speak Dutch, but developed their own languages and cultures. After 1775, when a serious economic crisis hit the colony of Suriname, absenteeism among plantation owners rose. The number of white women also declined dramatically, and these white families were replaced by white directors and managers, who preferably were single. It was official company policy of the Society of Suriname, the owners of the colony, that its employees were discouraged from marrying women from the Netherlands.

They were threatened with being dismissed if they expressed such a desire. As in the Indies, where "local women were enlisted to provide the services that allowed civil servants and planters to maintain a European standard of living and were acclimatized to the tropics at little cost" (Stoler 1995, 45), sexual relations between European men and local women were thus encouraged by the colonial state in Suriname, too. Notwithstanding the official prohibitions on "carnal conversations" between white men and black (and Amerindian) women, as recorded in the West Indian *Plakkaatboeken* (Placard books) (Schiltkamp and de Smidt 1973),[14] these men had free sexual access to enslaved and freed black women, and it did not really matter whether it was against or according to the latters' will, and the widespread institution of so-called Surinamese marriage, concubinage arrangements of various kinds, blossomed. No wonder that van Lier describes this frontier society and the interaction among its inhabitants, after 1775, as typically male and controlled by men: an extremely individualist, hierarchical, race- and gender-inflected society.

Among the striking psychological traits of the colonizers that van Lier ([1949] 1977, 38, 39) mentions are, from the colonizers' youth on, an unlimited hubris, pride, an extravagant feeling of self-worth, an excessive fear of the "multitude of slaves," coupled with cruelty toward them and a loss of respect for the value of human life. John Gabriel Stedman, the Scottish mercenary who went to Suriname (1772–1777) to defeat the Maroons, runaway slaves, and who became immortal through his relationship with the enslaved girl Joanna, tells a story that he witnessed himself. In front of a guest on a plantation, the ten-year-old son of the planter hit an older enslaved woman in the face, because she had touched his powdered hair when serving at the table. When the guest expressed his dismay and astonishment about this behavior, the father said with a smile that the child would not bother the guest much longer because he would leave by boat the next day for Holland, to further his education (Stedman 1974). I have never forgotten this story, since I first read it in 1984, because of the contradiction between this treatment and the deference on the basis of age that the older woman must probably have enjoyed in her own community. Van Lier speaks of a universe in which sadism on the part of the masters and masochism among the slaves—which is not very strongly supported by evidence—kept each other in balance. The system of slavery was an environment that was conducive to the emergence of psychopathological personalities. Even in normal personalities it led to psychopathology (Van Lier [1949] 1977, 45).

A second, encompassing and fruitful perspective is offered by those post- and decolonial scholars who indeed place metropole and colony in one analytical field and who understand the emergence of the nineteenth-century metropolitan bourgeois self as a racialized self: "race became the organizing grammar of an imperial order in which modernity, the civilizing mission and the 'measure of man' were framed" (Stoler 1995, 27). Thus, race is a constituting presence not only in the colonies, but also principally in the metropole, where all kinds of class, national, and sexual differences are thought of in terms of race, as I lay out in detail in chapter 3, when I try to understand five white women who claimed in 1917 that they had Hottentot nymphae, the term used at the time for the enlarged labia minora ascribed to black women. Postcolonial insights lead scholars to ask a different set of questions: How would it be possible to think of the white self under slavery, that system of madness, that pathological psychic and libidinal economy, instilled and set in motion in personality structures at very young ages, as containable and quarantinable to the geophysics of the colonies? Globalization, the travel of people, ideas, images, and personalities, was the order of the day as much in the sixteenth century as it is today, with other forms and intensities. The Netherlands was a diasporic space (Brah 1996) from the early days of imperialism, when the cultural archive of the Dutch was filled, from various sites, with images in which blackness was suffused with sexuality. Knowledge of the other got transmitted to the metropole by travel and narratives of imperial citizens in the colonies; by photography and racial images on all kinds of colonial products, soap, cocoa, coffee, sugar; by the world exhibitions of "savages" in which a sexualized other and an asexual self could be constructed (Nederveen Pieterse 1990, 188–210; Moore and Wekker 2011, 249–50). At the same time—and this is habitually overlooked in traditional approaches to historical knowledge production—these knowledges found fertile and looping ground in the metropole, where ideas about a healthy, vigorous, bourgeois body, full of self-mastery and self-control, were already predicated upon racialized, sexualized other bodies. One of Stoler's main points is that the ever-threatened, anxious superiority of the white self needed to be stabilized, that anxious white identity needed to be strengthened incessantly, and this is connected to the excessive physical and psychic violence perpetrated against blacks (Stoler 1995). This volatile concoction of putting the self in a superior position, a position reinforced by the sexualization of the other (among other strategies) is still at the heart of Dutch racism. At the same time, it is the least acknowledged dimension.

While there is a widespread self-flattering understanding that insists that the Netherlands is naturally and historically nonracist, some of the most immediate expressions of racism are overlooked. Images of black—in the sense of African-Diasporic—bodies, male and female, are daily, automatically, and immediately aligned with sexuality. In the next section, which presents an analysis of the novel *Negerjood in Moederland*, I discuss a case in which a black female protagonist is sexualized and criminalized, but also how, in this representation, racialized, sexualized discourses strongly determine the intimate relationships between marriage partners, and, finally, how they play a role in white male bonding.

Negerjood in Moederland (Negro Jew in Motherland)

In *Negerjood*, Surinamese Dutch author Ellen Ombre (2004) tells the story of the Surinamese Dankerlui family, which has migrated to the Netherlands in the early 1960s, consisting of an Afro-Surinamese father, Jewish mother, their son Richenel—who is largely an absent presence—and daughter Hannah, who is twelve years old when they settle in Amstelveen, one of the posh suburbs of Amsterdam. It is significant that the family chooses to settle in this suburb, an unusual one for Surinamese families and indicative of their aspirations to a better life than they actually get. The father is a public servant who, although the specifics never become entirely clear, has lost appreciable status in the professional sphere by migrating to the Netherlands and as a consequence is treated as a second-class citizen by his wife at home. His hobby is to collect books in secondhand bookstores, but his wife does not allow him to keep them in the house, condemning him to a life in the cellar, where he spends his leisure time reading and smoking. The mother is a complaining, unhappy, domineering housewife, eager to see her daughter married at the youngest possible age, so that she does not get pregnant first. Hannah depicts herself as her father's daughter, eager to learn and ambitious, while she shares a keen interest in Jewish matters with her mother. When she is fourteen, she starts working in a Jewish home for the elderly in Amsterdam, becomes a member of a Jewish youth club, and starts to frequent the American Hotel, home to bohemians, intellectuals, and rebels. It is here that she meets a white Jewish anthropology student, Chaim, who starts courting her, even though she is thirteen years younger. The narrative jumps back and forth in time and chronicles, with Hannah as the focus, her coming of age, her marriage to and breakup with Chaim, who eventually becomes a professor of anthropology.

This rather transparent roman à clef is the portrait of an upper-class mixed marriage of a black woman and a white man not unlike that of Ombre herself. It brilliantly shows this marriage's wear and tear, inflected by race politics, over the years. Especially noteworthy in the framework of sexualized racism is a scene in which Hannah and Chaim, after seeing the movie *Apocalypse Now*, walk on the Rembrandtplein, arms about each other's shoulders. Suddenly a police van grinds to a halt and Hannah is addressed by two policemen:

> "You, get in, yes, you!" They roughly took ahold of her, one on each side.
> "Why, what is the matter?" she asked, alarmed.
> "Shut up! Get in!"
> She was pushed into the bus. She resisted. A third policeman who was sitting in front, next to the driver, came to his colleagues' help. The arrest caused a crowd to gather.
> "Serves her right. Let them go whore around in the Red Light district," somebody shouted. "The city is going to the dogs."
> "She is my wife," Chaim shouted, bewildered.
> "I bet," one of the officers responded. "That's what they all say." (Ombre 2004, 114, my translation)

In the nightmare that follows, Chaim has to wait outside the van. He beseeches Hannah not to put up any resistance, because they will knock all her teeth out of her mouth. In this moment of crisis, he seems to think first and foremost of her beauty that should not be destroyed, while Hannah is interrogated in the van. When Hannah mentions her profession as a community worker, the feverish enthusiasm of the policemen to arrest her dissipates and she is released, after a threat not to show her face in that neighborhood any more. Once they are home, Chaim calls the police, although he thinks that Hannah should get over it. After all, the square where the incident took place has become a meeting place of prostitutes, who are addicted to heroin, and of course when the policemen saw a black woman. . . . The next day, at Chaim's insistence, the two policemen come to the house to apologize.

I will make two remarks about this vignette. First, it is important to keep in mind that this is a narrative, a representation of a mixed marriage by the author. Her literary imagination induces her to make particular choices and not others, to represent a woman like herself, a man like her former husband, and the micropolitics of a mixed marriage in particular ways. In this light, it is striking how the themes of sexualization and criminalization return in this narrative, just as criminalization was a major theme in Narrative 3 that I cited above. Essed (1984, 1990) has noted that the experience of many black women in the Netherlands is that they are seen as prostitutes. In this passage—until she mentions her profession—again, it does not matter at all to which class Hannah belongs. In combination with the location and her white male companion, the policemen perceive her as a sex worker. Chaim's presence signifies and heightens Hannah's being read as a prostitute. Class dissipates in view of the combined package of her gender/race and her sexualization/criminalization. We recognize how class falls out of the picture when white officers are arresting blacks. It is only in the last sequence, when, through the intervention of Chaim, the policemen come to apologize, that her class status is acknowledged. For many white people, there is an automatic equivalence between being black and being lower class; these two axes of signification are closely related, quasi-identical. Retaining the connection between whiteness and class superiority, that is, securing white superiority, requires automatically assigning blacks to lower-class status. In the anxious white mind, which is operating according to the nineteenth-century racist logic that black people are closer to the body/sexuality on a scale ranging from body/sexuality to mind/rationality, and on the basis of projection, one of the sure ways to accomplish white superiority is to keep the chain of associations between lower-class status, blackness, and sexuality, which for women comes together in the figure of the prostitute and for men, as we saw in Narrative 1, in being overendowed, in place. Thus, it is understandable that this complex figuration shows itself both in real life and in literary artifacts.

Second, it is striking that Chaim is represented as essentially understanding the policemen and thinking that they acted correctly. At the very least, he thinks that it wasn't a big deal. This is all the more noteworthy since Chaim is both a professor of social sciences and Jewish and, on both counts, the reader suspects that he knows about processes of exclusion. The narrator thus suggests that knowledge of racism and the experience of belonging to a threatened group are no guarantees for understanding everyday racism, much less for antiracist action. It is worth contemplating whether the narrator wants us to understand that Chaim's way of coping with this intolerable situation is to distance himself psychically from Hannah and, in order to be considered as one of the good old white boys, to deny the racism. Thus, it can be concluded that a form of white male bonding on the basis of sexualized racism is being represented here and that even one's closest kin can go along with that strategy to secure their own safety. The operative mechanism is that someone who in one or more major respects deviates from the normative, unmarked position is invited to go along with the dominant discourse that proclaims egalitarianism, that is, to deny the racism, sexism, or homophobia present, even though he or she might be targeted. In *Terrorist Assemblages*, Jasbir Puar explains how this works for affluent white gay men, who, in exchange for acceptance by dominant, heterosexual society, are encouraged to embrace an Islamophobic discourse. The fact that, in the Netherlands too, a poll of the readers of *Gaykrant*, the largest (mainly white) gay magazine, resulted in the choice for the rising, extreme-right, racist PVV as the most popular party, calls for a similar analysis.[15] Later, during the elections of 2010, white gays indeed overwhelmingly voted for this party. I analyze the simultaneous disgust with and sexual attraction to young Muslim men in chapter 4, focusing on Pim Fortuyn, the flamboyantly gay politician who was on the verge of becoming prime minister when he was murdered on May 6, 2002.

Conclusion

My analysis has only just started to scratch the surface of this enormous terrain that has lain fallow for such a long period. Disconcertingly, the difficulty was not lack of pertinent material, but its abundance. We are confronted with the tenacity of forces that have shaped dominant white self-representation over a long period of four hundred years of imperialism. Projection, denial, and disavowal with regard to race are the main mechanisms driving that self, while sexualization, criminalization, and relegation of black women (and men) to an inferior, dependent status are the main images that are available. The connection with sexuality is made, no matter what the class background of black women (and men). Some of the mechanisms that bell hooks, Toni Morrison, and other black American authors have described for the representation of black women in the United States are also operative in the Netherlands. Yet there is also a specificity to Dutch racism, which includes the Dutch inability so far to seriously work through and come to terms with the Dutch colonial past, its strong attachment to a self-image that stresses being an innocent and just, small ethical nation, being a victim rather than a perpetrator of violence; the lack of strong emancipatory, antiracist movements, which I connect to the specific nature of black Dutch double consciousness; the Dutch fascination with the black female body and a specific kind of Dutch whiteness, which establishes itself by rekindling ancient and derogatory images of blacks. Notwithstanding most reasonable claims to equal treatment by blacks, this variety of whiteness persists in imagining itself as either always already non-racist or finds an exquisite and unabashed enjoyment in holding on to its white privilege.

We need to work at making an inventory of the stock of images, scenarios, and scripts involving black women (and men), and to see to it that the sexualized chains of association are no longer circulating.

CHAPTER 2

The House That Race Built

I have never lived, nor have any of us, in a world
in which race did not matter. Such a world, free of
racial hierarchy, is usually imagined or described as
dreamscape—Edenesque, utopian, so remote are the
possibilities of its achievement. . . . How to be both free
and situated: how to convert a racist house into a race-
specific yet nonracist home. How to enunciate
race while depriving it of its lethal cling?

Toni Morrison, "Home"

Government and the academy, the two sites where I have worked for the past three decades,[1] are important locations where knowledge and meanings about different social groups are produced, more specifically where discourses with regard to gender and race/ethnicity are articulated and disseminated into the public sphere. In this chapter I am interested in the silent and seemingly innocuous discursive patterns at the background of and simultaneously at the heart of these bureaucratic organizations, which both, among many other issues, direct their attention at women and blacks, migrants and refugees.[2] These silent patterns express a number of commonalities, based on race in both sites, which are too stark not to be part of a strong and systematic configuration that, as I argue, is part of the cultural archive. These patterns are based on commonsense thought about race, and they are expressive of the way that race is done in the Netherlands, even in enlightened circles. Race in my understanding is not only a matter of ideology, beliefs, and statements about a particular group of people; race also becomes transparent in practices, in the way things are organized and done.

I do not focus very much on the content of emancipation policy or knowledge production with regard to women and blacks, migrants and refugees per se, over the past three decades and the ways they have evolved; only necessarily so. I am more interested in the understudied, taken-for-granted, hidden discursive and organizational principles, which, however much change of different natures has occurred in the two sites under scrutiny, have remained frozen, immobile, invisible, and thus not discussed. These principles or patterns are so common that—with the exception of an article by Essed and Nimako (2006)—in none of the prolific literature on women's or ethnic minority policy have I ever seen a discussion or even a mention of the toxic substructures upholding the worlds of policy making and academic knowledge production.

This chapter is a critical race theoretical enquiry into "the house that race built" (Lubiano 1998) in the Netherlands. Race critical theory "exposes how taken for granted claims of race neutrality, color blindness and the discourse of tolerance often hide from view the 'hidden, invisible, forms of racist expressions and well-established patterns of racist exclusion'" (Essed and Nimako 2006, 282). The chapter consists of three parts: I first sketch how the policy interest in women and in ethnic minorities was organized on the governmental level, as it was operative from the early 1980s, when I started working for the Ministry of Well-Being, Health, and Culture, until now. Although many changes took place in the course of time, practically at every change of government, it is not my ambition to follow each of these changes blow by blow. In the second part, I look at knowledge production about women and ethnic minorities in the sphere of the academy. I briefly highlight the current organizational state of affairs in both domains, in the middle of the second decade of the twenty-first century. Third, I zoom in on the discipline of women's/gender studies and explore how it has handled the diversity of axes of signification—such as race/ethnicity, class, sexuality, and religion—that, under the ever-increasing prominence of the theoretical school of intersectionality, have become inevitable and pressing subject matter.[3] Whereas the government and the academy at large could afford to overlook and dismiss the cogency of intersectionality, that was not possible for gender studies, which, after the largely unresolved battles around the status of race in the discipline in the 1970s and 1980s, had to find a way to come to terms with race/ethnicity and other axes, not as an afterthought but as a central ingredient of its mission. Within gender studies, intersectionality is widely considered the most important theoretical and methodological innovation and development in the discipline (McCall 2005; Davis 2008). I want to explore a general ethos of avoidance, fear, and displacement around the axis of race/ethnicity in Dutch women's studies, which is made up largely of white women. Because they are potential allies, I want to delve deeper into what this avoidance and anxiety consist of, how it manifests, and what could be the reasons for its hold on women's studies practitioners. Whereas in chapter 5, when I describe and analyze the reactions of people who love and defend the racist figuration of Zwarte Piet/ Black Pete, we will see an overriding affective economy of anger, aggression, being under siege, and strong feelings of loss, here among potential allies, fear and avoidance of the axis of race/ethnicity are dominant. How do these various affects relate and what does all of this mean for race as a guiding organizational principle cemented into the cultural archive? This excavation is necessary, for if this attitude of anxiety and avoidance is so widespread among potential allies, then how much more difficult will it be to take cognizance of race for others, in the academy, in government but also in society at large, who are not as deeply and consciously motivated by an antiracist ethos? This chapter should result in insights in the silent work that race does in the public sphere, but I hope that it will also offer tools to break through the impasses that we are stuck in with regard to race in women's/ gender studies and beyond. This exercise may also have significance beyond the Netherlands, for other European gender studies departments, where race often also is conspicuously absent, despite the usual mantra that a dedication to intersectionality calls up.[4]

Starting Out

At the end of 1981, I was a fresh graduate in anthropology from the University of Amsterdam. As was usual in those days with rather depressing labor market prospects, I had taken my time to finish my studies by engaging in antiracist feminist activism. Even before I graduated, I applied for and landed my first serious full-time job as a public servant, working for the Ministry of what was then termed WVC, Well-Being, Health, and Culture, in The Hague.[5] I was one of the representatives of the ministry in the field of ethnic minority policy, as it was then called, in the province of South Holland, and my job consisted of advising the ministry, the province, local municipalities, and organizations of ethnic minorities, the so-called self-organizations, on that policy. My job also included establishing and maintaining contacts with budding Turkish, Moroccan, Surinamese, Antillean, Moluccan, and other minority women's self-organizations.[6] From my office on Raamweg, a stately street in the center of The Hague, I traveled to the ministry in Rijswijk, a suburb of The Hague where the headquarters were, to report on how ethnic minority policy worked out in the field, which parts of the policy were effective, and where tensions arose and changes were needed. This was the time when it was finally acknowledged by the government that the majority of colonial and labor migrants from the circum-Mediterranean area, who had come to the Netherlands as guest laborers from the end of the 1950s/ early 1960s, would not go back to their countries of origin and that a longer-term policy was needed. Another immediate antecedent of the rise of ethnic minority policy in government was the armed actions and hijackings of young Moluccans in 1975 and 1977 (Essed and Nimako 2006; Nimako 2012). They protested against the predicament of their parents; their fathers had been soldiers in the Dutch colonial army in the East Indies. Fighting against independence for Indonesia, they faced an untenable situation and had been demobilized in the Netherlands. After thirty years in the Netherlands, mostly living in secluded, temporary camps, this group was still waiting for repatriation to their original islands, as had been promised to them, and wanted the Dutch government to intervene on their behalf with the Indonesian authorities. Eight young Moluccans hijacked a train in the north of the country, and this action was forcibly put down by Dutch marines, killing two train passengers and six Moluccan youths.[7] This event was followed by the establishment of the bureaucratic apparatus for ethnic minority affairs, initially in the Ministry of Home Affairs, which led to the first policy paper for ethnic minorities, which came out in 1983.

The first draft of the policy paper, the governmental Draft Policy Paper on Ethnic Minorities (1981) was conceived and circulated internally in the ministry and externally among municipalities and sociocultural organizations, for comment. The aim of the policy was formulated as "the development of a society in which the members of minority groups who live in the Netherlands will, separately and as a group, have a commensurate position and fully fledged chances for development" (1981, 35). This main aim was subdivided into three focal points: (1) creating conditions for emancipation and participation of minority groups in society, (2) lessening of the social and economic backwardness of members of ethnic minority groups, and (3) preventing and battling against discrimination and—where necessary—improving the legal position of these groups. A strange amalgam of groups had been brought together as targets of the policy paper: besides the usual suspects, Surinamese, Antilleans, Turks, Moroccans, southern Europeans, and Moluccans, also people permanently dwelling in mobile homes (*woonwagenbewoners*) and Roma had been rounded up, "for practical reasons," as the Conservative Democratic (VVD) minister Rietkerk phrased it.

I imagine that my colleagues who recruited me had foreseen that they would in the near future need expertise on multiculturalism that they were lacking, since ethnic minority policy was such a new field. Freshly hired and fired up, I was asked to write the commentary on the draft policy paper of behalf of the South Holland office. With no strategic experience, I took no prisoners and fired away at the underlying assumptions, the questionable notion of "backwardness" (*achterstand*) instead of "deprivileging" (*achterstelling*), which I preferred, the lack of transparency between aims and measures proposed and the one-sidedness of the policy paper, in which it was very clear which part of the population was supposed to do the adjusting and the integrating and which part was the norm: That is, I paid attention especially to how power differentials between outsiders and established were constructed. It was only years later that I learned that my colleagues at the Bureau South Holland were aghast and scandalized at the radical nature of my commentary. With the benefit of hindsight, in the current climate of supposedly failed multiculturalism and in light of the increasingly punitive and constricting content and tone of national ethnic minority policy over the next thirty years, I am surprised at how generous the initial policy papers actually were.

The infrastructure of the Ministry of Well-Being, Health, and Culture, where ethnic minority policy was located at the time, with its branches in every province as its eyes and the ears in the field, has vanished now, due to a succession of cutbacks, and along with the many name changes of the ministry itself, the location and the content of ethnic minority policy have also changed fundamentally. Currently, since 2012 and the coming into office of the Cabinet Rutte-II, a coalition between Conservative Democrats (VVD) and the Labor Party (PvdA), the policy is organizationally located at the Ministry of Social Affairs and Labor,[8] under Labor Minister Asscher (PvdA). Over the years, the policy has been termed "migrant policy," "policy for the allochthonous" (those who are not from here), and finally "integration policy." Although the content of the policy, its continuities, and changes are not the subject of this chapter (see Roggeband and Verloo 2007; Roggeband 2010; Bouras 2012; Ham and van der Meer 2012), I do want to broadly point out some striking shifts that have taken place in the past thirty years. In the first place, the earlier aims of "commensurate participation in society" and later "integration, while holding on to one's own identity" have given way to an emphasis on participation and to putting boundaries in place for youths from ethnic minority groups and educating them and, importantly, to the central insight "that for successful integration it is necessary that we can build on a foundation of *shared values*. Migrants should not only know the key values of Dutch society, but should also *internalize them*" (Ministerie van Sociale Zaken en Werkgelegenheid 2013).[9] These values involve, among other matters, the acceptance of homosexuality and the equality of women, and ending forced marriage.[10] The—in hindsight—generous and liberatory ethos of the early years has given way to a much meaner and leaner disciplinary regime. In general, the earlier focus on socioeconomic issues, such as employment, education, housing, and political participation, has shifted to a preoccupation with the unassimilability of the different and backward cultures of migrants, with a narrowing down of the earlier, broader allochthonous groups to a focus on Turks, Moroccans, and Antillean young men. The culturally inferior other has increasingly come to be embodied by Muslim men and women, while Surinamese and southern Europeans, the latter having returned in large numbers to their countries of origin, have—inch by painful inch—worked their way out of the category of allochthonous people.

Second and simultaneously, two important movements have taken place: from the late 1990s on, a decentralization of national ethnic minority policy to the municipal level, which is closer to the ground where the target groups of the policy actually live, was initiated. Moreover, earlier responsibilities that the state assumed in facilitating the emancipation of ethnic minorities have dwindled and it is now their own, individual responsibility to integrate, which is underlined and punctuated by an integration exam that is almost impossible to pass, even for native Dutch, which tests one's competency in Dutch language and cultural mores. The earlier emphasis on holding on to one's own cultural identity, which was facilitated by subsidies for self-organizations and cultural activities and which was seen as a fruitful take-off point for participation in society, has changed into an undiluted policy preference for assimilation. In a marked turn, a strong cultural identity is now seen as the cause of the lack of integration of ethnic minorities.

Third, while lip service is being paid to everyone having the same chances and opportunities in Dutch society, no substantial measures are taken against discrimination and racism. Again and again for the past twenty years, the Netherlands has been chastised by international human rights bodies, such as the European Commission against Racism and Intolerance (ECRI 2013), for its casual practice of racism.[11] Politicians of different hues, asked for comment on this sorry state of affairs, cannot be bothered and wave it away lightheartedly.

VIGNETTE 1: "I AM NOT THE CLOAKROOM ATTENDANT"
Among the many noteworthy experiences I gained at the Ministry of Well-Being, Health, and Culture, I want to share one particular event, which besides showing a daily instance of everyday gendered racism also serves as an introduction to the analysis of the policy fields—the emancipation of women and that of ethnic minorities—that I want to discuss in this section.

In 1982 there is a meeting of a broad working group, consisting of officials of the province, several municipalities, and volunteers and staff of social work organizations about the cutbacks in social work, somewhere in South Holland. All in all, about thirty people are present, almost all white, predominantly male. They are standing together, talking in small groups, before the meeting starts. The center municipality has called the meeting and sounds the alarm: All of the municipalities are feeling the effects of the cutbacks of the past years in toddler care, in after-school activities for youngsters, in the care for troubled youths, in language and schooling work, in women's work, and in care for the elderly. A black woman enters, hangs up her coat on the pegs on the wall, walks toward one of the groups, and extends her hand to one of the men standing closest to her. He bends over the chair where he has just hung his jacket, takes it, and hands it to her. The moment seems frozen in time. Then she says, "I am not working in the cloakroom. I am the representative of the Ministry of Well-Being, Health, and Culture and my name is Gloria Wekker." The white man is no longer white; fiery-red tongues of embarrassment leak from his head (Wekker 1998).

This event, one of those countless, painful moments when one clashes with a dominant, gendered, and racialized chain of associations and its concomitant social expectations, serves as a take-off point for my analysis of the work that race does in the public sphere. Rather than, as I did in this vignette, focusing on the (inter)personal sphere, I want to investigate the institutional level; that is, I am interested in the silent and taken-for-granted discursive patterns that are behind the conceptualization and organization of the object of attention—women and ethnic minorities—in public policy and in the academy.[12] One noteworthy feature is that, in the framework of emancipation policies, the state engages women and ethnic minorities not as individuals but as collectively organized groups, who through their organizations interface with the state (Roggeband 2010). This again is related to the history of pillarization, a sociopolitical structure dating from the beginning of the twentieth century, in which conflicts between native religious and political groups—Protestants, Catholics, socialists, and humanists—were managed and contained (Koopmans 2003). When I was growing up in the 1950s, pillarization meant that we went to Catholic schools and listened to Catholic radio programs, while my parents read a Catholic newspaper and voted for a Catholic political party, and social work also was organized along denominational lines. Although my siblings and I were abused and called *bruine poepchinezen* (brown poop Chinese) during my primary school years,[13] interestingly, since denomination was the overriding trait by which people were defined, after school the main battle was with Protestant children of the nearby school in Amsterdam West, who were embroiled in parallel organizational structures. My brothers and one of my sisters would regularly come home battle scarred, but it was first because we were Catholic, and secondarily because we were racially marked.

This pillarization model has, although it has waned in importance since the end of the 1960s, also become a blueprint to deal with ethnic minorities: ethnic groups could request the government to help them in establishing their own sociocultural organizations, churches, schools, and media.

As a welfare state, the Netherlands has, since the 1970s, given much attention, first to the situation of ethnic minorities (1970) and subsequently to that of women (1976),[14] which has demanded an organizational structure in which that attention could materialize: policy making and implementation, the development of subsidizing instruments, monitoring of developments, and the production of statistical data all need to take place within that framework. Along comparable lines, an organizational structure for the interest in women and ethnic minorities needed to take shape within the academy. As has been remarked by some authors (Essed and Nimako 2006; Nimako 2012), government and the academy are not two separate, watertight spheres of public interest; on the contrary, there is a lot of traffic in ideas, government-sponsored research executed by academics, overlap in personnel on advisory boards, civil servants becoming researchers and professors, and vice versa between the two. This is especially marked in the case of ethnic minority affairs, but it is also true in the sphere of women's emancipation. In fact, in both spheres, virtually all research is funded directly or indirectly—through funding agencies like NWO and KNAW[15]—by the government. In general, it is not too much of a stretch to say that research about ethnic minorities (Nimako 2012) follows governmental policy. This is a highly deplorable, claustrophobic, and interdependent situation, where one again and again meets the same people, sometimes in the role of advisor in allocating research funds, who the next time is in the position of the research applicant. This is a more or less closed circuit, in which it is hard to get independent, innovative research plans approved and funded. I am arguing that the pillarization model, important as it is in streamlining the relationships between the government and specific ethnic minority groups, is preceded by and builds on a deeper structure, that is, the cultural archive in which long-standing ideas about and practices with regard to race are always already assigning differential meanings to different people.

The Governmental Organization
of Attention for Women and for Ethnic Minorities

I want to illustrate how race operates in a policy context through an imaginary case study involving women. Suppose a relative outsider is interested in starting a project to improve the economic situation of all women in the Netherlands and she would like to have governmental support for her activities, in the form of advice and possibly a subsidy, to accomplish this. Until a few years ago, before the huge cutbacks in government spending set in, this would not have been considered a preposterous desire at all, and chances were that she would get such support, like other national women's organizations such as Atria, the National Women's Council NVR and Women Inc.[16] Hers would not be a superfluous project, since only about 40 percent of women are economically independent from their partner and the dominant division of labor is the so-called 1.5 model, where one partner, often the male, works full time (1.0) and the woman part time (0.5) (Roggeband and Verloo 2010). The first information this person would need is in which part of the governmental infrastructure she would find appropriate interlocutors. Counterintuitively, this interest in women generically is not situated in one location, since women's issues are spread over three different ministries. After some searching, it will become apparent that the organization of the knowledge about and the attention for the category of women is split at the root. While the Directorate for the Coordination of Emancipation Affairs, currently located in the ministry of Education, Culture, and Science,[17] is nominally concerned with women generically, in reality it is white women who silently occupy a privileged and colonizing position here. There are numerous illustrations of this practice: I have heard several public servants, over time, say to me in meetings that this directorate is concerned with gender and not with ethnicity, and that I should be addressing my concerns about women of color to another directorate, the Directorate for the Coordination of Minority Affairs. In this seemingly innocent remark, which is always delivered in a manner that bespeaks white innocence, several instances of epistemic violence (Spivak 1987) are encapsulated: In the first place, it is conveyed to the outsider that gender is taken to be an absolutely separate axis from race/ethnicity. "Here, we deal with gender (meaning women), over there is ethnicity (meaning folks of color), so do not speak to us about women of color" is the clear message.

This means, second, that the gendered position of white women is seen as race free; whiteness is not seen as an ethnic positioning at all. It is seen as *gewoon* (ordinary), as nothingness. In other terms, this stance was confirmed during a public lecture, the George Mosse Lecture, on October 1, 2013, given by the minister responsible for women's (and, increasingly, men's) emancipation, Dr. Jet Bussemaker, when she said, "Equality (between men and women) trumps diversity."[18] I return to this statement and what it means in chapter 4.

And third, looking at the last policy paper of this minister to parliament, on May 10, 2013, in which she unfolds her plans for the period 2013–2016, I am confirmed in my assessment that the directorate and the ministry narrowly conceive of their task as only pertaining to race-evacuated gender.[19] The general aim of emancipation policy is that "the government strives toward a pluriform society, in which everyone, irrespective of gender or sexual identity, can shape his/ her life" (Ministerie van OCW, 2013, 4). Since 1985, equality, independence, freedom of choice, and responsibility have been central in emancipation policy, while for the period 2013–2016 four focal points have been designated: (1) economic participation in light of the economic crisis; (2) social safety of girls, women, and LGBTs; (3) the differences between boys and girls (are girls successful or do boys have a problem?); and (4) international polarization, which is about the defense and propagation of women's and LGBT rights abroad (Ministerie van OCW, 2013, 7–9). Promising as all of this may sound for everyone, in practice the implicit subject of the paper remains white girls and boys, women and men. This is so because blacks, migrants, and refugees are explicitly named and specific measures mentioned in only five instances.[20] Several feminists have pointed to a significant shift in emancipation policy, whereby migrant women, especially Turkish and Moroccan women, have become the focal point of emancipation policy in recent years (Roggeband and Verloo 2007; Bijleveld and Mans 2009), where they are invariably connected to problematical issues such as sexual violence, unemployment, and lack of economic independence. I agree with that assessment insofar as especially migrant women have discursively been positioned as intensely problematical and lagging in their emancipation, but not, as I have shown, insofar as they would have become the central subject of that policy.

Fourth, and importantly, the discourse in which gender and race/ ethnicity are firmly dissociated is an important way of doing race. In other words, by considering women as a race-free category, race accrues only to black, migrant, and refugee women. This phenomenon is also evident in the quite common practice that when the directorate introduces a new policy paper on emancipation, which is often prepared with the help of women's studies practitioners and which invariably takes only gender as its theoretical starting point, several meetings are called to consult "the field," that is, white women's organizations, about its intentions. Then, almost as an afterthought, a final meeting is called for allochthonous experts on the same subject matter (Wekker 1996a).[21] This is a perfect illustration of the collusion in the dominant discourse with regard to race between the ministry and the dominant form of gender studies in the Netherlands, whereby it is clear who gets constructed as the norm, the self, and the other.

Let us return to our expert who is truly interested in supporting all women in becoming economically independent. She has now learned that, in order to include black, migrant, and refugee women in her project, she needs to turn to the Directorate for the Coordination of Minority Affairs, which aims at the integration of ethnic minorities and is currently located at the Ministry of Social Affairs and Labor. This directorate is concerned mainly with the integration of men, but also with women from these groups. Thus, Surinamese, Antillean, Turkish, and Moroccan women, and women from other ethnic minority groups, are catered to here. It bears pointing out that the object of concern of the two directorates, Coordination for Emancipation and Coordination of Minority Affairs, is not equal and commensurate; they are in a hierarchical position. This again became abundantly clear when the then minister of emancipation affairs, Christian Democrat de Geus, declared in November 2003 that the emancipation of women was finished and that it was now only allochthonous women (i.e., women coming from elsewhere, black, migrant, and refugee women) who needed to work on their emancipation. This remark indicated that he had an extraordinarily rosy picture of the emancipation of "women." This picture allowed him to disregard the many indicators—whether they concerned women's employment and representation in the higher regions of the labor market, the disparities in income and pensions of men and women, child care facilities, or domestic violence[22]—that point to the still deplorable inequalities in the positions of men and women. In assigning allochthonous women an unemancipated position, two power moves are evident: First, there is a homogenizing of all allochthonous women, not taking into account the widely varying differences between different categories, as far as their labor market position is concerned, for instance, where Surinamese Dutch women have traditionally worked more hours than white Dutch women. Second, the statement installs a naturalized, hierarchical, colonial difference between "women" and allochthonous women. One of the more practical agenda points behind de Geus's statement was the justification to fundamentally cut back on the resources and institutions of the women's movement, evident in the process of decimation and endless fusion of women's organizations that became apparent in the following years.

The third ministry, finally, that the imaginary protagonist of women's economic position will have to access in order to accomplish her goals is the Ministry of Foreign Affairs, the Directorate of International Cooperation, where the interests of Third World women are served. In recent years, a human rights discourse has become leading in this ministry, and it has prioritized its policy focus on equal rights and opportunities for women, and the right to sexual and reproductive health. Additional resources have been pledged for programs to combat violence against women. Earlier priorities such as water management, food security, safety, and the legal order remain in place. The same is true for crosscutting themes like gender, environment, and good governance (Regeer Accoord 2012, 15, 16).

Two major changes that have taken place under the current government, a coalition between Conservative Democrats and Labor, is that foreign trade and development cooperation have become intimately linked under Minister Ploumen of the Labor Party. Much emphasis is given to the initiation of a fund meant to facilitate trade relations of Dutch medium and small companies with businesses in developing countries, while at the same time the budget for development cooperation has been cut to one billion euros until 2017 (Regeer Accoord 2012, 15). These cutbacks became very clear in the summer of 2015, when well-known organizations active in the Third World, such as OXFAM, NOVIB, ICCO and HIVOS, were cut back up to 90 percent of previous subsidies. Whereas previously the Netherlands prided itself on automatically reserving 0.6 percent of the gross national product for development cooperation, that percentage has been rather quickly and silently abandoned, under the onslaught of rightist parties that insist on "our own people first." All of this does not bode well for women or gender issues.

What the initiator of this project has thus learned is that governmental policy attention for women in the Netherlands is divided over three different ministries and three different directorates, whereby race is used as the silent, but meaningful dividing criterion. While "women" (i.e., white women) are the norm, the distance to them decides the location of other women, and they are again subdivided into allochthonous and Third World women. Culturally determined blind spots lead to this hierarchical, colonial division of labor: We are dealing here with a toxic heritage, the epistemic violence of a colonial discourse in which white people have silently and self-evidently assigned themselves a normative and superior position, the teleological axis or endpoint of development, and other women are always already located in relation to them. The "naturalness" and self-evidence of this division of labor in the policy attention for women inexorably reminds me of situations under colonial rule in Suriname, when the differences between various categories of women were constructed and enforced by rules and practices, such as *cordons sanitaires*, enforced areas of white safety, for instance in and around the house, where only a select number of people of color were allowed to come; rules prescribing how white women in particular were to behave socially and sexually, whom they should associate with, and who was absolutely to be shunned, which tasks they should perform and which were beneath them, how much closeness to abject, unclean, matter and people was allowed, and so on, drawing intimately on simultaneous repertoires of gender, race, class, and sexuality (Schiltkamp and de Smidt 1973; Stoler 2002; Wekker 2001b).[23] Likewise, in that universe the construction of enslaved women as capable of the same hard labor as enslaved men, but unlike white women; as always already sexually available, again unlike white women, drew on the same repertoires.

This ordering of women is also highly reminiscent of Johannes Fabian's insights on how anthropology has constructed its others: "The anthropologists are 'here and now,' the objects of their discourse are 'there and then' and the existence of the Other—'the savage,' 'the primitive,' the 'underdeveloped world'—in the same time as ours is regularly denied" (Fabian 1983). The fact that other women are kept "there and then," are locked in other sections of the governmental bureaucracy, is a reflection of deepseated racialized ordering principles.

This silent ordering of people, which is at the same time vehemently denied when it is pointed out—or rather, bad intentions or consequences are denied, since the sorting itself cannot be—is so much part of commonsense thought that it automatically and immediately presents itself in organizational and discursive principles in the Dutch context. Yet the exclusionary consequences of the dissociation of gender and race/ethnicity, the evacuation of whiteness as a racial/ethnic positioning, and the hierarchization of racial/ethnic positionings are far-reaching, felt on a daily basis by members of ethnic minority groups. These ordering principles ultimately confirm again and again who belongs and who does not belong to the Dutch nation. Gender, in its intersection with race/ethnicity, is an important mechanism that determines and orders the opportunities and chances people will have in their lives. In short, dominant views make use of asymmetrical, hierarchical binary categories that enable the dominant gender and the dominant racial group to represent themselves as neutral, nongendered, and nonracialized/ethnicized. That is how issues connected to power are normalized and hidden from view.

I have paid attention to the delineation and location of the category of women in the organizational structure of the government, and its splitting into three different subjects, which are divided over three different ministries. Even though each subcategory of women has migrated to different ministries in the course of the years, the deep, commonsense notion that there should be a split, that they cannot possibly be housed in the same organizational structure, has, as far as I know, never been questioned. I argue that this makes sense on the basis of a cultural archive, in which an imperial and "natural" hierarchy between different women has been firmly installed, with white women at the apex. In its latest incarnation, we are told that the emancipation of white women is complete, in spite of many indicators to the contrary. Black, migrant, and refugee woman are not there yet; they/we still have a long way to go and ought to actively follow the example set by their white sisters (Wekker 1996a), while Third World women are, of course, even further removed from the teleological endpoint of development. Thus, in a strange, dazzling, and neonationalistic turn, the emancipation of women and gays has become the litmus test for modernity (see chapter 4), and those who want to belong have to embrace these values—"Migrants should not only know the key values of Dutch society, but should also internalize them!"—while those who reject this gesture are doomed to be excluded and outsiders. Tradition is ostensibly placed in another time, one that is not contemporaneous with our own (Alexander 2005, 190). I have also dealt with the location of ethnic minorities, men and women, in the Directorate for the Coordination of Minority Affairs of the Ministry of Social Affairs and Labor. Here, men and women are supposedly dealt with on an equal basis, but in practice, based on the unmarkedness of masculinity, it is men who are the norm.

The Organization of Attention
for Women and Ethnic Minorities in the Academy

The same principles based on an imperial cultural archive that are discernible within government are present within the academy, when it comes to knowledge production about women and ethnic minorities. At its inception in the 1970s, the discipline of women's studies was chiefly a maneuver to chart the lives, accomplishments, and thoughts of white women, which were deemed unimportant by traditional scholarship or were described in stereotypical ways. Sex was the key concept of the new discipline, and dominant versions assumed implicitly that masculine ideology was suppressing all women in the same way. Sharing female gender implied that other differences, such as ethnicity and class, were not of vital importance. Later on, with the acceptance of gender as the key concept of the new discipline, and still later with the innovation of intersectional thought, which brought other simultaneous personal, institutional, and symbolic axes of signification into view (Scott 1986; Crenshaw 1989), new, dynamic, and more inclusive conceptualizations of gender were made possible.

The following vignette (Wekker 1996a) lays out a sign of change in the traditional division of labor with regard to women, which occurred when I had just started to work at Utrecht University:

VIGNETTE 2: WOMEN'S STUDIES AND BLACK CRITIQUE
I started working in the Department of Women's Studies in the humanities at Utrecht University in March 1994, and fairly soon I was asked whether I would be interested in teaching a class in the introductory course in women's studies. The course, taken by about five hundred undergraduate students in the humanities and social sciences each year, is meant to get students acquainted with the discipline and offers sessions, given by different teachers, on women's history, film criticism, semiotics, literary criticism, philosophy, and cultural studies. The task that was offered to me was to teach the class on black critique.

In the first instance, I was baffled by so much ethnic innocence. Such a request would have been untenable in the context of the North American universities UCLA and Oberlin, where I had previously taught anthropology and gender studies. I immediately knew that I was home again. The image that presented itself to me was that the caravan of women's studies consisted of the thoughts and theories of white women, while behind that caravan a horde of black creatures was running, who did not agree with that body of thought and was just formulating critique, but did not put forward their own theories, their own constructions of reality. In this worldview, there apparently were no black and Third World feminisms, but moreover such a take on reality was only possible from the situated and privileged universe of a white subject. This simple request caused me great distress about women's studies, making it so clear who the Eurocentric norm was, the silent imaginary subject.

Which course should I chart here? I had hoped that my entry into women's studies would be a bit more tranquil. Should I go along with this and, if so, under which conditions? I was all too aware of the dangers of being held accountable for the "black aspect" as the only black teacher in the department, as an addition, as a variation, as a reaction to the white canon. If I did accept the invitation and if I did not mark the blind, but hierarchizing spot with regard to the dominant race/ethnicity, the women's studies canon could stay as it was, the so-called add black women and stir method. I wished that I could teach about a subject that was also dear to me, such as the construction of female subjectivities. Then I would also inevitably have to confront issues of difference, the simultaneity of gender and race/ethnicity, but in a less central way than would be the case with black critique. On the other hand, this was a unique opportunity to utilize the podium that was offered me to make it clear to students that there are different feminisms and that the dominant form of women's studies, which was presented to them as the only kind, was situated and needed to be complicated. Ultimately I decided to teach the class, with inclusion of all my criticisms on the conceptualization of the course and the thought that supported it. Feminist analyses that take only gender as their key concept do not offer a satisfying starting point to understand complex realities and they are, moreover, the privilege of those who do not personally experience oppression on the basis of race/ethnicity or class (hooks 1984).

Parallel to my findings in the previous section, in the Dutch academy too, there is a division of labor ordering the study of women. When I came back to the Netherlands in 1993 and started working in the Department of Gender Studies at Utrecht University in 1994, it struck me that there were at least three sites where women were being studied, again with race at the basis of the distinction.[24] I was now the imaginary outsider like the one encountered in the previous section, seeking her bearings in an unfamiliar system. While this division of labor was stark in the mid-1990s, some of its sharpest edges have softened, but in principle the same division of labor is still operative: the imaginary subject of each subfield is racially differently conceived.

Thus, white women are the object of study in several women's/gender studies departments, among other places at the universities of Amsterdam, Maastricht, Groningen, Nijmegen, and Utrecht. Black, migrant, and refugee women are mostly studied in departments of ethnic or migration studies, while Third World women find their niche in women and development studies programs. Since there is not much interaction between these three sites of knowledge production, each of them functions in splendid isolation and neither the division of labor nor existing power relations are questioned. Again, we see an automatism in discursive and organizational patterns, whereby it makes utter and silent sense to split the category of women into three racialized subdivisions.

While I return to the way that race/ethnicity is interpellated in a gender studies department in the next section, I now first want to look at the academic spaces where other women are being studied. In order to take cognizance of black, migrant, and refugee women, we need to zoom in on ethnic or migration studies, the core of which is located in three main institutes in the Netherlands: IMES at the University of Amsterdam, ERCOMER at Utrecht University, and ISEO at Erasmus University in Rotterdam (Essed and Nimako 2006).[25] The immediate antecedents of the rise of ethnic studies in the academy were, as I indicated before, the armed actions of young Moluccans in 1975 and 1977. These events were followed by the establishment of the bureaucratic apparatus for ethnic minority affairs within the government and subsequently of the study of ethnic minorities in the academy. The oldest of these institutions is IMES, the successor to the short-lived CRES, Center for Race and Ethnic Studies, 1984–1991 (Essed and Nimako 2006), at the University of Amsterdam, under the directorship of black Briton Chris Mullard, where for a tantalizingly short period critical race studies were engaged with. Currently IMES, along with ERCOMER and ISEO, engages in comparative research in the field of international migration and ethnic relations within a European context.[26] Two characteristics come to the fore in reflecting on the studies done within these institutions.

First, black, migrant, and refugee women have a precarious position here, judging by the number of publications devoted to them or to gender. Just as within ethnic studies gender is not a systematic, critical object of research, race/ethnicity is—with the exception of the work of some particular individuals (e.g., Prins and Saharso 1999; Prins 2004; Ghorashi 2006) and expertise centers—not given the attention it deserves within women's studies. Thus again, we encounter the by-now familiar dissociation of gender from race/ethnicity and the foregrounding of masculinity. Second and strikingly, the concept of ethnicity, which is central in all three institutes, is conceptualized in a dazzlingly narrow way: it is "we" studying "them." Ethnicity refers exclusively to the other, to ethnic minorities; whiteness is not recognized or acknowledged as a racialized/ethnicized positioning and thus as a worthy object of study. The feature that we encounter here, again, is the evacuation of whiteness out of race, which means "mostly (but not always) problematizing ethnic minorities while generally downplaying the influence of racism, the ramifications of the colonial history, and concomitant presuppositions of European (Dutch) civil and cultural superiority" (Essed and Nimako 2006, 285).

Thus, the institutes manufacture a never-ending stream of often government-sponsored studies on the identity and the social, political, educational, and economic integration of ethnic minorities in Dutch society, which Essed and Nimako (2006, 284) refer to as the "Dutch minority research industry," in which people have—until recently—had access to appreciable amounts of research money and which they oppose to "Race Critical Theory." The division of labor between women's studies and ethnic studies in the academy follows lines comparable to the ways tasks are allocated within ministries and it illustrates dominant thought about gender and race/ethnicity in the Netherlands.

Finally, the third category of women, Third World women, are—with few exceptions when they are paid attention to in anthropology or in some departments of women's studies—located in gender studies units at the Agricultural University of Wageningen and the Institute of Social Studies in The Hague. Their funding lifelines are in the Ministry of External Affairs in the Directorate of Foreign Trade and Development Cooperation. The hierarchization of "women," again with white women at the apex, is metaphorically but also really felt in the distance between the three disciplinary fields—women's studies, ethnic studies, and development studies—that do not entertain many contacts or networks. The atypical situations in which practitioners from each of these fields meet would be expert meetings on, for instance, sustainability (cf. Braidotti et al. 1994) or when a feminist star such as Vandana Shiva, Chandra Mohanty, or Joan Scott gives a keynote speech in the Netherlands.

Let me try to sum up what the main racialized characteristics and underpinnings are, based, as I have argued, on an imperial archive in which race plays a vital but unacknowledged role, when one wants to think about women and ethnic minorities in the Netherlands. Dominant thought with regard to gender and race/ethnicity, whether in governmental, academic, media, or other discourses in the Netherlands has the following characteristics: First, gender and race/ethnicity are dissociated. Something either has to do with gender or it has to do with race/ethnicity, not with both at the same time. Second, the concepts of gender and race/ethnicity often are translated into understandings of women and ethnic minorities respectively, thus evacuating the unmarked categories within each concept, that is, men and whites. Moreover, supposedly the categories of women and ethnic minorities have clearly defined boundaries that do not overlap. Anyone giving this subject some thought will realize that this cannot be the case: the category of women contains white, black, migrant, and refugee women, and the category of ethnic minorities contains both women and men. What is going on here? Is this just sloppy thinking?

We could of course call this approach careless or thoughtless, if it were not so systematic in nature. Something else is going on: a seizure of power that includes separate subcoups. Disassociating gender and ethnicity means, in the first place, that the ethnic positioning of white people is made invisible; a white ethnic position is supposedly not important and worthy of mention but is at the same time elevated as the norm. Thus, there are "women" and then, separately, women of color. Belonging to the white ethnic group or to the group of men is the norm that does not have to name itself or analyze itself. That is exactly the way in which power is executed and reproduced. As a second part of this discursive power play, masculinity is elevated to the norm in terms of both gender and race/ethnicity. Both masculinity and whiteness are unmarked categories while being black, migrant, and refugee are marked categories, like femininity. A characteristic of unmarked categories is that they do not have to name themselves; the power position they represent speaks for itself. That is the reason why "women" really refers to white women; when other women appear, the latter are specifically mentioned. On the other hand, often no distinction is made between men and women in the case of ethnic minorities, as a result of which men become the implicit subject and women disappear from view. In both cases the dominant pole of a pair is reinforced and elevated to the norm; in the case of women, a category that consists of different ethnicities, whiteness is dominant; in the case of ethnic minorities, a category that consists of different genders, masculinity is the norm. Another way of putting this is that gender relates as much to men as race/ethnicity does to white people, but this intersectional insight is not part of dominant thought. Therefore, we are not talking about carelessness or sloppy or lazy thinking here, but about the effects of power.

The Different Axes of Signification in Women's/Gender Studies

While sex and later gender was its initial object of interest, increasingly women's studies has had to engage with the other axes of signification, such as class and sexuality, but especially with race/ethnicity. The desire to consider gender as always already coconstructive with race was, in a Dutch context, put on the feminist agenda by Philomena Essed in 1982 in her article "Racisme en Feminisme"[27] in which she pointedly asked white feminists whether they could agree that feminism by definition has to be antiracist. It is not within the scope of this chapter to give an extensive overview of the main developments pertaining to antiracist thought within gender studies (but see Loewenthal 1984, 2001; Wekker and Braidotti 1996; Hoving 1996; Botman, Jouwe, and Wekker 2001). Worth mentioning explicitly is Troetje Loewenthal's (1984) classic article "De witte Toren van Vrouwenstudies" (The white tower of women's studies), which sharply analyzes the Winter University of Women's Studies, held in 1983, laying bare the unreflected whiteness of the discipline. Feminists of color, influenced by U.S. and U.K. feminism of color, developed their own analyses of reality, in which gender, race, and class figured prominently. Although very few feminists of color ever worked in the academy, their movement was inclusive, comprising Surinamese, Antillean, Indo-, Moluccan, Turkish, and Moroccan Dutch women, while, contrary to the men from these groups, a joint analysis based on gender, race, and class was thought through (Deekman and Hermans 2001). An influential figure that needs to be mentioned in this context, for the sheer power and influence of her intersectional and transnational thought, is Audre Lorde, who visited the Netherlands twice in 1984 and 1986 (Wekker 1992; Hermans 2002; Ellerbe-Dueck and Wekker, 2015).

The long and often acerbic debates about racism in Dutch society, the Dutch women's movement, and women's studies, during the late 1970s and 1980s, resulted in a stalemate, whereby members of the latter two constituencies—with very few exceptions—were reluctant to firmly commit to or actually engage in an antiracist feminism. These debates were interrupted only by the introduction of the innovative body of thought of intersectionality (Crenshaw 1989, 1991). Twenty-five years after its introduction, I have to conclude that, even though intersectionality has nominally come to be widely embraced in gender studies, as in the well-known mantra, even though Dutch researchers have published about or along intersectional lines (e.g., Phoenix and Pattyanama eds., 2006; Buitelaar 2006; Verloo 2006, 2013; Prins 2006; Eijberts 2013), even though it has become a buzzword (Davis 2008) and has been called the most important theoretical and methodological innovation and development in the discipline of gender studies (McCall 2005), intersectionality has not blossomed to become the radical and inclusive intervention it initially promised to become, if an equal engagement with race, as is the case for gender, is taken as a criterion. It is still quite feasible and respectable to do gender studies as a single-axis endeavor, without ever paying attention to its intersections with race or one of the other axes. Most Dutch intersectional work deals with the female other, increasingly embodied by Turkish and Moroccan women. Too little work has been done on the meanings of whiteness as a racialized position and on the power configurations in which it is embedded and which sustain it (but see Hoving 1996). In fact, I am arguing that the introduction of intersectionality came at an opportune moment not to continue, much less resolve, the debates about race in the feminist movement. These battles were immediately and abruptly discontinued, because the dominant interpretation of intersectionality was that, depending on context, it was optional which axes one had to engage with seriously. And since race as a prime ordering and discursive mechanism, always already intersecting with gender, had never been wholeheartedly embraced by the dominant versions of gender studies, it should have been no surprise that it was race that continued to be shunned. This gesture stayed in line with commonsense understandings of race in society, in which race had been declared as missing in action, as a nonpertinent analytical toolbox, as the praxes and thought of the extreme Right. Understandings of racism as everyday (Essed 1990, Essed and Nimako 2006), as systemic and institutional, as part of the practices of the elite (Van Dijk 1993), have never gained widespread currency. Thus, the professed embrace of intersectionality, whether taken as theory, methodology, concept, or heuristic device (Lutz, Vivar, and Supik 2011; Lewis 2013) is, speaking from a black Dutch feminist perspective, a rather hollow feat, as I further show in the remainder of this section, when I consider praxes with regard to race, always termed ethnicity and/or culture, in the department of gender studies to which I was connected.

In addition, I am also arguing another point: that is, that the reluctance of the Dutch feminist community to engage with and commit to antiracism is deeply connected to the widely felt, general self-representation that we are not racist and that four hundred years of imperial past have left no traces in the present. Racism is, as Lewis (2013) also argues, displaced onto others elsewhere, such as the United States, South Africa, and possibly the United Kingdom, but it does not take place here. Other internal displacements are operative where racism is imagined to be a characteristic of the Far Right, of populist parties, basking in resentment against "foreigners," or of the working- or underclass only. The both personal and collective claim to an inherently nonracist position, even when there are many indications to the contrary, has deep cultural reverberations and repercussions, as I also try to lay out further through the material that follows.

Before I take up the analysis of attitudes of women's studies practitioners toward race/ethnicity, I want to briefly think back on my years in the academy. Although I cannot possibly provide a full, rounded picture of my experiences there as the only black teacher in the department, and one of only two in the entire faculty of the humanities, I do find it important to call attention to my feelings of isolation, of being displaced, of being both the moral conscience and the primary problem solver of the department on issues of race, whether it concerned either students or other teachers, or the curriculum. This has not been an easy ride, to put it mildly, and I was often painfully struck by everyday occurrences with regard to race/ethnicity. My main reason for laying out some of these experiences is that such writings by other female faculty of color from the United States, Canada (Bannerji et al. 1991; Alexander 2005), the United Kingdom (Ahmed 2012; Lewis 2013; Phoenix et al. 2010), Germany (Arndt et al. 2009; Kilomba

2010), and Sweden (Sawyer 2006; Habel 2012) have often been a lifeline, and they have made me feel connected to colleagues in comparable positions elsewhere. In addition, as Adrienne Rich states, "revision, the act of looking back, of seeing with fresh eyes, of entering an old text from a new critical direction—is for women more than a chapter in cultural history: it is an act of survival. . . . We need to know (the writing of) the past, and know it differently than we have ever known it; not to pass on a tradition but to break its hold over us" (1979, 35).

Teaching as a black female teacher in virtually all-white female classrooms, is a topic that has been addressed by several scholars (Essed 1987 Bannerji et al. 1992; Habel 2012). For most of the students, this is the first time that they are confronted with a black teacher: "a black woman in an intellectual, officially powerful position appears as a contradiction in terms to them" (Habel 2012, 109), which sets a whole array of contradictory affects in motion: disbelief, being looked at as an impostor, as being out of place.[28] In addition, as Philomena Essed writes about teaching in the Netherlands:

> Sometimes my students complained that they felt alienated by the language and by the concepts in which certain theories were developed. To give an example, the denial of racism hampered Dutch development of theories in this area for a long time. In classroom discussions, students had to swallow before they could say "Black," "race" or "racism"—terms that were used in the English-language articles but that were taboo in Dutch. Yet the students recognized many of the practices referred to as racism in the English-language articles from their own observations or experiences in the Netherlands. (1987, 133)

All of this is highly recognizable to me. The following event also comes to mind (Wekker 2002).

VIGNETTE 3: "ARE YOU A PROFESSOR
BECAUSE YOU ARE GOOD OR BECAUSE YOU ARE BLACK?"
Years ago, a black male colleague, Professor Jonathan Jansen, at the time dean of the Faculty of Pedagogy of the University of Pretoria, came to Utrecht University to give a presentation about the transformations in the South African educational system, after the abolition of apartheid.[29] While Professor Jansen was visiting a colleague at a Utrecht teaching institute,

this person asked him, without batting an eyelid, "Are you really the dean of the pedagogical faculty? Is that so because you are good or because you are black?"

When Professor Jansen recounted this event to a circle of mostly white bystanders, during an interval at the conference, a gasp of dismay and disbelief rippled through the group. But I was not that surprised, because, when I became a professor, that was also the most constant question I was asked in interviews: "Is your appointment a real one or is it just a politically correct gesture? Aren't you just an *excuus-Truus*?"—that is, the female version of a token appointee.

I have become increasingly interested in the question as a self-reflexive one, that is, in the landscape that underlies the question, the cultural archive, and what it tells us about the continuities of the imperial construction of a dominant white Dutch self and the implicit or explicit way in which whiteness is bound up with it. It is a complex configuration, because, in the first place, a hyperdirect style of interviewing poses as modern, fast, and sexy, expressing, "I dare to state things as they are" and "I cannot be bothered by political correctness." We might be dealing here with a Dutch habitus. In anthropological studies of the Netherlands by outsiders, since the eighteenth century, characteristics of its inhabitants that have been mentioned time and again are bluntness, rudeness, and coarseness (Van Ginkel 1997), often interpreted by the Dutch themselves as their praiseworthy directness. This directness has found new purchase in the past decades in the social and political domain through the rise of the new realist discourse (Prins 2002), propagated by the political Right but with the deplorable tendency to move across the political spectrum. But there is more going on.

Second, being black, whether male or female, and learned are apparently hard to think together; they exclude each other. Being black is associated with being athletic (Van Sterkenburg 2011), with low literacy, with stupidity, with being amusing, an entertainer, and with naturally occupying a place on the lowest rungs of the social ladder. There is a long academic tradition within scientific racism that has created, invoked, and defended this natural order; these images circulate widely; they surround us; we—both black and white—are constructed by them as inferior and superior. Representations of race that were common in the nineteenth century have also been preserved in the academy, that bastion of objective knowledge, and in the media. That is sobering and it drives those sighs of dismay and disbelief.

In order to make sense of the engagement of women's studies practitioners with the axis of race/ethnicity, it is good to keep in mind that intersectionality in all programs, the one-year MA, the two-year MA, and the PhD, is highlighted as one of the trademarks of gender studies at Utrecht University. I will make use of my own experiences and of the MA thesis of Maartje Meuwissen, an alumna in the one-year program that was then called Comparative Women's Studies in Culture and Politics at Utrecht University, written under my supervision.[30] In her (2011) thesis, titled "The Impact of Women's Studies," Meuwissen set herself to do a qualitative investigation of how three generations of practitioners of gender studies—staff, alumnae, and current students—deal with work, ethnicity, sexuality, and relationships under the influence of their women's studies training. She compares the characteristics of the women's studies community with general surveys and research on the female population of the Netherlands. It is noteworthy that Meuwissen herself is white, as are all of her interviewees, which conforms with the overall population characteristics of the discipline: largely white women. With the help of interviews with five respondents from each subgroup, Meuwissen paints a collective picture of women's studies practitioners that is noteworthy in general, and especially with regard to race/ethnicity. Although it is a small population and I have no ambition to generalize these findings (as the author does not either), a number of meaningful trends can be discerned in the work.

In general, students experience an atmosphere of growth during their studies, in which they can discuss many different topics with teachers and each other. The group picture of teachers and (ex-)students that emerges is one in which hard work is a shared value: it is "not the feeling that you should work hard for your boss, but for a certain moral good," as one of the teachers remarks. The women's studies community differs from average Dutch women in that they are more ambitious, are confident in their own skills, and all want to participate in the labor market, finding work that they feel passionate about and where they can make a contribution to society (Meuwissen 2011, 16). A feeling of responsibility and being accountable for one's privileges is a strongly held value among the staff and is transmitted to the students (Meuwissen 2011, 19). As far as race/ethnicity is concerned, students and alumnae state that their awareness of their own privileged ethnic positioning was raised by their training; Peggy McIntosh's (1992) "invisible knapsack" has had a particular impact. Students nonetheless express that they have difficulty with addressing these issues. Because of their raised awareness, they experience feelings of unease, guilt, and fear of excluding, generalizing, and discriminating. The two central concerns that they mention are that they have to deal with their own prejudices and that they are uneasy with the vocabulary in this domain. For example, in ways that are reminiscent of Essed's experiences, previously quoted, words like *allochthones*, Moroccans, Turks, *uitgeprocedeerde asielzoekers* (asylum seekers who have exhausted their legal possibilities to stay in the Netherlands), even terms like *blank*, or *zwart* give rise to great discomfort, which in my experience often translated to lack of engagement of the white Dutch students, while the foreign students and the Dutch students of color were very vocal. The Dutch word "blank," translating to "white," as opposed to *wit*, a political term, carries strong, positively evaluative overtones. In the general population as well, many white as well as black and migrant people are also equally deterred by the political term *zwart*/black, and would prefer *allochtoon* or even its diminutive, *allochtoontje* (see chapter 5). The fear of and insecurity about dealing with race/ethnicity have been displaced onto the concepts that I used in the classroom to talk about different categories of the population.

Eventually, many of the students decide that not addressing race/ethnicity at all is preferable to speaking about it (Meuwissen 2011, 25–26). The alumnae are, in various ways, engaged with race/ethnicity in their work (24). While the teachers all agree that race/ethnicity should always be present in the training of students, there is a strange disjuncture in that several of them do not think that that is the case in research. Some want to decide on the importance of race/ethnicity in context, while for others class is a priori always more important. All respondents strongly indicate that they have become "intolerant toward racism" because of their training, inciting them to speak up against racist utterances in their family or circle of friends.

I want to reflect a bit more on the following themes that transpire from the material: the terminology to talk about race/ethnicity in women's studies, the value of hard work, and the mechanisms of displacement and disavowal.

Above, I noted that students in women's studies report having problems with what they experience as the in-your-face terminology for race/ethnicity, to the point that they rather would not engage with these issues at all. This may be the first time they hear terms like *wit* instead of "blank," *zwart en migrant* instead of "allochtoon." In general, the supposedly innocuous terms that generally circulate in society in the domain of race/ethnicity are deconstructed; the tensions of using racializing terms in a society that prides itself on the absence of racism are shown up, and the unearned privileges of whiteness are foregrounded. Growing up in a supposedly color-blind society, in which the term "race" is taboo, and often, especially if they are from outside the big cities, not having been exposed to many people of color as peers in their immediate environment, these terms must sound to them like, as an old saying has it, *vloeken in de kerk* (cursing in church). My colleagues and I encountered even more unease with the terminology in a research project on adoptees of color in our introductory class in women's studies (Wekker et al. 2007). The adoptees reported that one of the most prevalent, not very helpful, reactions from their white adoptive families, when they remarked on their experiences with race, was, "Whether you are yellow, purple, or blue, we love you anyway." In light of their experiences of having been raised as white, the contrast with their racialized experiences as they grew up made the women's studies classroom into an even more charged environment for them than for white students.

I understand the unease with terminology to stand as pars pro toto here: It stands for the entire shift in worldview and outlook that exposure to insights in women's studies, generally but especially in the domain of race/ethnicity, affords students. In other words, BA students experience culture shock after entering a women's studies classroom. I am interested in the changes that occur between generations of women's studies practitioners. Whereas the students indicate strong feelings of guilt, unease, fear, and anxiety at being confronted with their own prejudices and only a minority deploys the concepts of race/ethnicity in their work, these feelings are not reported on by the alumnae and the teachers. While the latter two subcategories may or may not actually address race/ethnicity in their research—and for most of them that does not seem to be the case—they do not speak about their affective economies. I understand this phenomenon as a socialization into the required professional mores, coinciding with general societal attitudes, whereby the older generations have apparently found ways to deal with the initial shock experience of learning about the work of race/ethnicity in texts, artifacts, and society. This does not necessarily mean, however, that the affective economy has changed fundamentally, only that the older generations are better able to deal with it. One of the ways to accomplish that is to assign an optional nature to race/ethnicity, which is in line with the anxious shunning of students. A gendered sequence is institutionalized, whereby anxiety/fear is followed by avoidance, amounting to disavowal, the simultaneous affirmation and denial of a thought or desire. This is an important mode of dealing with race in the academy. It strikes me as significant and as highly sobering that in this microcosm of potential allies, this is the royal road taken by most practitioners of gender studies. I return to the gendered nature of this sequence below and subsequently in chapter 5.

HARD WORK

For many Dutch people, especially progressive ones, much is at stake in keeping intact a self-representation at whose core is a deeply antiracist claim. Although in the past decade or so, neorealist discourse has made such a claim largely superfluous and even seemingly undesirable, even among many people who have a conservative political agenda, not exposing oneself to an accusation of racism is vital. It is a no-go area from both sides, an utterly untenable accusation, and, equally, an utterly untenable position to be placed in. Witness the frequent instances when an employer, caught red-handed in racist actions, hastens to declare that he is not racist and, anyway, he did not mean it that way. And even goldilocks Geert Wilders of PVV does not stand for being called a racist, after he incited his followers, on the evening of the municipal elections (March 19, 2014), to a shout-out about . . . "fewer, fewer, fewer Moroccans" in The Hague and in the country. Why are antiracism and egalitarianism in the domain of race/ethnicity, such a vital strain in the stories we Dutch like to tell ourselves about ourselves? Referring back to the series of paradoxes evident in Dutch self-representation that I outlined in chapter 1, here I want to briefly point to the important ingredient of our self-image as a hospitable nation receiving foreigners since time immemorial and offering them a safe haven in a hostile world.

I would like to add a layer to this self-image here. The widely shared, cross-generational value placed on hard work that transpires in the interviews with women's studies practitioners, is strongly reminiscent of the Protestant ethic (Weber 1930), in which hard work, deferral of enjoyment to an afterlife, and work for the common good are central building blocks. Although secularism has long replaced overt forms of religiosity, it is not at all unthinkable that this set of values has remained alive in the cultural archive. Another paradox presents itself here: If one is working hard for the common good, how can one possibly be accused of racism? In addition, an accusation of racism runs deeply counter to the strand of egalitarianism that is also such a strong ingredient of the Dutch sense of self: Not only is the person uttering the charge placing herself above her peers, thus breaking with egalitarianism and putting herself above "us," but it means excising the accused from the egalitarian tapestry, as well. Neither position, both of which are considered extreme, is tenable, because they deeply break with this supposed egalitarianism. This configuration is also operative in other postimperial nations, such as France, which have a strong egalitarian strand that supposedly makes them blind to race.

GENDERED DISPLACEMENT AND DISAVOWAL

Displacement takes place in commonsense understandings that race is missing in action in the Netherlands, essentially by acclamation, because we say that that is the case. Race is done elsewhere—in the United States, in South Africa, in Britain—but not here. Another form of displacement is the idea, widespread in many European societies, that class takes precedence over race/ethnicity and that the latter does not need to be taken into separate account. Taken together, what is pointed up here is a bracketing of race.

What has struck me in the course of writing this chapter is that there are gendered responses to discussions about race and racism. As we will see in chapter 5, when I discuss the reactions of the general public to accusations of racism in the figure of Zwarte Piet, mainly white male responses to such allegations are anger, aggressive dismissal, and even death threats. Here, among highly educated white women, we find anxiety, fear, avoidance, and feelings of guilt. Fearful avoidance and aggressive ignorance are archetypical female and male responses, and I will delve deeper into these bifurcated patterns.

Conclusion

Against a rather general consensus that race does not play a part in the Netherlands, several moves with regard to race/ethnicity have been showcased. First are the systematic but silent ways in which discursive and organizational repertoires sort women on the basis of their racialized positions, both in government policy and in the academy. Subsequently, in a discipline where race/ethnicity has been explicitly designated as an important axis of signification, the concept is again by and large evacuated, bracketed, and "ghettoized" in Gail Lewis's (2013) terms. There is anxiety and fear among the youngest practitioners of women's studies when they are first exposed to the work that race does, in texts, in artifacts, and in society. Among older generations there is a bracketing of race, making it into an optional variable, either because of fear and unease with the category or because of a faulty and color-blind assessment that it is not a pertinent axis of signification, and that others are more pressing.

"We are a small nation, innocent; we are inherently antiracist; we do not have bad intentions" is shorthand to sum up this white sense of self. These defense mechanisms serve to preserve this ideal image of ourselves as deeply color-blind and antiracist. Questioning this most dearly held core of the Dutch sense of self means putting oneself above "us"; it also runs deeply counter to another strand in the Dutch sense of self, egalitarianism.

CHAPTER 3

The Coded Language of Hottentot Nymphae
and the Discursive Presence of Race, 1917

Likewise, while many groups of African blacks
were known to Europeans in the nineteenth century,
the Hottentot remained representative of the essence
of the black, especially the black female.

Sander L. Gilman, "Black Bodies, White Bodies"

In this chapter, I present a little-known, tantalizingly short, Dutch psycho-analytical case study from 1917, which, as I argue, has far-reaching conse-quences for our understandings of the place of race in the Dutch cultural ar-chive.[1] Three Dutch women, apparently white and upper class, in treatment with the psychoanalyst Dr. J. H. W. van Ophuijsen in The Hague, claimed to possess "Hottentot nymphae." This term was the coded, contemporary one used to refer to the supposed morphology of black women's genitalia; the three women are implying that they possess overdeveloped labia minora. Several features of this case study are intriguing: First, while the women understand themselves in terms of a racialized discourse, the psychoana-lyst Dr. van Ophuijsen dismisses their claim and understands them to be suffering from "masculinity complex," a concept that he developed and that was later taken over by Freud. Masculinity complex frames the women in terms of gender. I want to explore the meaning of this substitution of gender for race; what is at stake for the women and for the psychoanalyst? What is the nature of the world that these women and the analyst inhabit and what kind of knowledge pertaining to race, bodies, sexuality, and gen-der circulates in it? A second feature that this case study brings to the fore is that, contrary to what is commonly assumed, race was firmly present as a discourse, at least in upper-class circles of the metropole. The fact that these women used a racialized discourse to make sense of themselves runs counter to the dominant view that race, whether used as a reference to specific—often black—people, or as a way of ordering and understanding the world, was absent in the Netherlands until the first postcolonial migrants—Indos and Moluccans—started to arrive from the Dutch East Indies after World War II.

I want to investigate where this racialized discourse, glimpsed in "Hottentot nymphae," came from and what it consisted of. Apparently, it was shared by the analysands and their analyst, even though he disagreed with them. In what domains of society would the discourse have circulated and what was its significance? Ultimately, I analyze the case study in terms of what it can tell us about Dutch society at the time and about the cultural archive.

The chapter is organized as follows: The first section traces the first appearance of the women in the minutes of a meeting in 1917 and the subsequent 1918 article in which they take center stage, where I lay out the main points of its content. I follow the fate of the article, which is little known and regarded as underrated (Grigg, Hecq, and Smith 1999), and, finally, I sketch what is known about its author, Johan Wijnand Hendrik van Ophuijsen. The next section places the case study in two contexts: historical and scientific. These contexts are pertinent to a more probabilistic understanding of what it was the women and their analyst had on their minds, in terms of race. In the historical context I place the case study against the backdrop of the first feminist wave and the widespread tendency in society to suffer from neuroses, especially in upper-class circles, and I inquire in which sites in society a discourse about race circulated. Given the scarcity of material on the women, ultimately the chapter will be an in-depth reading of society at that time and the places where race inserted itself. The scientific context allows me to inquire into the understanding of female genitalia that was circulating among medical doctors, sexologists, biologists, and anthropologists, and which phantasmal place the genitals of African women occupied in that representation. Having woven an ever thicker contextual tapestry, in the third section I use postcolonial and intersectional approaches to lay out what I see as the content, significance, and context of the case study for a novel reading of the role of race in white female subject formation, a reading that undoes the determined and dogged excision of race from mainstream conceptualizations of the Dutch self.

An inspiration for this chapter was Jean Walton's (1997) illuminating article "Re-Placing Race in Psychoanalytic Discourse: Founding Narratives of Feminism," in which she argues that race has been a sorely missing aspect of early psychoanalysis and that this is the case until today, in both the fantasy lives and the subjectivity formations of psychoanalytic clients. She briefly mentions and analyzes the case study of five Dutch women in treatment with van Ophuijsen, and I immediately saw the possibilities of this tantalizingly thin case study to illustrate for the Netherlands a key insight within postcolonial studies, that the concepts of self and other that came into being in Western modernity were dependent on the politics of colonial relations. I want to stress the rare and possibly unique, yet fleeting, glimpse that the case study offers us of white female upper-class subjectivities that were produced in Dutch diaspora space (Brah 1996) in the 1910s and the role that race played in those psychic economies. The centrality of race in this particular case study has wider implications for our understandings of Dutch society and subjectivity.

How is it possible and what does it mean that these women enunciate an "I" that intertwines gender and sexuality with race? In order to answer the many questions that the case study raised, I had to learn more about Dutch psychoanalysis in its formative years, the 1920s and 1930s, about the analyst, and about the rare cases in psychoanalysis that brought up race as a meaningful factor. My trajectory to rediscover psychoanalysis, which I had shunned since my graduate school days because of its universalist claims, "its blindness to most of the earth" (Derrida 1998, 66), its active aversion to race, led me to eventually conclude that psychoanalysis is deeply steeped in the racial common sense of the day.

Finally, let me say something about the theoretical stakes of this chapter. Underlying my work is an attempt to read metropole and colonies as one analytical field, as Frantz Fanon, Edward Said, Ann Laura Stoler, and Anne McClintock, among other postcolonial and psychoanalytical scholars, have urged us to do; to seek insights into how knowledge was produced along trajectories that were embedded in a web that spanned metropole and colony. In the Netherlands, this mutual dependency between knowledge production and self-production has been studiously avoided, which points to one of the ways the dominant attitude of white innocence could be maintained. One notable exception to this state of affairs has been the work of African American historian Allison Blakely; in his very useful *Blacks in the Dutch World* (1993, 2), he makes an impassioned plea that the study of the images of blacks in Dutch history and culture has to include the empire as well as the homeland. It is noteworthy that it is North American scholars, Blakely and Stoler, with their focus on the Netherlands, who have first practiced these postcolonial insights in a Dutch context. The majority of Dutch historians have persistently abstained from seeking colonial connections, meanwhile musing that it is remarkable that postcoloniality has had so little purchase in the discipline of history (Oostindie 2010). Susan Legêne is one of the first Dutch historians to have taken up the challenge put forward by Stoler (1995);[2] Stoler asks why Dutch historiography, unlike other European historiographies, has put the colonies in quarantine. By so doing, it does not consider that social and economic developments during empire worked in one transatlantic field and should thus be treated in one analytical field. Legêne's (2010, 8) work is based on an assumption that is very similar to mine, that is, that Dutch culture developed in many respects as a colonial culture and that the traces of this are discernible in our contemporary society. My focal point is Dutch self-representation, which, as I understand it, was formed in active interaction with overseas others. I am interested in the question of how this Dutch colonial culture manifested in representations of the other and the self. Finally, I turn to van Ophuijsen's description of the women with Hottentot nymphae.

Case Study: The Masculinity Complex in Women

In March 1917, thirteen men, all medical doctors or psychiatrists, founded De Nederlandsche Vereeniging voor Psycho Analyse (NVPA), the Dutch Society for Psychoanalysis (Brinkgreve 1984). The NVPA was the Dutch branch of the International Psychoanalytical Association. In the early decades of the twentieth century, the Netherlands had 200 to 240 psychiatrists, a highly respected professional group with much social status; about 10 percent were members of the NVPA (Stroeken 2009). Brinkgreve (1984) insightfully describes the never-ending conflicts and jockeying for position that took place in the small, tightly knit world of Dutch psychoanalysis in these and its ensuing formative years. The atmosphere that she calls up resembles a slightly dysfunctional family, in which dissent with the Great

Father, Freud, was strongly frowned upon. This and the largely exaggerated feeling of being under siege by outsiders that did not accept them functioned as a shield to keep the psychoanalytic family together. Striking also about the early psychoanalytical world was the apparent readiness with which analysts exchanged analysands; once a patient reached the end of the line with one analyst, she might easily take up with another. We will see an example of this in Patient H.

At the second meeting of the NVPA on June 23, 1917, in Amsterdam, the psychiatrist Johan Hendrik Wijnand van Ophuijsen, a founding member, delivered a talk titled "Casuistische bijdrage tot de kennis van het mannelijkheidscomplex bij de vrouw" (Casuistic contribution to the knowledge of the masculinity complex in women). In the minutes of the meeting, August Stärcke (1918), another founder and secretary of the new association, reported as follows on the gist of van Ophuijsen's talk: Freud has found, and others have confirmed that in the infantile imagination there exists the possibility for the woman to possess male genitalia, and that this is at the core of an unconscious complex. Van Ophuijsen calls this complex "the masculinity complex." According to the very short summary of the lecture, sixteen lines in the journal, the complex expresses itself in different ways:

> Embitterment not to have been born as a man. The anxious expectation on the part of the woman that she will at some point in the future still obtain the male organ;—depression, as if the male genitalia, whether by her own fault or not, has been lost (castration complex, etc.). With those women who have this complex in a strong degree, one seldom finds masculinity in behavior and appearance, and homosexuality is seldom manifest, but one does find a kind of competitiveness with men, in intellectual and artistic respects, and in relation to their own gender. On the basis of fragments of a number of cases and analyses, van Ophuijsen tries to argue that the masculinity complex is correlated with, resp. is based on that part of infantile sexuality which is tied to the functions of clitoris and bladder, and the lust feelings that are connected to them. (Stärcke 1918, 1428; my translation)

We do not get a good idea of the discussion that followed van Ophuijsen's presentation, only that van der Chijs, also a cofounder, asked about the nature of the musical pieces that one of the patients composed during her childhood, since they might give pertinent information for her treatment.

This particular patient turns out to be Patient H., who will return in the article that van Ophuijsen wrote later.

The article, based on the lecture, was first published in German in 1917 as "Beiträge zum Männlichkeitskomplex der Frau" (Van Ophuijsen 1916–1917), and then in Dutch in 1918. It was not until six years later, in 1924, that van Ophuijsen published the English version in the *International Journal of Psycho-analysis* (Van Ophuijsen [1924] 1966).[3] In an intense engagement with Freud's work, van Ophuijsen opens his article by stating that he has recently come across a number of patients in his practice who exhibit the precise symptoms that Freud has described for all women, that is, that they have been "hurt in their infancy, and that through no fault of their own they have been slighted and robbed of a part of their body; and the bitterness of many a daughter towards her mother has as its ultimate cause the reproach that the mother has brought her into the world as a woman instead of a man" ([1924] 1966, 61).

Van Ophuijsen's case study consists of five women who are in analysis with him—four for an extended period, one for only a short time—all of whom have a strong memory of having observed the male organ of their father or brother in their youth. He offers a frame in which to understand the women when he explains the difference between the masculinity and the castration complexes, which closely resemble each other. In the latter case, women experience a feeling of guilt because the loss of the genital organ is supposed to be the result of wrongdoing, the punishment for a sexual lapse. In the former, the unconscious wish to be a boy engenders a feeling of having been ill treated, and thus of strongly developed bitterness and protest. In psychoanalytical fashion, van Ophuijsen ([1924] 1966, 63) understands the early confrontation of the little girl with the male organ as a repressed memory, which in later life is the starting point for a new fantasy system in which the repressed wish returns.

Van Ophuijsen then describes, albeit still summarily, some of the individual cases, indicating the women merely by their first initials. Thus, he writes, "[Patient D.] tells me quite clearly that the wish to be a boy developed from the desire to be able to urinate like a boy, after she saw a boy perform this act. This incident has determined till today the manner of her sexual satisfaction through masturbation. Another patient H., was able to observe her father and uncle, who were not ashamed to urinate before her" ([1924] 1966, 62). Patient H. had the expectation that an organ would grow out from within, based on her Hottentot nymphae (70), the over-developed labia minora attributed to black women. Furthermore, several of these patients behave as if they had male genitals; that is, they urinate while standing up or sit like men, with their legs spread, "as if they want to prevent their genitals from being crushed." We do not learn much about these women. Patient H. is described most elaborately, it is mentioned that she is musically gifted, a composer and a piano player since she was very young;[4] but no information is given on the activities, occupations, or ages of the other patients.

One of the several ways in which one can discover the masculinity complex in analysis, as van Ophuijsen says, is if women express a desire to take possession of a person "instead of devoting and subjecting themselves to him, or they have the feeling that they wish to penetrate someone else, instead of themselves being penetrated or they remark that a state of tension would disappear if they could but give out something instead of taking something in" ([1924] 1966, 64). He mentions that one of the three women experiences "homosexual coitus dreams" (67); another developed strong homosexual tendencies (70); and the last one had homosexual fantasies (72). Homosexuality looms large as an absent and contested presence in the text, and I return to the significance of female homosexuality later. Van Ophuijsen diagnoses them as suffering from psychasthenia with obsessions, otherwise called "obsessional neurosis" (62).

One passage in the article is of key importance for my endeavor: "It might perhaps be not without significance that *three of the five patients informed me of their own accord that they possessed "Hottentot nymphae"*: this fact, which they had already noticed very early in their lives, led them to the conviction that they were different from other women" (emphasis added). This is the first time the term "Hottentot nymphae" appears; it was not used in August Stärckes minutes of the meeting in 1917. Van Ophuijsen does not explain "Hottentot nymphae," which appears in inverted commas in the article, making it seem probable that it would have been familiar to the intended audience: psychoanalysts, doctors, and an educated lay public interested in the discipline. By the 1910s and 1920s, psychoanalytical insights had reached a more general, educated audience in Dutch society (Bulhof 1983).

Van Ophuijsen's motivation to publish the article was that he was convinced of the value of what he had seen in his clinical work, the "intimate connection between the masculinity complex, infantile masturbation of the clitoris and urethral erotism" ([1924] 1966, 72). In this condensed phrase we find encapsulated some vital Freudian doxa, taken-for-granted knowledge (Bourdieu 1977), about the sexuality of women. However, in 1926, Freud famously stated in "The Question of Lay Analysis," "We know less of the sexual life of little girls than boys. But we need not feel ashamed of this distinction: after all, the sexual life of adult women is 'a dark continent' for psychology" ([1926] 1990, 212). It is no coincidence that Freud compares adult women's sexuality to the European explorers' impenetrable, unknown, African continent; it is a metaphor rich in connotations calling up heroes who "struggle through enchanted or bedeviled lands toward a goal, ostensibly the discovery of the Nile's sources or the conversion of the cannibals. But that goal also turns out to include sheer survival and the return home, to the regions of light. These authors move—against a dark, infernal backdrop where there are no other characters of equal stature— only bewitched or demonic savages" (Brantlinger 1985, 195).[5]

The coincidence of the period of high colonialism, with its heroic roles for men, and the rise of psychoanalysis resonates in Freud's statement. Indeed, Khanna (2003, ix), among other critical psychoanalytical scholars, understands psychoanalysis as a masculinist and colonialist discipline that promoted the idea of Western subjectivity in opposition to a colonized, feminine, and primitive other. An embedded layer in Freud's statement is that the accomplishment of "true femininity"—normal, vaginal, maternal— remained an equally difficult, hazardous journey, whereby the dangers of masculinity or, worse, homosexuality, were forever rearing their ugly heads. Indeed, central to Freud's and van Ophuijsen's initial theories about female sexuality is the primitive masculinity of the little girl, who is a little man, before she changes object and wishes to acquire a child from her father as a substitute for the unobtainable penis.[6] This is seen as the normal and most desirable outcome of women's quest for femininity, but there are two other female responses to the shock every little girl experiences when she discovers that she is different from the little boys she encounters. In the second model, the girl/woman recognizes the absence of the penis and abandons hope of obtaining any external love object as substitute. The third model, finally, which van Ophuijsen foregrounds in his article, is the woman's unconscious wish to possess a penis and its attendant masculine pleasures, such as her inappropriate sexual preference for the clitoris and the bladder, and their sexual responsiveness. This active, clitoral, and urethral sexuality clearly does not conform to the desirable Freudian feminine mode of passivity and vaginality. Freud emphasized the connection between strongly developed urethral erotism and ambition in women (Ruitenbeek 1966, 10).

The importance of van Ophuijsen's article is, first, that it inaugurates the classical psychoanalytical debates about female sexuality during the 1920s and 1930s (Grigg, Hecq, and Smith 1999); second, it is van Ophuijsen who, albeit on the basis of and strongly connected to Freud's work, first coins the term "masculinity complex," and Freud later acknowledges his intellectual debt to van Ophuijsen in his 1919 (1993) paper "A Child Is Being Beaten" and in later work.[7] And finally, the article engages with one aspect of the theory of penis envy, that is, that it derives from a woman's sense of having been injured in infancy through no fault of her own, and hence her blaming of her mother for having brought her into this world as a woman instead of a man.

Finally, let me briefly say something about the psychoanalyst. Johan Hendrik Wijnand van Ophuijsen was born in the Dutch colony of the East Indies, in Padang, Sumatra, in 1882, and, after an eventful life, he died in New York City in 1950.[8] At the age of thirteen, he came to Leiden, in the Netherlands, for his secondary studies. Although van Ophuijsen published many articles and book reviews and gave numerous presentations on important themes, including the masculinity complex, sadism, and the feeling of being persecuted, among others, he never published a book and did not make an important contribution to psychoanalytic theory. However, before World War II, he was easily the most influential Dutch psychoanalyst, due to his ties to the Freud family and his roles in the early organizational life of the psychoanalytical movement in the Netherlands and in the International Psychoanalytical Association, for which he acted as the Dutch intermediary. He held several important national and international positions, such as treasurer of the NVPA, was a member of curriculum committees both nationally and internationally and active in the organization of conferences, including the Sixth International Psychoanalytical Congress, held in The Hague in 1920.

Van Ophuijsen looked like an Indo-European person, an Indo, that is, a descendant of the racially mixed population in the colony of the East Indies; he was handsome and distinguished, with a generous shock of hair. After studying in Zürich, where he was in analysis with Jung, he settled in

The Hague, to this day known, as a popular song has it, as "the widow of the Indies." The Hague was, at the beginning of the twentieth century, the chosen place where the Indo community settled, and where Dutch civil servants who had worked in the colony spent their furlough in the Netherlands. It is thus no coincidence that he chose The Hague as his residence, *the* colonial city in the Netherlands at the time. According to the census of 1920, out of a total population of 355,000 in The Hague, 7,500 originated "uit eene der Nederlandse kolonieën," from one of the Dutch colonies, that is, almost 2 percent. [9] The majority of those migrants would have been from the Dutch East Indies, as opposed to migrants from Suriname and the Dutch Antilles, who were in general less prosperous and thus less capable of travel than the Indo population. [10]

I want to take into account the characteristic mind-set of the Indo population, which in later decades came to be called a "model minority" in the Netherlands, when speculating about van Ophuijsen's worldview with regard to race. While both the mixed descendants of Dutch and Indies people and white Dutch people having lived in the Indies for generations, *tótoks*, had developed a particular Indo-European, creole culture, they also were known for a pronounced preparedness to assimilate to Dutch metropolitan culture; to put Dutch language, culture, and the royal family, the house of Orange, on a high pedestal, with a conservative political streak and a tendency to be more Dutch than the Dutch themselves (Van Leeuwen 2008, 2009). Importantly, identification with the Dutch, first in the Indies and later in the Netherlands, consolidated the erasure of race among Indo-Europeans (Captain 2014). Is it too far-fetched to assume that van Ophuijsen might have been painted with the same brush, compounded by the circumstance that in his professional circles race was likewise evacuated?

In the strife between Freud and Jung, which resulted in their lasting estrangement around 1912, van Ophuijsen chose Freud. Through his second wife, Ans van Mastrigt, who had been "engaged" to one of Freud's sons, van Ophuijsen was intimately connected to the Freud family, even to the extent that when he had marital problems with Ans, Freud would write soothing letters to her, apologizing for van Ophuijsen, who, after all, was in essence a good man. In psychoanalytical fashion, this mini portrait would not be complete without providing a sketch of his personal problems. According to Stroeken, who wrote an elaborate biographical portrait, van Ophuijsen had two main issues. One was with money: He continuously writes about his debts in his correspondence, asking friends and colleagues for financial help, loans, and advances. It is not clear why he, with his more than ample income, was constantly in need of money. Stroeken suggests that he might have had a gambling problem. Second, he often fell in love with his female patients and had a total of four marriages, besides affairs, all with former patients.[11]

A Historical Context for the Case Study:
In Which the "Unhappy Few" Are Exposed to Imagery about Race

What was the nature of the world that these five women and the analyst inhabited and what kind of knowledge pertaining to race, bodies, sexuality, and gender circulated in it? If we consider Dutch culture as a colonial culture, what are the sites where these women would have been exposed to race? Although it is of course impossible to really gain access to their thoughts and ideas, we may approach it by closely reviewing some important sites where pertinent bodies of such knowledge circulated. In order to gain an image of that early twentieth-century world, I first sketch what inevitably has to be a selective picture of what was happening in Dutch society at the time.

The Netherlands had 6.6 million inhabitants.[12] The first feminist wave was under way, which did not take the intense forms it had in Great Britain, Germany, and France. The Dutch feminist movement engaged with marital law, access to education, and suffrage and objected to the double moral standards for men and women (Braun 1985). In 1919, parliament legalized the right of women to vote, which the Vereeniging voor Vrouwenkiesrecht (Association for the Women's Vote), founded in 1894 by Aletta Jacobs and Wilhelmina Drucker, had fought for (Bosch 2004). The fight for the vote revealed unprecedented changes in the relative positions of men and women. In a European framework, Philipp Blom (2009) characterizes the years between 1900 and 1914 as the "dizzying years," which formed the input for the ensuing important intellectual, scientific, and emotional changes in Europe during the twentieth century. The earlier characteristic emblem of the virgin, as the principle of female fertility, gave way to the masculine principle of the dynamo, giving an enormous speed to development, a nervousness, an insecurity about things to come, making life seem like treacherous quicksand. Even if this general European fevered pitch of life was at a lower frequency in the Netherlands, it still made itself distinctly felt. The industrial revolution, at the end of the nineteenth century, had brought about a transformation in manufacturing, manifest among other things in the advent of the airplane, the automobile, and other kinds of machineries and technologies, and the pure strength of mechanical power had set in motion an insecurity among men, especially of the middle classes, regarding what their traditional superior strength might still mean. In 1910, girls formed only 10 percent of the total school population at the five-year secondary Hoogere Burger School (van Essen 1990). For the first time now, a handful of women was able to study and to make a living wage on their own; many gained a basic education and some were able to limit the number of children they produced; their newfound freedom was feared and often vilified. There was a keen interest in female homosexuality as a response and (in part) as resistance to the suffrage and early women's movement. In those years, all women's lives were touched and changed by the movement, whether they were feminist or not.

The general insecurity led to a high incidence of neuroses, general nervous states, both among men and women working with the modern technologies, such as telephone operators and typists, railway workers, engineers, factory workers, operators of fast machines, and the businessmen and managers who were at the heart of the new economy, and who mainly dwelled in cities (Blom 2009, 343). Psychoanalysis was an expensive affair that the less wealthy simply could not afford: "It was the prerogative of the 'unhappy few'" (Brinkgreve 1984, 102). The problems that they presented were marriage problems, clashing characters, phobias, sexual problems, melancholia. According to contemporaries, the increase in neurasthenic complaints came predominantly from educated people, "those working with their heads and the so-called higher classes" (Brinkgreve 1984, 47). Generally, the many emotions to which they were exposed in modern society and intellectual overexertion were blamed for their predicament. Women of the higher classes also formed an important group of patients, suffering from exhaustion, tightness of the chest, and overexcited nerves: neurasthenia had become a sign of good taste, of possessing a sensitive nature, a means by which the hard-working middle classes and upwardly mobile could distinguish themselves from others. Working-class people and their complaints mostly came into view after the 1920s. They were easily locked away in asylums or treated with suggestive, highly directive therapies (Foucault 1964). By the 1920s, psychoanalysis had become the leading school of thought within the world of therapy.

Against this background of changing gender roles and intense nervous states, my key question in this historical section is this: What were the sites in Dutch society where these white, female patients would learn about black women and their bodies? After all, dominant common sense has it that with Dutch "colonialism of the exterior," race had, until the middle of the twentieth century, pertinence only in the colonies, not in the metropolis. Race, in the sense in which it was (and sometimes unfortunately still is) understood, that is, as blackness, was something that played out over there, not here. Race was blackness and seemed to have nothing to do with the civilized white human subject.

Next I describe five sites where the protagonists of this narrative were exposed to knowledge about black women and their bodies.

FIVE SITES IN SOCIETY

First, there is the domain of education, especially education in geography, the subject par excellence in which students learn about the world, with its different races and cultures, and, often implicitly and sometimes explicitly, about their own place in that world. In the social Darwinist and evolutionist geography curriculum that was taking shape in the heyday of imperialism students were invited to identify with a "natural" positive self-image and a civilizing mission (Mok 1999). They received ideas about the superiority of Europe and the Netherlands, as the highest-ranked racial group, and an unassailable power position in the world was offered. Development was a key concept, and its hallmark was the capacity and the duty to "spread beyond one's own domain," as Said (1993, 52) also indicated in his definition of the nineteenth-century European cultural archive, to uplift and civilize other peoples. The curriculum, moreover, built on polygenetic principles, a position that defended the separate and independent development of the different races, which allowed for, even demanded, ranking. Among the geography texts Mok analyzes is the famous Bos text with an accompanying atlas.

A SHORT EXCURSION

Reading about the Bos Atlas took me back to my own school days. The Bos Atlas was, at the time when I went to secondary school, between 1962 and 1968, and is still today the most popular geographical tool, both in and outside school. The principles that Mok (1999) outlines, with Europe as the powerful center of the world and developing countries as needy appendages, were still very much the heart of the curriculum, when I was in grade and secondary school. At the Catholic all-girls nuns' schools I attended in Nijmegen, the overriding sentiment was symbolized in two activities: the daily drive to save the blue and red aluminum caps of school milk bottles and the little blue container in which we could as often as possible deposit money *voor de arme negertjes* (for the poor little Negroes). These were stern reminders of the envisioned relationship: a benevolent, rich "we" magnanimously giving to a backward, poor "them." This "politics of compassion" is what Markus Balkenhol (2014) refers to in his dissertation, *Tracing Slavery*, when he contrasts compassion, the Dutch attitude toward racial others, which is based on a hierarchically superior position, with solidarity. Along the same lines, Dienke Hondius's (2014b) paternalism fits well as an explanatory model.

In the fourth grade of primary school, when I was ten years old, I decided to give my yearly class presentation on three Surinamese freedom fighters, Kodyo, Mentor, and Present, who had set the capitol city of Paramaribo, Suriname, ablaze in 1821 in an attempt to put an end to slavery. I had learned about them from my grandfather, my mother's father, a proud Afro-Surinamese man, a carpenter by trade, who was full of historical tales and songs, accompanying himself on the guitar. He had moved in with us from Suriname when I was nine years old (Wekker 2002a). I remember that I was nervous giving the presentation, because it was so different from other girls' topics: dolls, a visit to the zoo, a sick hamster. But I was also determined to put my topic on the table because I already felt that I, my family, and Suriname were, on the one hand, hyperinvisible in the classroom and, on the other, visible and perpetually framed as needy, as undercivilized, as unequal, although I certainly could not have used these terms at the time.

A second site is the domain of art. Blakely (1993) suggests that from an early admiring and positive depiction of black figures in religiously inspired art of the fourteenth century, gradually as Dutch empire expanded in the seventeenth century, more negative imagery came to the fore. He characterizes the imagery of blacks in Dutch art, over a period of seven centuries, as highly ambivalent and ambiguous, with familiar negative stereotypes dominating—stupidity, inferiority, servility.[13] The early twentieth century marks the beginning of an era in which black models, black music and dance, black history and literature, and black people were hot in Paris, Brussels, and Amsterdam (Schreuder 2008, 122); new types like the boxer, the female dancer, and black male and female nakedness became en vogue, under influence of the desire, against naturalism, to explore and delve into the "primitive, the authentic, the pure, the primary and the magic" (Schreuder 2008, 109). In The Hague, the well-known artists' association, the Pulchri Studio, presented black models to its members. It would have been hard for women of an interested, educated upper class to escape these widespread modernist manifestations. The desire to embrace authenticity, primitiveness, closeness to nature, and an unbridled sensuality was driven by the idea that modern (i.e., white) humanity had lost these qualities, and African and Pacific people became the projection screen by which these desirable states could be recuperated (Essed and Hoving 2014b).

A theme that is often avoided in mainstream studies of this early twentieth-century enamoration with blackness is sexualization. Sander Gilman notes that a complex configuration is operative in medical and artistic Western discourses, in which the black female, specifically the Hottentot, comes to occupy the same spaces as the prostitute and the lesbian: They are all sexually active, pathological, prone to sexual disease, and constructed as a danger to the body politic, that is, white men. "The 'white man's burden' thus becomes his sexuality and its control, and it is this which is transferred into the need to control the sexuality of the other, the other as sexualized female. The colonial mentality which sees 'natives' as needing control is easily transferred to 'woman'—but woman as exemplified by the case of the prostitute. This need for control was a projection of inner fears" (Gilman 1985, 256). According to Gilman, it is the figure of the black servant, which is so ubiquitous in European art of the nineteenth and early twentieth centuries, whose main function is to sexualize the society in which he or she is found and who marks illicit sexual activities.

Another, third, domain was the world, colonial, and anthropological exhibitions, sites where blacks and Indies peoples—in all shapes and forms— could be gazed at. The five colonial exhibitions between 1880 and 1931 were meant to secure and advertise the status of the Netherlands as an imperial power, meant to impress an amazed public with the efficacy of colonial governance and entrepreneurship, and to firmly install the hierarchical relations between the West and the Rest (Bloembergen 2002). In another genre, throughout the nineteenth and the beginning of the twentieth century, bearded women, giants, dwarfs, and women with other anomalies were put on display at fairs. African women were exhibited in Europe as examples of a primitive sexuality (Buikema 2009). The infamous case of the South African Khoi woman Sarah Baartman comes to mind here. She is but one in a long line of unknown others who form part of the cultural archive of the five patients. She was put on display in museums in Paris and London in the early 1800s, to be gazed at because of her protruding buttocks, steatopygia. Baartman died in Paris in 1815, after which her genital remains stayed on display throughout the twentieth century, until she was brought back to South Africa in 2002 (Ferrus 1998).[14]

Between 1825 and 1913, there were thirty-four exhibitions of "exotic people" in the Netherlands (Grever and Waaldijk 1998; Sliggers 2009). Meanwhile, large collections of exotic artifacts and photographs of people from around the world had been amassed by local anthropological associations, museums, and scientific institutions, with the aim of showing the human diversity that was embedded in immutable racial hierarchy. Photographic postcards, whose circulation ran into the millions each year, displaying black and Middle Eastern women in erotic poses were another variation on this theme. Apart from the racial hierarchy apparent in all these different artifacts, there was also a deep desire for the "vital force" that was increasingly thought to be on the wane in Europe; a supposed sexual freedom that was available only in the Orient, Africa, and other non-Western places. Various exotic populations had their own stereotypes, which were repeated again and again: the sexually potent Arab with his harem, the phlegmatic, sensual Asian, and the African with his savagery, barbarism, cannibalism, and immorality (Corbey 1989).

A fourth site of (pseudo) knowledge was the popularization of medical and anthropological research in magazines, prominently featuring the examination of black female genitalia, such as the Hottentot apron or enlarged labia. It is noteworthy that it was black women with their genitalia and pelvises and not black men who held obsessive fascination for white European and American biological and medical scientists.

A fifth site was commercial advertisements, where images of blacks were displayed on the covers of products from the colonies—soap, tea, coffee, tobacco, liquor, cocoa, candy, and sugar (Nederveen Pieterse 1990). Anne McClintock (1995) has insightfully shown the colonial obsession with cleanliness and soap as a yardstick of civilization, which, in a Dutch context where cleanliness had always already been remarked upon historically by foreign observers as a favorite national pastime (Schama 1987; Blakely 1993), took on a more intense meaning, filtered as it was through religiosity. Simon Schama makes that connection between cleanliness and godliness: "To have been slaves was to have been dirty. To be free is to be clean" (1987, 379). If, as Allison Blakely (1993, 206) notes, black skin increasingly, from the sixteenth century on, became a sign of evil, and if for Calvinists cleanliness was one of the conspicuous signs of being one of God's elect, this placed all blacks in compounded peril, in an inferior light and in association with dirtiness. This sense is conveyed by a series of old, sometimes biblical, expressions like "washing the Moor" or "Can the Nubian change his skin, or the leopard its spots?" (Jeremiah 13:22–25), meant to convey the futility of an endeavour (Blakely 1993, 205).

Other products, such as shoeshine, metal polish, and toothpaste, for obvious reasons, were brought into association with blackness. The "Toothpaste Negro," Joseph Sylvester, a.k.a. Menthol, was born on St. Lucia and somehow wound up in Hengelo, the Netherlands, and married a Dutch woman, Roosje Borchert, a model. He started his own toothpaste brand, which he sold at local markets, and was a well-known and popular figure in the east of the country, around the 1920s (Altena 2008). All these manifestations of blackness in Dutch commercial culture were brought together in the Negrophilia collection, assembled by Antillean artists Felix de Rooy and Norman de Palm, and exhibited in an Amsterdam exhibition, Wit over Zwart (White about Black), in 1989.

Thus far, I have been arguing that there were many sites and discourses in the Netherlands in the early twentieth century, where the female patients came in contact with blackness and the pejorative images it invoked. There are many more sites I could have named, travel literature, encyclopedias, and other reference books, for example, often accompanied by prints, drawings, and allegorical pieces of Africa: "No people have been more fascinated by serious travel literature than the people of the Low Countries" (Blakely 1993, 148).

It seems fair to conclude that the patients were exposed to images, ideas, ideologies, and representations of race and black women in many different domains of everyday life, apart from psychoanalysis. In an earlier exercise on this subject, my coauthor Henrietta Moore's position was that the women would have been exposed to racial fantasies only in the analytical context, mirroring back the racial fantasies of the analyst (Moore and Wekker 2011). I do not agree with that position. Moreover, the different sites I have just outlined also illustrate the fruitfulness of considering metropole and colonies in one analytical field, showing the imbricatedness of cultural productions here and there.

A Scientific Context

The end of the nineteenth century and the beginning of the twentieth was a period of high colonialism and nationalist conflict in Europe, which coincided with various other important developments such as the rise of photography, of psychoanalysis, and of modern science. In particular, a distinctive separation of the human and natural sciences was in process that bore the marks of increasing professionalism based on the findings of nineteenth-century science (Moore and Wekker 2011). In this section I want to provide an answer to the question that has thus far been implicit: Where did this obsession with black female genitals come from? How do we understand this special interest in black women's genitalia and pelvises, which is apparent from the foregoing and that also speaks from the coded language embedded within the term "Hottentot nymphae"? How are race, gender, and sexuality imbricated in this concept? My aim is not, cannot be, to provide a full-fledged intersectional rereading of early twentieth-century science, but is to throw more light on the backgrounds of the use of the term "Hottentot nymphae."

My central understanding in this section is that race, as the prior fundamental scientific object of study, has inexorably been central to the conceptualizations of sex/gender and of sexuality that later evolved in the development of the sciences, and that this must also have been the case in the Netherlands. Since there are no analyses specifically for the Dutch development of sciences that take race, gender, and sexuality into account, my work here builds on critical thought in cultural studies in the United Kingdom and the United States, assuming that it will, in its main contours, also be applicable here.[15] It is mainly gender-conscious accounts that have been undertaken in the Netherlands.[16] I am arguing that it is necessary to think through how race was imbricated and articulated in Dutch sciences in order to see the (dis)continuities in the development of science as a transnational endeavour. Dutch sciences, in this case the fields of medicine, biology, sexology and anthropology have traditionally been open to academic developments elsewhere. It seems futile to claim a space of exceptionalism for the Netherlands as being outside these transnational, mutually connected knowledge circuits.

This is a complicated narrative that showcases a deep obsession with blackness, and specifically with black female genitalia, on the one hand, and, in subsequent epochs, an active disappearance of this interest, on the other. Race as a fundamental social and (pseudo)scientific concept preceded sex/gender, sexuality, and class, and this manifests in various conceptualizations taking race as their point of departure. It is not just that in temperament, intelligence, and physiology, the so-called lower races have often provided a metaphor for women and, vice versa, that women have stood in for the lower races (Stepan 1993; Markowitz 2001). The unfortunate tendency to still speak in terms of masculine and feminine races, where, for example, exoticized Indonesian men are seen as feminine versus hypermasculine Dutch men, is another instantiation of this powerful metaphor at work. The concept of sex/gender, lying at the heart of the discipline of gender/women's studies, which seems so innocuous, neutral, universally applicable, and race free, has been fiercely criticized as being suffused with race from its inception (Markowitz 2001). Sex/gender difference has from the start, in the eighteenth century, been conceptualized as racially marked: The more pronounced the sex/gender dimorphism in a particular race, that is, the outward differences between men and women, the more advanced that group of people is considered to be. A scale of racially coded degrees of sex/gender difference has silently been installed, culminating in the manly European man and the feminine European woman (Markowitz

2001, 391). Of course, whites figure as the most advanced race in this ideology and all others are found wanting: Men and women supposedly resemble each other too much. The consequences are far-reaching: when sexual dimorphism is envisioned as being embodied only in European races, true femininity and masculinity are white. Markowitz doubts the usefulness of the sex/gender concept, as long as the racial dimensions of sexual dimorphism remain lodged below cultural awareness.

Along other lines, decolonial feminism arrives at a similar conclusion that gender is not an innocent concept: This school of thought points to gender as a colonial introduction. As a concept, gender did not exist among indigenous and black people; more fluid categorizations prevailed (Wekker 2006), but the nonexistence of gender led to the categorization of colonized people as animalistic, nonhuman. The freedom that was allowed the colonized to construct themselves sexually came at an enormous cost: unbridled sexual abuse (Lugones 2007, 2010).

Continuing the line of thought that race as a scientific concept is prior to other concepts, race has often provided a way to understand and speak about class, as is evident in the case of Irish working-class men and women, working under deplorable conditions, who were seen as a different race. Finally, in the domain of sexuality, race has been the leading concept, too: The mere concept of sexual races, in terms of heterosexuals and homosexuals, that was widespread during the opening decades of the twentieth century alerts us to a more or less implicit theory that couples race with sexuality (Halperin 1990). Kobena Mercer and Isaac Julien have also remarked upon the historical and theoretical links between race and sexuality: "The prevailing Western concept of sexuality . . . already contains racism. Historically, the European construction of sexuality coincides with the epoch of Imperialism and the two inter-connect. . . . The personage of the savage was developed as the other of civilisation and one of the first 'proofs' of this otherness was the nakedness of the savage, the visibility of its sex" (1988, cited in Somerville 2000, 5).

But let's take a step back and look at the scientific archive that is at work here. The idea that biological characteristics, the outward appearances and the interiority of bodies, are legible made race and (race-infused) sex/gender and sexuality important building blocks in the classificatory activities that came to characterize the subject matter of the evolving sciences, and it is central to this narrative. The scientific structures and methodologies, as practiced within the disciplines of comparative anatomy and physical anthropology, drove the earlier dominant ideologies of race and also fueled the pursuit of knowledge about the homosexual body. Gradually, as Somerville suggests, both the nonwhite body and the nonheterosexual body were, to greater or lesser extents, constructed as pathological. The backdrop of these scientific pursuits is an intellectual climate that increasingly leaned toward polygeny. Polygeny, as we have seen earlier in this chapter, held that different races were actually different species with distinct biological and geographic origins. This theory came to be accepted widely among American scientists in the 1840s and 1850s. The other major school in the field of scientific racism was monogeny, which had been the prevailing theory in the eighteenth century, and held that all so-called races were related to each other, were members of the same species, and had descended from common ancestry. It would be a mistake to assume, however, that monogenists generally advocated racial equality. Mok (1999, 86–89) has noted for the Netherlands that Darwin's *On the Origin of Species* (1859), with its belief in progress and natural selection, gradually won in influence and that, although there were appreciable differences in the way the theory was interpreted, especially because of the pressure it put on the teachings of Christianity, his work eventually acted to cement preexisting ideas about the superiority of the fittest races.

During a sustained moment, starting in the eighteenth century but continuing well into the twentieth, female genitalia and pelvises became the obsessional markers of evolutionary progress toward civilization. In the pseudo-science that was practiced, many different indicators—skin, skulls, facial angles, and brain mass, but also the pelvis and genitalia—were used to prove the hierarchical ranking of the different races, while diverse measuring methodologies were tried within the disciplines of comparative anatomy and physical anthropology. Hence the excessive attention to black women's primary (the genitals) and secondary characteristics (the buttocks), as exemplified by various Hottentot women, who after their deaths were dissected and taken as proof of the primitive sexuality of black women. As opposed to the normative sexuality of white women, the prim, beautiful, maternal, and exalted angel of the house, big clitorises and their attendant unfeminine sexual desires were presumed to be the domain of lesbians, prostitutes, and women of color.

In the framework of this transnational obsession with black women's pelvises and genitalia, the work of several Dutch scientists has been kept in the transnational scientific archive and transmitted to us. Medical doctor Willem Vrolik played a noteworthy part in 1826 that had reverberations well into the twentieth century.[17] Markowitz notes, "On the one hand, some early anthropologists and physiologists claimed that the wide female pelvis . . . signified racial 'primitivism,' since a generous pelvis seemed to promote the ease in childbirth supposedly enjoyed by beasts—a convenient justification for continuing to drive hard-laboring female slaves of 'lower race' even when they were pregnant" (2001, 393). Willem Vrolik, on the other hand, advanced the view that a wide pelvis was a sign of racial superiority, a view that was later taken up by sexologist Henry Havelock Ellis, who insisted that "as races become more advanced, their increased head size required a wider maternal pelvis to accommodate the larger skull of the racially superior infant" (Markowitz 2001, 393). Another Dutch protagonist who has survived in (transnational) scientific memory is forester Herman Bernelot Moens (De Rooij, 2015), because he proposed in 1907 to conduct experiments meant to produce offspring by mating black men and female anthropoid apes, gorillas and chimpansees. This experiment, luckily, never came to fruition. Finally, there is German Russian gynecologist Carl Heinrich Stratz (1858–1924), who—like van Ophuijsen—practiced and lived in The Hague and, having practiced five years on Java, published *Die Frauen auf Java, eine gynäkologische Studie* in 1897, which also appeared in Dutch in the same year.[18] I am not inclined to see his pornotropical work, with its racist overtones, as exceptional, but I firmly place it within the normal scientific quest for racial hierarchy.

All these scientists were preoccupied with black or Asian women. Why was it black women who were singled out for medical, sexological, and anthropological attention and not black men's sexual endowments? One might be tempted to assume that in disciplines overwhelmingly consisting of white men that it might have been black men who would have held their primary attention, yet on the basis of overviews provided by Sander Gilman (1985) and Siobhan Somerville (2000), posthumous dissections of black men are conspicuously absent in U.S. medical and anthropological journals. I read this gendered phenomenon as, in part, driven by racist scientific ideology seeking to establish hierarchy between races, and also by the power relations operative, which positioned black women at the farthest remove from the subjects of science. Such research must have provided appreciable sexual pleasures to the white men engaging in it. Is it too far-fetched to see the relationship between the white male scientist and his black female objects of study as analogous to the relationship between male colonists and colonized women? The scientific task to be accomplished, as it was seen at the time, was to maintain a cross-racial hierarchical sex/gender classification, one that installed differences between men and women universally (and was most pronounced, as we have seen, between white men and women, as a sign of advanced civilization), as well as an intraracial hierarchical ordering between the genders (cf. Markowitz 2001). In other words, white men and women were to be installed as superior in terms of race, and men as superior to women within races. Thus, black women's pelvises and genitalia were instrumentalized as the lowest, the most uncivilized, in terms of race as well as gender, in the quest for racialized, gendered hierarchy.

Something Is Happening Here, but Do We Know What It Is?

I have been moved to read this case study as telling us something meaningful about the ways that the bodies of the white upper-class female analysands were requisitioned and interpellated by black female bodies, as well as about the resulting psychic economies of these women, and, finally, about what van Ophuijsen's substitution of gender for race meant. I will ask three questions about this case study, coupling, as I am doing throughout the book, a postcolonial framework with a cultural archival and an intersectional perspective.

My first question is: Did the patients themselves use the term "Hottentot nymphae" or was it J. W. H. van Ophuijsen who came up with it? Preliminarily, given the Dutch demographic structure in 1917, I have been assuming that the women in this case study were white, and, given the costs attached to psychoanalytical treatment, that they had a middle- or upper-class background. I am arguing that the term is not meaningless nor coincidental, but that its use says something meaningful about understandings of gender, race, sexuality, and subjectivity in Dutch society at the time. A discourse was available to these women to express their problem, that is to say that more than a mere idiosyncratic way of speaking and understanding themselves was at stake.

While there is no way to know for sure, I am inclined to think that the women actually used the literal term "Hottentot nymphae," that is, that they were interpellated, in an Althusserian sense, by the term as inviting them to identify with the conditions described under it: feeling clear, "This is me." It is as if, across this century, the women are calling out to van Ophuijsen and to us: "See me for who I am. Take seriously how I describe myself."[19]

That the women might have used the term to describe themselves is underscored by the fact that van Ophuijsen uses inverted commas around "Hottentot nymphae" but especially by his phrase: "They informed me *of their own accord* that they possessed Hottentot nymphae." Would he not have used another phrase, something like, "I concluded on the basis of their descriptions that they possessed Hottentot nymphae," if *he* chose the term? As we saw, Sander Gilman has pointed out that by the 1920s it would have become a commonplace to associate sexuality, and in particular a sexuality that exceeded or contradicted a clearly heterocentric model—as in the case of the prostitute, the lesbian, or the hysteric—with the image of the Hottentot, the stereotype of black female sexuality, the lowest of the low (Gilman 1985). Furthermore, van Ophuijsen clearly does not agree with the diagnosis of Hottentot nymphae, which is all the more reason to assume that he was not the one to have brought it up.

Ultimately, however, what matters more than who actually used the term, is that it circulated among a professional and an educated lay public and that there were ample other everyday sites in society, as I have shown, where the women would have been exposed to racial imagery and representations. While the women call on Hottentot nymphae, thus on gendered race, to make a statement about themselves and on what is wrong with them, van Ophuijsen does not pay any attention to it. He actively dismisses it and substitutes gender for race: Their neurosis is that they are suffering from rivalry with men, from masculinity complex. We are confronted then with a situation where van Ophuijsen, in line with dominant psychoanalytical and social common sense, does not want to hear anything about race, and is most preoccupied with gender and sexuality.

Furthermore, we need to ask what is at stake when these white women adopt the coded language of Hottentot nymphae? It would seem that it is impossible for them to speak directly about their gender and especially about their active sexuality—geared as it supposedly is toward clitoral and urethral pleasures—because doing so would place them, in psychoanalytical understandings to which they might very well have been privy, in the unfavorable category of possessing an immature, inappropriate sexuality: not passive, not receptive, not focused on the vagina. Thus, they need to displace those feelings onto black women. But these women are also displacing themselves in the colonial, gendered, racialized, and heterosexualized order of things; they seem to be embracing a racial grammar that has assigned a particular, fixed place to particular actors. Specifically, they have embraced a more intense libido and affective states that are the domain of black women, thus shunning the normative, receptive sexuality that is assigned to white women. The excessive, aggressive, more masculine sexuality ascribed to black women must have held appeal for them: still officially feminine, but with a masculine tinge. While their identification—if we could call it that; appropriation might be more apt—with black women might, on the one hand, be read as a transgressive gesture, on the other, it leaves the supposed purity and putative passivity of white female sexuality intact and thus reinstates the binary nature of the sexualities ascribed to black and white women. Thus, in the Dutch cultural archive of the era, an intermediate gender position and a strong libido cannot be claimed by white women and is racialized as black and feminine.

The second set of questions is, why is it that van Ophuijsen discards the women's own racialized understandings of their situation and prefers to frame their predicament in terms of gender? What is that substitution about? Also, what's up with van Ophuijsen himself? Does his East Indies background play into choosing the particular stance that he does? Contextually, it is important to keep in mind that in Western Europe this was a time of huge social changes, especially in terms of gender relations, and gender and sexuality were foremost on people's minds, both among the general public and among medical professionals. In the early decades of the twentieth century, there was both in the United States and in Europe a keen interest in female homosexuality as a response and (in part) as resistance to the suffrage and early women's movement (Martin 1993). Against this background, it would seem reasonable that van Ophuijsen was more motivated by the grammar of (race-evacuated) gender than by that of race. Coupled with the fact that race as a category pertaining to whites was evacuated and that thinking both categories simultaneously was unthinkable, he did not pay any attention to what his patients were telling him. I read the fact that he was from the East Indies, with its own, pronounced racial grammar erasing race in Indos, and his position as an alien body in a professional, overwhelmingly white psychoanalytical environment as underlining his inability to hear the racialized grammar the women used to speak about their predicament. Gilman offers an additional consideration, when we think about van Ophuijsen's position as an invader within his profession: "As virtually all of Freud's early disciples were Jews, the lure of psychoanalysis for them may well have been its claims for a universalization of human experience and an active exclusion of the importance of race from its theoretical framework" (1993, 6). His East Indies background is parallel to the Jewish positioning within psychoanalysis: these positionings need to be erased. This converges with a professional ethic in which race was evacuated and made void, thus making it more difficult for him to surmount the already present barriers to deal with race.

Given the chain of associations that is set in motion by the women's appropriation of black women's sexuality, its lasciviousness, its excessiveness, the overdevelopment of labia minora and the clitoris, which may very well lead to those excesses that are called "lesbian love," the "unhealthy attention" to the clitoris at the expense of the vagina, and, generally, a too-active sexuality, it stands to reason that van Ophuijsen has to dissociate, and "cannot acknowledge that these white women are enacting a specifically cross-racial, rather than cross-gendered, identification" (Walton 1997, 234).

Finally, my third and most overarching question: What is the significance of this case study for psychoanalysis, for subjectivity, and for the exploration of the place of race in the Dutch cultural archive? While black people were largely an absent physical presence in the Netherlands at the time, the case study shows that the explicit discourse on gender and sexuality of the period was informed by implicit assumptions about racial difference. A rereading of this case study along intersectional lines throws new light on the presence of race in the Dutch cultural archive. The concepts of self and other that came into being in Western modernity were dependent on the politics of colonial relations, and a postcolonial approach to the study of subjectivity has to take that into account. It does not make sense to understand white female subjectivity in abstraction from race. More generally, the analysis of this case study again shows how the still-dominant practice in the Dutch academy of keeping metropole and colonies apart in separate analytical fields results in the maintenance of significant racial blinders about practically all things, but significantly about (sexual) subjectivity. In order to produce inclusive knowledge about the Netherlands, it is essential to consider race as an equally important grammar of difference as gender.

So, in summing up, what does the expression "Hottentot nymphae" code and hide? What is its meaning? I have been arguing that the three female patients were eroticizing their own gendered and sexual states; they were projecting these states onto black women, who were not actually present in society and whom they might never have met, but whose imagery figured ubiquitously as an absent presence. This projection allowed them to inhabit (what was seen at the time as) a less than feminine gender and an active, clitoral, nonheterocentric sexuality. Central to the code is the silent ubiquity of race, that is, black women with their abject, supposedly unfeminine, excessive sexuality.

CHAPTER 4

Of Homo Nostalgia and (Post)Coloniality
Or, Where Did All the Critical White Gay Men Go?

"Haunting," the way in which abusive systems
of power make themselves known and their impacts
felt in everyday life, especially when they are
supposedly over and done with.

Avery F. Gordon, *Ghostly Matters*, 2008

Our times are suffused with nostalgia; from different corners our desires for the past, for better, clearly delineated, and "normal" times, are kindled. The Netherlands has attractively been constructed and represented as free, emancipated, tolerant, a beacon of civilization in the rising tide of Islamic and immigrant barbary coming ever closer. There is nostalgia for a time when religion faded from the public sphere and an autonomous, neoliberal self could be constructed. The sudden confrontation with Islam in the public sphere reminded the Dutch painfully of the Christian religion that they had just, within one generation from the end of the 1960s, gotten rid of, and they did not want to return to it (Van der Veer 2006). Others cherish a nostalgia for the 1950s when demographically the Netherlands were still unproblematically white and gender relations were clear, with men as breadwinners and women staying at home. In gay circles nostalgia is rampant, too: for the times when we were safe, could kiss and hold hands in public, before Muslims came and rained on our parade. When we could still live in our neighborhoods without being harassed by Moroccan boys, when the inexorable march of progress toward sexual liberation could proceed, without being hampered by uncivilized others. In none of these versions of nostalgia is there any remembrance or accounting for an imperial past. The lament against Muslims was summed up by Pim Fortuyn (2002), icon of many white gay males, when he said in a much-quoted interview in *De Volkskrant*, headlined "Islam Is a Backward Religion," that he "does not feel like doing the emancipation of women and gays over again." It is clear at whose doorstep the blame is laid for the backlash against gays and lesbians, and the gains of women's emancipation are also deemed to be in grave danger.

I, too, am plagued by nostalgia. But it is not imperialist nostalgia that I long for (Rosaldo 1989). Imperialist nostalgia is a condition in which colonizers mourn the passing of what they themselves have altered, destroyed, or transformed; "it uses a pose of 'innocent yearning' both to capture people's imaginations and to conceal its complicity with often brutal domination" (Rosaldo 1989, 70). Imperialist nostalgia is so effective because it invokes a register of innocence; the responsible imperial agent is transformed into an innocent bystander, masking his involvement with processes of domination. Rather, I am driven by a critical nostalgia, with nonnormative sexualities as a basis upon which a politics of solidarity can take off, and for which hard work will be required. This nostalgia longs for a time when there was critical reflection and action upon the question of which alliances could be made between different categories of minority groups, migrants and gays, hetero women and lesbians. That attitude now is hard to come by, when we witness the retrograde and Islamophobic statements even at academic conferences, such as one held at the University of Amsterdam in January 2011, dedicated to the exploration of various sexual nationalisms (cf. Haritaworn 2012).

This chapter addresses gay politics in the Netherlands in the past decades, but also attempts a more in-depth excavation of homosexuality's genealogy, that is, its entanglement with race. A driving force for writing this chapter, one that has widely been swept under the carpet, was the—to me—jolting realization that at the national parliamentary elections on June 9, 2010, white gay men voted overwhelmingly for PVV, the Party for Freedom, under the leadership of Islamophobe and xenophobe Geert Wilders. The most popular political party among white Dutch gay men was PVV, while white lesbian women tended to vote more traditionally for leftist parties, like the Labor Party and the Green Left.[1] The strongest characteristics of PVV are an anti-European agenda, opposition to multiculturalism, especially advocacy for anti-Islamic measures, policies, and understandings, and support for women's and gay rights. Apart from its rare, antidemocratic political structure, which concentrates power in the hands of Wilders alone,[2] PVV stands out for an extraordinary coarseness in its political-rhetorical style, "telling things as they are," expressly seeking to insult and humiliate Muslims by using derogatory expressions like *kopvoddentax*, which is a tax on the wearing of headscarves,[3] "hate palaces" to indicate mosques, and "street robbers and bandits" to refer to young Moroccan Dutch men. By constantly proposing ideas for the solution of the "Muslim problem" that are, as Wilders well knows, unconstitutional—such as his often-repeated proposal to send young offenders of Moroccan descent back to Morocco, though they have Dutch citizenship—he effectively helps to produce an atmosphere of fear and exclusion among Moroccan Dutch people, and he feeds the mind-set among the white Dutch population that finds Muslims inassimilable in the Netherlands and that favors their deportation. On March 12, 2014, on the evening of the municipal elections, Wilders asked his followers: "Do you want more or fewer Moroccans?" "Fewer, fewer, fewer," the crowd chanted. Wilders: "Then we are going to arrange that." In December 2014, The Public Prosecutor decided to sue Wilders for this statement.[4] PVV is Fortuyn's electoral heir, after his murder in June 2002, and it supports gay and women's liberation since these issues have become the litmus test for modernity, for who qualifies as belonging to the nation. In their electoral program of 2012, PVV stated explicitly, "We defend our gays against advancing Islam."[5]

In 2010, PVV showed enormous growth, expanding from nine to twenty-seven seats in parliament, thereby becoming the third largest party at the time. This electoral success led PVV to give extracoalitional support to the new government Rutte-I, consisting of VVD, Conservative Democrats, and Christian Democrats, which stayed in office until April 2012. The fact that these parties accepted PVV support in order to govern was unprecedented, lending credibility to this party, which had hitherto been politically shunned in a quasi-*cordon sanitaire*. After PVV wreaked considerable political havoc, putting pressure especially on Gerd Leers, the Christian Democrat minister responsible for immigration and integration policy, the upshot of this experiment was a swing to the right of the entire political spectrum.

I am interested, first, in tracing the history of the Dutch white gay movement in comparison with the women's liberation movement. These two major social movements of the second half of the twentieth century form the backdrop of the developments I want to describe in this chapter. The existing historiography of these two movements is largely white, although women and gays and lesbians of color were already present when they took off.[6] To a very limited extent, I suggest some material that would have to be included in an inclusive gay and lesbian history. This will lead me, second, to explore governmental gay policy and which understandings of homosexuality it privileges, embraces, and defends. In other words, not just any form or manifestation of homosexuality will do, to be recognized by the government. Third, I want to investigate the political economy of desire that Pim Fortuyn was embedded in. One of the most forceful explanations is that gay liberation became entwined with Islamophobia through homonationalism, which forcefully foregrounds the acceptance of homosexuality as the litmus test for modernity, while rejecting Islam (Puar 2007). My exploration is a different one, a cultural archival one, although it will eventually also invoke homonationalism. I am interested in the figure of Pim Fortuyn with his contradictory desires—rejecting Muslims and at the same time allegedly preferring them as his sexual partners in dark rooms. I am arguing that Fortuyn's contradictory desires are not uniquely and idiosyncratically his; they are more widespread among white gay men. They come straight from the colonial past and connect intimately to the Dutch cultural archive. This chapter also and obviously is an exercise in thinking gender, race, sexuality, and nation together, in a country that prides itself on its progressive sexual politics.

Major Social Movements

As a general backdrop to this chapter, I want to zoom in on the two major Dutch social movements for emancipation that have been operative since the 1960s, the women's movement and, somewhat later, the gay liberation movement. Traditionally, the government has played an important role in emancipation movements, such as those of Catholics and Labor earlier in the twentieth century, which took place on a massive scale in the framework of pillarization. Actually, coalition governments were the expression of the balancing act between various societal groups, whereby power was divided for the sake of equality between the groups. From the end of the 1960s, the government also supported women and gays and lesbians, on a much smaller scale, by subsidizing their activities, doing research, and designing policies to stimulate the aims of the groups. For the movements, the connection with the government not only means recognition but also a legitimization of their issues. When the black lesbian literary group of which I was a cofounder, Sister Outsider, asked the Directorate of Emancipation Affairs in 1984 and 1986 to incidentally subsidize the journey and visit of African American poet, essayist, and activist Audre Lorde to Amsterdam, it meant a major recognition of our activities (Wekker 1992; Hermans 2002; Ellerbe-Dueck and Wekker 2015).

A Short Excursion

Audre Lorde arrived on Friday, July 13, 1984, and all of Sister Outsider went to welcome her at Schiphol Airport. We had an elaborate lunch at my place. I had set the table with linen and a giant bouquet of sunflowers; we had white wine and I had baked coconut and chocolate pies. Audre was not supposed to eat rich foods, but she did anyway, displaying naughtiness and willfulness and making it clear that she was in charge of her own life. What struck me most about her was how full of life and joy she was. Whether it was good food, smart conversations, dancing, gossiping, taking notes, as she was continually doing, she was totally present. When she encountered someone, she gave that person the feeling that she really wanted to know her, without delay, as if she was saying, "Tell me your story; there is no time to lose." She had an incredible intensity and focus. It felt like basking in her light, and she made me feel beautiful and smart. On Saturday morning she had woken up early, before me, and had taken inventory of my bookshelves. When I woke up, she was ready to be enlightened about the history and sociology of Suriname. I talked to her for hours, while she was taking notes. I had just finished an article on "beautiful Joanna," a light-skinned enslaved woman who has been immortalized by her lover, the Scottish captain John Gabriel Stedman ([1790] 1988), who had come to Suriname to defeat the Maroons, who, in the view of the colonial government and the planters, were bringing the colony to ruin. During his sojourn in Suriname (1772–1777), Stedman kept a diary, in which Joanna features prominently; he also made numerous sketches of her, with her curly locks. Joanna refused to go to Europe with him after his period of service was over. Audre was mesmerized by the story and later wrote in her diary, "Learned more about Suriname in an hour with Gloria Wekker" (based on my diary and on Ellerbe-Dueck and Wekker 2015).[7]

Returning to government funding of activist groups, the downside, of course, of this dependency on government funding is that organizations may cease to exist when policy changes, which is what happened to the larger women's movement, lately to a host of cultural institutions, and, as we saw in the introduction, to NiNsee, the National Institute of Dutch Slavery and Heritage. Thus, the government has considerable power to keep movements intact, to slow them down, or even undermine them.

The hegemonic Dutch reading is that the women's and gay movements have largely accomplished their aims, as is abundantly clear from the national pride taken in their accomplishments by politicians and the media, and in everyday discourses. One does not have to engage in the hyperbolic rhetoric of Pim Fortuyn (1997, 69–70) that the liberation of women and gays is "the greatest mental and cultural achievement after the creation of the welfare state in the modern history of mankind" to ascertain that this general sentiment has broad purchase in Dutch society and even that national identity, from left to right in the political spectrum, is bound up with a progressive, ultramodern, liberated self-image, in which the embrace of women's and gay liberation has increasingly become pivotal. In debates about Dutch multicultural society, there is in general a self-congratulatory national tone that the Netherlands is a paradise of emancipation. In order to sustain this fiction, one needs to overlook the still widely divergent income levels of men and women; the widespread sexual violence against all women, and the disproportionate presence of women from the south and eastern Europe in sex work.

It is striking that a vocal part of the women's movement was inspired, certainly in the early decades, by a radical difference agenda, an *Umwertung aller Werte*, a rejection of the reigning sexual morality, against monogamy and marriage, and against the limiting roles of men and women. Against the background of a very traditional division of labor between men and women, where women were supposed to be full-time homemakers, giving up paid work after marriage so that only single women worked outside the home, which lasted well into the 1970s, paid work became a spearhead of the women's movement. Other issues that were embraced and that, to this day, still have not been satisfactorily resolved include a more equitable participation of women in the higher sectors of business and in the academy, equal pay for equal work, affordable child care, and combating sexual violence against women. In fact, it takes an exceptionally rosy outlook to claim that the emancipation of women has been accomplished, especially when, to consider but one indicator, paid work, we take into account that the usual 1.5 model, with men working full time and women usually half of the time, has increasingly become unassailable and the sign of progressive gender relations. Many women defend it as their personal choice, expressive of a neoliberal, hyperindividual outlook on life that has distinct blinders. It overlooks the often steep loss of income that they will suffer in case of a divorce, which happens in one out of every three marriages, and, in addition, the almost negligible pensions they will have built up over their working lives. In the case of black, migrant, and refugee women, the combination of divorce and pension loss takes even more dramatic forms (Wekker 2009b). The current minister of emancipation affairs, Dr. Jet Bussemaker, stresses the importance of women working (as close to) full time as possible, not only to avoid such a deplorable economic future, but also to encourage women to benefit society with their education, until recently largely financed by the state. The minister reaps mostly disdain and rejection, which points to the metamorphosis that emancipation has undergone in the past decades: from a collective struggle to increase women's autonomy in all domains of life, to emancipation as an individual choice, in which the government is seen as undesirably meddling in people's personal lives, which is experienced by many as superfluous.

Importantly, inserting an intersectional perspective, the women's movement was more prepared—at least in principle—than the gay movement to reflect on race as a social and symbolical grammar as important as gender. Although the debates about race in the women's movement, from the end of the 1970s on, were never satisfactorily resolved, and many black, migrant, and refugee women split off from the larger (white) women's movement in their own organizations, the introduction of intersectionality in the Dutch context acted as a dea ex machina; a dominant part of the women's movement and women's studies now interpreted race as a voluntary axis of signification: one could engage with it but did not have to. Meanwhile, (a part of) the women's movement accommodated itself to government policies and was able to erect an elaborate patchwork of women's institutions during the 1970s and 1980s. In the first decade of the twenty-first century this quilt was all but destroyed, when the government in the person of Christian Democrat minister de Geus declared in 2003 that women's emancipation, except for that of black, migrant, and refugee women, was accomplished. Notwithstanding the many indications to the contrary—whether in terms of income and pensions, sexual violence predominantly directed at women or the steeply gendered yearly lists charting powerful and influential persons in the Netherlands—this move not only allowed the government to cut severely into women's subsidized organizations and networks, it also firmly reinstalled and reaffirmed racialized hierarchizations among women: It again positioned white women at the apex of emancipation, with their less fortunate "sisters," women of color and Third World women, in a lower station, as we saw in chapter 2. Many of the debates in the domain of women's emancipation, and the most heated ones, are dialogues between men about topics that have to do with black, migrant, and refugee women and their sexuality: clitoridectomy, the veil, the burka, the locking up of women, young women forcefully being married to men of their parents' choice, rather than reflecting on the usual subjects: equal pay for equal work, and so on. A subtext of these debates is a desire on the part of men to control the sexuality of women, including lesbian women of all hues. Or, as Gayatri Spivak famously remarked in "Can the Subaltern Speak?," the debates are about "white men rescuing brown women from brown men" (1994, 93).

The gay movement—and white men have populated this movement more thickly and thus have been at the forefront here—has from its inception been more interested in equality: equal rights, gay marriage, the right to adopt children, the right to copious consumption of all manner of material goods, and has pursued a more assimilationist agenda with the social, political, and cultural powers that be. It is noteworthy that the largest gay organization, COC, publicly supported the position of PVV as extra-coalitional partner to the government in 2010. Its chairperson, Vera Bergkamp, stated, "We will not be hijacked by the left or the right, but we look where our interests are best met. PVV indeed touches a chord with gays. We cannot afford to look the other way when people are under duress. Violence against gays has increased according to the police in the past years. Among the perpetrators Moroccan boys are overrepresented" (Akkermans 2011). With this statement, which rehearses and reproduces "common knowledge," COC, whose task supposedly is to defend the interests of all gays and lesbians, made it abundantly clear in which limited way it conceives of its duties. Implicitly, gays are conceived as white, while the perpetrators are Moroccan. The pernicious binary "the homosexual other is white; the racial other is straight" is reinstalled. Misrepresenting and stressing the role of Moroccan gay bashers overlooks the part of white attackers, who, according to research by the police, are in the majority: 68 percent (Politie 2013, 33).

Race was never a significant part of the agenda of the gay movement, although it has always seemed to me that there were more than enough reasons to look into issues like the self-flattering erasure of race in policy and everyday understandings about homosexuality; the widespread but never interrogated number of interracial relationships, with partners of color from either near or far, which repeat traditional dependency patterns; the unproblematized adoption of black children by white gay couples;[8] the sexualized imagery that surrounds gays of color. The move to the right, evident in the overwhelming vote for PVV in 2010, may be less improbable if we see it in light of the blindness to race and the depoliticization that had always already characterized white gay politics.[9] I fully agree with Mepschen, Duyvendak, and Tonkens, who state that "paradoxically, it is the depoliticized character of Dutch gay identity, 'anchored in domesticity and consumption' . . . that explains its entanglement with neo-nationalist and normative citizenship discourses. Dutch gay identity does not threaten heteronormativity, but in fact helps shape and reinforce the contours of 'tolerant' and 'liberal' Dutch national culture" (2010, 971).

Turning to gay organizations, including the AIDS industry, gendered and racialized relations often go unnoticed. Within COC, which is largely white in personnel, board, and directorship, race is dealt with by subsidizing several youth organizations, such as Respect2love and Foundation Malaica, to cater to gays of color. In another part of the gay organizational world, the HIV/AIDS conglomerate, white gay men, in collaboration with the Dutch state, were able to carve out some significant institutional niches in the struggle against HIV/AIDS, which still exist to this day (Duyvendak 1996). Oftentimes in research studies in the field of sexual health, attention is only or predominantly paid to how STI/HIV can be prevented in men, not in women. Questions like who is deemed qualified to work as an official employee in an organization and who can only render services as a volunteer need our attention. A division of labor often takes place in the

AIDS organizational field in which people of color are the objects of care, not independent knowers, and white people are the subjects of knowledge, the experts, even when the target populations are people of color. However, such questions hardly ever surface in the gay movement.

In comparing the two movements, I arrive at some of the same conclusions as Foucault does: homosexual movements had no choice but to focus on the "sexual centering of the problem, since it was their sexual practice which was attacked, barred and disqualified as such, the need to limit their claims to their sexual specificity made it much more difficult to escape the 'trap' of power. Women's liberation movements, on the other hand, had much wider economic, political and other kinds of objectives" (Foucault, cited in Scott 2011, 16). The long march through the institutions of the respective movements has, measured in the terms they themselves have set, been more successful for the gay movement, in that they have been able to reach more public visibility, attention for their specific problems, and a separate niche, the HIV/AIDS conglomerate and events like the Gay Parade, which have become firm power bases. Especially the Gay Parade has become thoroughly enmeshed in commercialism and self-congratulation. The women's movement, while initially much more massive, radical, and visible, has also made important strides, but its main goals have not been reached, and institutionally it has not proven too difficult to break it up, fuse it into two remaining national bodies and some local and regional agencies.

Public visibility of gay life has its limitations. The dominant representation of homosexuality after sixty years of intense postcolonial, labor, and refugee migration to the Netherlands still is that gays and lesbians belong to the dominant racial group; that is, in the public eye gays are white. Diversity in sexual cultures, including same-sex cultures, has, by now, with the multiracialization of Dutch society, become an irreversible fact, but there is no diversity in dominant representations of gay and lesbian life. Most visible in the public domain, through media content, a commercial entertainment industry, and yearly events like the Gay Parade, are white gay men of a certain type—entertainers, TV personalities, businessmen, politicians. In the past decades, as evident in polls, they have come to be embraced and accepted by the majority of the straight population. Black, migrant, and refugee gays, the gay Other, do not get much attention, but Islamic gays—for instance, the visitors of the first Arab gay café in the world, Habibi Ana in the center of Amsterdam,[10] who also participate in the Gay Parade—are cherished too, because they seem to adhere at least to some of the do's and don'ts of the habitus of white Dutch gays: They have, to a certain extent, come out of the closet. Furthermore, they are embraced because they need to be protected against their barbaric, aggressive hetero brothers.

White and black, migrant and refugee lesbians are virtually invisible in the current landscape. This has not always been the case. Under the influence of black lesbian thought from the United States and the United Kingdom, in the early 1980s a movement became visible that was predominantly made up of Indo, Moluccan, Surinamese, and Antillean Dutch lesbians. We developed our own organizations and activities, having come to a heightened consciousness regarding cultural and political differences with the white lesbian movement and the racism extant within it. Black and migrant lesbians realized that their relations with the white lesbian movement were characterized by power differences. Those who organized in the black, migrant, and refugee (BMR) lesbian movement were mostly women who had been born or raised in the Netherlands and had studied there, but there were also Afro-Surinamese mati in the movement, who had arrived after the independence of Suriname in 1975 (Wekker 2006), and kapuchera from the Antilles (Clemencia 1996). Mati and kapuchera are working-class African diasporic women, who have erotic relationships with men and with women, either simultaneously or consecutively, and they typically have children. The construction of their same-sex sexuality, based on West African "grammatical principles" (Mintz and Price [1976] 1992), should not be equated with Western homo- or bisexuality (Wekker 2006). Later, other groups presented themselves—more or less vocally and visibly—in the Dutch sexual landscape. Almost all these cultures, including those who have their roots in Turkey and Morocco, have hardly been studied (but see Kursun and El Kaka 2002; Hira 2011). Ghanese supi (short for "superior") as well, who often start their love lives with other girls at boarding school and sometimes continue them when they are married and have children, were and are with us. Supi are a Ghanaian variation of what Judith Gay (1986) has described as "mummies and babies" in the context of southern Africa, where boarding-school girls with an age difference between them have loving and flirting relationships with each other. Supi are mostly located in the southeast of Amsterdam,[11] and I understand them and their sexual practices as thoroughly related to Afro-Surinamese mati (Wekker 2006).

The history of these other lesbians in the Dutch landscape remains largely unwritten.[12] A remarkable difference from the white women's movement, from my perspective as an Afro-Surinamese lesbian activist who came of age in that movement, was that the divisions that were so characteristic there—no men, that is, no boys above the age of twelve allowed—were largely absent in the BMR-lesbian movement. Indeed, the presence of men was often a bone of contention within the women's movement at large, with BMR women wanting men present, as fellow warriors against racism. The joint analysis of our situation that BMR women undertook, a fledgling intersectional analysis, was done by women of various sexual stripes, since the distinction homo/hetero was not as significant as in the white women's movement. Many BMR lesbians found the unproblematized normativity of the white lesbian position, with its accompanying patterns, untenable to participate in, because those dynamics diverged from the ways in which we wanted to shape our desires to be with women. Among those patterns were, first, the lack of consciousness in many white women about their own, dominant racialized position and the "unearned privileges" that whiteness carried (McIntosh 1992; Frankenberg 1990). Second, the prescribed scenario of coming out of the closet rubbed many BMR women (and men) the wrong way, because it did not conform to our cultural behavioral understandings. And third, the other prescription to operate separately—socially, politically, and erotically—from men did not find many adherents either.

Inclusive descriptions and analyses of the gay male movement are also sorely lacking. According to one of my black gay informants, there was a sizeable community of male and female mati couples in southeastern Amsterdam, a.k.a. de Bijlmer, from 1975 on. At some moment, he estimates, there were around five hundred black gays, whose number was decimated by HIV/AIDS. Because black gays were discriminated against in the discos in the center of Amsterdam—where only well-known black gay men like the writer Edgar Cairo and radio journalist Robert Wijdenbosch were welcome—they had set up their own traveling circuit of living-room meeting spaces in the Bijlmer.

An important part of the dominant narrative about homosexuality that circulates is that everything was fine with gay and lesbian liberation until Islamic people turned up and made everything go downhill. They caused a rupture in the triumphant march of progress. This representation is possible only when a homogeneous and Eurocentric us-versus-them schema is in place, whereby everything that is progressive is attributed to us—that is, we accept the emancipation of women and homosexuality, the litmus test for modernity—while everything that is negative is ascribed to them, the backward barbarians, who got stuck in religious tradition.

Just Being Gay (2007–2011)

In 2007 the government released a gay emancipation policy paper, *Gewoon Homo Zijn* (Just being gay), which covered the period until 2011, followed in the next period by a Policy Note on Emancipation (2013–2016). Since 2007, the emancipation of lesbian, gay, bisexual, and transgender (LGBT) people falls under general emancipation policy, located in the Ministry of Education, Culture and Science, together with women's emancipation. I will make a critical analysis of the former policy paper, since it most clearly expresses the problems inherent in the conceptualization of homosexuality by the government and since these problems have not been addressed in the later policy note. Given the continuity of policies, I feel justified in assuming that these ideas are still present.

The main policy aim of *Just Being Gay* is to stimulate the social acceptance of homosexuality among the Dutch population (Ministerie van OC&W, 2007, 5) and there are five operational goals:

1. To stimulate conversation on homosexuality in different population groups
2. To counteract violence and intimidation against gays
3. To stimulate national and local alliances
4. To make an effort to produce gay-friendly environments at school, in the workplace, and in sports
5. To play an active international and European role in the acceptance of homosexuality

Let us stick with the main goal for a moment. The main goal, to stimulate the social acceptance of homosexuality among the Dutch population, has quickly morphed into one of the operational subgoals, that is, to stimulate conversation about homosexuality in different population groups. Fairly soon, this aim was completed by the following sleight of hand: The government wants to make homosexuality a topic of conversation among ethnic minority groups, among youth, and in religious circles (Ministerie van OC&W, 2007, 7). The Dutch population at large has thus effectively been cut down to three problematic categories. The main instrument is to stimulate a dialogue. All kinds of activities and subsidies have been set aside to facilitate this dialogue. Who could possibly be against a dialogue to discuss homosexuality from religious, cultural, and philosophy-of-life perspectives? It seems so self-evident and necessary that it is, to use a time-honored Dutch expression, like cursing in church to be critical toward this policy aim. However, I have two remarks to question the foundational assumption that speaking about one's sexuality is only natural and thus good for everyone. Underlying this assumption is the difference between speaking about homosexual acts and performing those acts, without necessarily claiming a homosexual identity (Wekker 2006). My second, and related, overarching remark refers to the lack of attention to differences within and between categories of gays and lesbians.

First, why is it unproblematically assumed that homosexuality is something that should be talked about? Foucault's ([1976] 1990) study of the history of sexuality is the history of sexuality in the West, and he meticulously shows how "a proliferation of discourses" about sexuality came into being through institutions like the church, medicine, and later therapies. Sexuality has become an object about which we need to talk and confess incessantly. What is striking about *Just Being Gay* is that no attention whatsoever is paid to the fact that the dominant manifestation of homosexuality in the Netherlands is a very specific historically and socioculturally anchored form. Ironically, homosexuality is presented as a homogeneous, natural way of being, while a multiplicity of forms of homosexuality present in society is obfuscated, as well as the status of the dominant form as one specific, albeit powerful social construction. Different cultures shape hetero- but also homosexuality differently. In a multiracial/-ethnic and multireligious society, we should think and speak about homosexuality in the plural: homosexualities. When it is desirable that different sections of society engage in dialogue, there should also be a deep consciousness of the dissimilarity and the different forms of various sexual cultures. Such consciousness is sorely missing, both in the policy paper and in society at large. Neither is there any analysis of the power relations between the different forms in which homosexuality manifests in Dutch society. The reality that is constructed is that there is only one model, and that happens to be the dominant model, which foregrounds speaking about homosexuality. This model is both desirable and self-evident. The dominant scenario, when one experiences feelings of attraction to someone of the same sex, entails "being in psychic distress—coming to terms with it oneself." Telling family and friends about one's sexuality, that is, coming out of the closet, is implicitly and explicitly represented as the natural, the desirable, the only correct and thus the normative way of acting. Underlying this scenario is a specific conceptualization of sexual identity as lodged in one's inner self, authentic and unchangeable (Foucault 1990). By coming out of the closet, that authentic, inner sexual self is brought to the outside, which is the symbolic act of emancipation of the high modern (neo)liberal individual. Dudink notes that for some the homosexual in the twenty-first century, through publicly displaying (especially) his pain and pleasure in coming out, has become the modern subject par excellence (Dudink 2011). The privileging of speaking on the individual level is continued on the social and institutional levels. That is to say that on the individual level, not only is it desirable to speak out, it is decidedly taken as a negative characteristic if a person does not do so. In the binary speaking/acting, silence about one's homosexuality carries connotations of tradition, of secretiveness, of being sly and untrustworthy, of being in denial, of leading a double life, and, in teleological/imperialist fashion, "not as advanced, evolved as we yet." This habitus does not deserve much appreciation from a dominant perspective. On a collective level, the dominant model finds expression, for instance, in the preposterous expectation that homosexual asylum seekers speak out, in their first interview by the IND, the Immigration and Naturalization Service, on their homosexuality.[13] If they fail to do so, they might as well forget their request to stay in the Netherlands. This model is so well entrenched that it has become virtually impossible to recognize alternative ways of imagining desiring modern subjects within a secular sociopolitical order (Ewing 2008). The entrenchment also speaks from the proliferation of popular TV shows in which young gay people are supported and coached to come out of the closet to their family and friends. We are confronted here with the deep-seated assumptions underlying the supposed opposition between secularism/modernity and religion/traditionalism, whose full weight these days is brought to bear on Muslims, although other others do not escape it either. Joan Scott has insightfully pointed out, "The most frequent assumption is that secularism encourages the free expression of sexuality and that it thereby ends the oppression of women because it removes transcendence as the foundation for social norms and treats people as autonomous individuals, agents capable of crafting their own destiny. . . . We are told, secularism broke the hold of traditionalism and ushered in the (democratic) modern age. However varied may be the definitions of modernity, they typically include individualism, which in some accounts . . . is equated with sexual liberation" (2009, 9).

This is not the only scenario that is possible within a multiracial society, however. In my research on Afro-Surinamese working-class women in Suriname and in the Netherlands, and the ways in which they construct and give expression to their sexual subjectivity, it was clear that speaking about one's sexual subjectivity is not the way to deal with the sexual self (Wekker 2006). As different informants have told me, "My mother has eyes to see." In the working class, in which different sexual repertoires circulate without a heavy social stigma attached to them, sexuality is mainly something one does, not necessarily something to talk about, to deeply identify with or come to terms with. The Afro-Surinamese working-class sexual self is not conceptualized as unchangeable and authentic, but as multiplicitous and dynamic, and same-sex sexual acts are associated with particular spiritual beings who carry that person. We are talking here, in Bourdieu's terms, about a difference in habitus, into which people in different cultures are socialized: In the West, the verbal is the sign of modernity, emancipation, and sexual liberation, versus the Afro-Surinamese performative, that does not have to claim an inner, fixed sexual being. In Dutch society the latter habitus is not appreciated nor taken seriously. The mati work, the sexual practices and understandings that mati engage in, is often associated with tradition, with "days gone by," and only lesbianism represents secular modernity, the pinnacle of civilization. The often explicit assumption is that if one spends enough time in the Netherlands, one will automatically become a bona fide lesbian.

In the policy paper *Just Being Gay*, speaking is the privileged form of dealing with homosexuality, while the power relationship to other forms is neither mentioned nor reflected upon. The minister responsible for emancipation, Dr. Jet Bussemaker, spoke implicitly yet in no uncertain terms about that power relationship in her Mosse lecture on October 2, 2013. She said, on the one hand, that the government has a role to play in the emancipation of women and gays, "to hold up norms, to protect the minority against the changeable sentiments of the majority, to influence behavior in the desired direction, but not to prescribe feelings" (Bussemaker 2013, 52, 53). On the other, the government also expects something from LGBT people themselves: "that you also ask from lesbians, gays, bisexuals and transgenders themselves to adjust to the Dutch secular norm that it is good 'to come out of the closet' and to show who you 'really' are" (54, my translation). The status she assigns to "not speaking" about homosexuality becomes clear when she talks about the complacency that might inflict itself upon us, if we take the emancipation of women and gays for granted. The biggest danger of our success is that we sit back and do not even notice, say around 2030, that equal treatment is actually not practiced: "So that we would hardly see it if homosexuals would simply 'choose' not to come out of the closet, not to get married, not demand their equal rights" (56).

While I had initially thought that these were mere possibilities, choices between different alternatives, it turns out that these options have transformed into normative expectations for the behavior of LGBT people. They need to conform to what the government conceptualizes as appropriate behavior. This stance is in line with another notable feature in her presentation: "the privileging of equality above diversity and other values: no matter one's ideas and lifestyle, equal rights and equal treatment of people go above diversity" (Bussemaker 2013, 53). This statement only makes sense from a historical background of pillarization, in which equality was deemed to be more important than all other considerations. When equality is given the same status in current, multiracial society, racializing processes are set in motion. Thus, if I understand her statement correctly, the minister defends the untenable position that equality, conceived as pertaining to women in relation to men and of LGBT people in relation to straight people, all the while taking whiteness as the unstated default position, trumps any notion of diversity. Diversity thus pertains to the other, to women and gays of color, whose cultural and racialized positionings are bracketed, formally declared to be of no account. This is not the practice of intersectionality and is all the more deplorable since the minister used to be a gender studies specialist herself.

My second remark is that there is hardly any differentiation in the categories under discussion: There are only a few times in the policy paper that I was able to ascertain that there are also lesbians in the world; that is, lesbians hardly are mentioned. It is stated that they have other problems, so the implicit subject of the policy paper, those who are centrally important, are gay men. Research shows, for instance, that lesbians are more inclined to internalize their problems, drinking and smoking too much, while gay men externalize them (Bos and Ehrhardt 2010). *Just Being Gay* explicitly states that it is important to pay attention to youths, but here again it seems that it is boys who experience problems; girls are nowhere to be seen. The dominant gendered position of masculinity is silently and self-evidently made central. When we pivot our gaze to race/ethnicity, the different positionings are not treated equally either. Again, the dominant racial positioning is not named nor interrogated, but silently installed as the normal, the normative positioning. This is evident, for instance, from the often-repeated injunction to have a dialogue between "gays and Muslims." Not only are sexual and religious positioning juxtaposed here, but simultaneously it is apparently deemed superfluous to name a racial/ethnic positioning for whites and a sexual one for Muslims. This creates the impression that on the one hand there are gays (read, white gays), and on the other Muslims, who evidently are all straight. This exclusionary and binary way of naming and categorizing, a zero-sum game, goes against the stated aim of stimulating discussion between groups.

At this point, I want to draw some conclusions. First, it is clear that policy in the domain of LGBT emancipation, as underwritten by the minister, lacks an intersectional analysis; equality is perceived as a more important value than diversity, foregrounding the privileged positions of white men. Against that stance and second, it is important to realize that homosexuality does not look the same in all cultures and that there are plural homosexualities circulating in Dutch society. Third, there is a power relationship between those different sexual cultures and also between the forms and conceptualizations shaping homosexuality. Fourth, our positionings at simultaneous different axes of signification necessitate a more complex analysis than has thus far been the case. When the dominant pole of a particular axis, such as masculinity, is allowed to stand without explicitly naming it or reflecting on it, a supposedly general policy note is only about men, not about women; when white gays are not named as such, relations of power toward other homosexual positionings are inadvertently kept intact. Fifth, and finally, a thorough and robust gay emancipation policy must be based on more fundamental research into the different sexual cultures present in the Netherlands. Research about sex is often policy oriented, with a central problem that needs to be solved, from the battle against HIV/AIDS to gay bashing and harassment.[14] Not so remarkably, these are often problems confronting white gay men. Research should not be driven only by the (justified) need to combat HIV/AIDS, but by an integral understanding of the cultural worlds different groups inhabit, and the understandings and categories that they use in the sexual domain.

Homosexuality and (Post)Coloniality

Delving into the homosexuality-(post)coloniality nexus, which, as I argue, is based on and fueled by a racist cultural archive, I am struck by the pivotal position of Pim Fortuyn, the gay politician, who was a trailblazer for Wilders's political party, PVV. Fortuyn was murdered on May 6, 2002, by activist Volkert van der G., just days before the national elections, in which Fortuyn promised to win a landslide victory, which in fact was twenty-four seats in parliament.

While much has by now been written about the man Fortuyn, the significance of his ascendancy in the political landscape, his murder, and the supposed loss of innocence of Dutch multicultural society at that juncture (Mak 2005; Buruma 2006; Scheffer 2007), I am intrigued by Fortuyn's entanglement in a racialized, gendered, and sexualized order, which thus far has not been made central to an analysis of his significance.[15] My interest in him is thus less as the victim of "the first political murder in centuries" than in the political economy of desire that he was bringing to the table and that he was embedded in. Analysis of this configuration will, as I argue, tell us something meaningful about the Dutch cultural archive. Fortuyn is pivotal in at least two senses: first, that he was the first politician to speak so openly about the incompatibility of a sexually liberated country, which had gone through two major revolutionary movements (i.e., the women's and the gay liberation movements), and a backward, sexually repressive Islam. While other politicians before him, such as VVD's Frits Bolkestein, had spoken in comparable terms, in the 1990s, the starkness and the accessibility with which Fortuyn approached the issue was new. In a much-publicized interview in De Volkskrant on February 9, 2002, he indicated his deep disgust with Muslims, who with "their backward culture are forcing us to redo women's and gay liberation one more time," which he absolutely refused

(Poorthuis en Wansink 2002). He compared Muslims to *Gereformeerden*, Christian Reformed people, a rather strict part of the Protestant Church, claiming they also always lie, because the demands of their religion are so fierce, unattainable, and not humanly possible. Aware that legally he could not make it work, he was in favor of the borders being closed: zero immigration, especially to Muslims. But for those who are here already, "onze rot Marokkanen" (our own rotten Moroccans), he said they are entitled to their rights, but should shape up and not import their brides from backward home regions anymore. He also said he did not appreciate when highly educated Muslim girls wore a veil, saying this was symptomatic that they were not showing any backbone in enforcing their emancipation from their fathers and brothers. Moreover, he claimed Muslim women do not help their sisters and mothers emancipate, as their (white) feminist predecessors had done with their mothers. Here, again we find the familiar trope in discourses about Muslims that agency is withheld from women, and they cannot possibly be imagined to make their own choice to wear a veil. The most objectionable statement in the interview was, "I am just going to say it, sir, Islam is backward, a backward culture," after which he was ousted from his party, Leefbaar Nederland, and started his own highly successful LPF, Lijst Pim Fortuyn.

The second sense in which Fortuyn is pivotal for my project is that he embodies a most glaring paradox and contradiction in the simultaneous disgust and desire that he displayed toward male Muslims. He had a long history of giving interviews about himself, in which he was not shy about his sexuality. In an early interview in the daily *Trouw* in April 1999, before he had begun his political journey, he seemed somewhat at a loss about what to do next in his life. He was asked to comment on what the Ten Commandments meant to him, as a man who was raised as a Catholic. He answered, about the commandment "Thou shall not commit indecency":

> It is absolutely not my intention to speak blasphemy, but I have to tell you that I find the atmosphere of the Catholic liturgy back in certain acts in the dark room of such a gentlemen's club. The dark room that I frequent in Rotterdam is not totally blacked out: just like in an old cathedral, the light comes in filtered. In such circumstances, making love has a religious aspect to it. Religiosity and merging—that you sometimes have in sex—can be two sides of the same coin. And the beautiful

thing about a dark room is that you find the whole range of emotions there that also exists within a relationship: from blowing your nose to the most intimate form of being together. (Visser 1999, 4)

This poetic sequence forms rich material and insight into Fortuyn's conflation of religion with homosexuality, perhaps playing into his desire for (supposedly religious) young Muslim men (Buruma 2006). For someone bathing in secularism, there is a remarkable degree and density of religiosity present, again pointing to the falseness of the posited dichotomy.

In an earlier interview, in the Amsterdam newspaper Het Parool of February 15, 1997, he laid out his experiences with having sex with male Muslims: "There is a remarkable extra weight attached to doing homosexuality, without naming it and with the connotation: 'Of course, we are really hetero.' There is something narrow-minded about it. I do not have sex with Muslim men anymore. Because their suppressed feelings make for a really strange kind of sex: very focused on fucking, without intimacy, a quick climax, no kissing. I hate that." This statement is intriguing because it alludes to understandings of both equality and inequality in sexual encounters and how Fortuyn skillfully positions himself in both discourses. Against the background of the highly valued norm of equality in society at large, including in gay and lesbian circles, inegalitarian sexual encounters cannot count on much appreciation. Thus Fortuyn, in a strategic move, distances himself from such inegalitarianism. One of the forms, however, in which gay male sex took shape in upper- and middle-class circles well into the 1950s was inegalitarianism: sex with a working-class boy or man; nowadays Muslims evidently embody what a working-class sex partner did before. Muslim boys are not former colonial subjects; they are less inscribed in the Dutch cultural archive, and thus they are extra different, extra unequal. While ostensibly Fortuyn says that he has had it with inegalitarian sex with Muslim men, and thus that he evidently now prefers egalitarian sex, the effect of the statement is that he can embody and be in command of both kinds of sexual encounters.

Fortuyn was an icon for many white gay men, with his eloquence and his flamboyance, with his Daimler automobile, with a driver, and his two King Charles cocker spaniels, Carla and Kenneth. He lived in his Palazzo di Pietro in Rotterdam and he had a villa in Italy. He represented freedom, luxury, the good gay life—the longed-for, desired, but never materialized acceptance by straight society. As the possibly prospective new prime minister, he embodied the promise that "we," gays, could come out of that closet and be taken seriously by society at large. He openly displayed a gay style in debates with straight and straitlaced politicians, who often did not have a satisfactory answer to his gay antics. He showed them up for being at least boring or, worse, falling short of his eloquence. The figure of Fortuyn is noteworthy because he held significant appeal not only for white gay men, who saw him as a symbol of their acceptance into straight society (Mepschen, Duyvendak, and Tonkens 2010), but also to a much wider cross-class audience, men and women alike, who, in embracing him, could feel part of the modern mainstream, which set "us," white moderns, apart from "them," backward Muslim barbarians.

How to make sense of his simultaneous disgust toward and attraction to young Muslim men, whether it was a thing of the past or not? I, at least, find it a remarkable combination, and I also find it remarkable and telling that no one, so far, in the Dutch context has found this deep contradiction worthy of analysis or even remark. One way in which innocence in the sexual domain can be maintained is by not delving deeper into the colonial antecedents of this peculiar combination. In informal conversations with white gay men, the common lazy and self-flattering conclusion one hears is that Fortuyn clearly could not have been a racist, since he fucked Moroccan Dutch boys. As far as I am aware, only Joan Scott has remarked upon Fortuyn's sexual preference: "Pim Fortuyn's comment about liking to fuck young Moroccan boys without interference from backward imams stands as a call for tolerance (of homosexuality), while its emphasis on the availability of brown bodies articulated in the language of colonial orientalism is normalized in the process" (2012, 17). I argue precisely that in order to make sense of this glaring paradox, we should inspect the Dutch cultural archive, in the deeper layers of which, both men and women perceived as others, like blacks, Arabs, and Asians, are always already sexualized, projected to be sexually available and pleasurable, wild and excessive, possessing a greater freedom in their bodies than whites, and thus maddeningly and deeply attractive. Earlier in chapter 3, I pointed out how in the early twentieth century the cure for the waning European life force, libido, was projected onto blacks and various racial others. But this combination must have been installed even earlier. Fortuyn's "idiosyncrasy" is highly reminiscent of sexuality between the master class and the subordinated in colonial times, when the volatile mixture of disgust and desire was installed.

Frankly, Fortuyn is in many respects reminiscent of Thomas Thistlewood, a British overseer on the Egypt plantation in Jamaica who later set himself up as an independent planter. He arrived there in 1750, at the age of twenty-nine, and died at sixty-five in 1786 (Beckles 1999). Thistlewood kept a diary during his thirty-six years in Jamaica (amounting to over 10,000 pages), in which he kept a record of his managerial duties, perhaps aware of the momentous nature of his work and in search of a West Indian fortune, but also and importantly, tracking his sexual exploits with enslaved women.[16] He had an ongoing relationship with the enslaved woman Phibbah for the full thirty-six years of his stay, setting her up as his wife, mother of his child, confidant, servant, but always slave (Beckles 1999, 41). Meanwhile, he was constantly seeking access to other enslaved women, even when he was plagued by venereal disease, which frequently infected the entire plantation, making slavery for women into what Hillary Beckles calls "a gendered form of tyranny." Thistlewood kept meticulous records of his sexual exploits on a daily basis, where and how he had sex, describing the women, their ages, their African origins, and the degree of his satisfaction. Over the course of a decade, he had sex with almost all twenty-seven women on the plantation and with fifteen of their daughters, with many of them repeatedly. Beckles provides overviews of his sexual encounters, for instance, between 1751 and 1754: 265 times (45). As Thistlewood grew older, he seemed to prefer young girls (48). Beckles describes him: "Thistlewood celebrated himself as a sexually promiscuous colonist. By his own record, he was a sexual sadist and a rapist. His sexual exploitation of enslaved black women was not peculiar but typical of the permissiveness that was endemic to the social culture of white slave owning males. He was confident in his violent masculinity" (40).

I know of no other material that gives us such direct and, frankly, sickening insight into colonial masculinity, with the sexual and power cards stacked entirely in favor of white men. Thanks to the elaborate record Thistlewood kept, and his frank admission that it was he himself who sought the women out, not invoking the widespread myth that it was black women who by their excessive sexuality seduced him, it is possible to get insights into what seems to be driving this attraction. First, Thistlewood makes it clear that he is not the only male colonist driven by this colonial economy of desire, by describing the life and sexual histories of the two white men clos-est to him: John Hartnole, a nineteen-year-old driver, and William Crook-shank, his assistant overseer (Beckles 1999, 44). It is not that white women are scarce or absent. These men are sometimes married to white women (or in any case are exposed to their companionship), but their preference is for "enslaved sexuality" (41).

Second, there is the intoxication of the unfettered ownership of en-slaved women (and men). The mere ownership of enslaved people, as Saidiya Hartman has insightfully shown, confers pleasure: "The fungibil-ity of the commodity makes the captive body an abstract and empty vessel vulnerable to the projection of others' feelings, ideas, desires, and values: and, as property, the dispossessed body of the enslaved is the surrogate for the master's body since it guarantees his disembodied universality and acts as the sign of his power and dominion" (1997, 21). Black peoples were envisioned fundamentally as vehicles for white enjoyment, and the extraction of sexual pleasure from enslaved women fit seamlessly into this vision, while excessive enjoyment of the sexual act was imputed to them. As we saw in chapter 2, "the white man's burden became his sexuality and its control, and it is this which is transferred into the need to control the sexuality of the other" (Gilman 1985, 256). As subjects, the enslaved were socially dead, not entitled to bear witness against any white person who harmed them. Hartman's main point is that white people were invested in disavowing the cruelty of the system by attributing enjoyment and pleasure to blacks. The enslaved were confronted with absolute power of all whites over them, including "the imputation of lasciviousness that dissimulated and condoned the sexual violation of the enslaved" (25). Men like Thistle-wood were able to convince themselves that the enslaved women volun-tarily consented to having sexual relations with them. He sees them as free sexual agents, which granted them an agency in this respect they, in truth, did not possess.

Third, the racial power differential in itself seemed to act like an aph-rodisiac for Thistlewood. In Imperial Leather, Anne McClintock (1995) has brilliantly described the fascination of a Victorian gentleman in the late nineteenth-century imperial metropolis, the barrister Arthur J. Munby, for Hannah Cullwick, a working-class charwoman, with red, roughened hands. The racialized class differential seemed the driving force for both of them. More specifically, it was the "peculiarly Victorian and peculiarly neurotic association between work and sexuality" (McClintock 1995, 77) that eroticized and racialized working-class women to Munby, whereby traditional gender relations also were undermined. McClintock points out the importance of working-class women in middle-class households, often those who took care of children, pampering, smacking, caressing, disciplining, punishing, and sexually arousing them (85). While the role of nannies and nurses has been displaced out of psychoanalysis and the holy trinity of the modern family, it is this formative attraction to working-class women that forms the bridge between work and sexuality. In parallel fashion, I suggest that under slavery, racial difference must have eroticized relations with enslaved women for white men in the colonies, because of the impossibility of black women refusing them. Thistlewood himself might very well have been raised in a home with a nanny or nurse, and certainly white men, born in the colonies, had black nannies and wet nurses. In addition, the work regime for black women was not gendered, making them to white men, in comparison with domesticated white women, probably somewhat androgynous, vital, powerful, and strong. The white masculinity that is on display here, "backed by the cannons of empire" (Beckles 1999, 41), is emotionally highly detached. On the same day that Thistlewood has sex with one or more of the women, he may have them whipped one hundred lashes for minor transgressions.

Before I expand my investigation into this male economy of desire to Suriname, it is important to, however briefly, pay attention to the compromised perspective of Phibbah. She was a respected woman on the Egypt plantation, even before Thomas Thistlewood showed up. She was aware of and endured his transgressions all of her life, in hopes of being set free. The relationship is one prolonged quarrel. She occasionally protests and sometimes manages to turn things to her advantage, by playing her owner against Thistlewood. Upon his death, she is manumitted, set free.

But it is not only in Jamaica that we find this colonial masculinity. Its contours can also be discerned in De Plakkatenboeken (The placard books of Suriname), where between the years 1761 and 1816 the colonial government tried to regulate the behavior of the colonizers and the colonized (Schiltkamp and de Smidt 1973). Among the regulations that are constantly repeated is an injunction to colonizers to abstain from carnal conversation with the enslaved women and the "Indianinnen" (the native female population). In the sheer repetitiveness over the centuries, one can read the depth in male colonizers of the drive to sexually possess their female enslaved. The wanton use of the black female body is memorialized in a song made during slavery and to this day transmitted to younger generations, called "Basia fon" (Overseer, whip her).[17] I learned the song from my grandfather. The song is still sung at parties in Afro-Surinamese circles, both in Suriname and the Netherlands, and the merry lightness of the music, a waltz, is in stark contrast to the cruelty of the text. The main speaking voice is that of Jaba, an enslaved woman, who has, for whatever reason, angered her white lover and has been abandoned by him; the other voice, in the refrain, is that of the master, enjoining the overseer to keep on whipping her:[18]

Basia fon (Overseer whip her)[19]
Meneri, meneri, da pikin, pardon.
Memre wan ten, memre wan tron,
Fa yu ben lobi mi so te
En fa mi lobi yu ete.

Basia fon! Basia fon!
A wentje mek' mi ati bron!

Te na kondre yu kon skrifiman,
Mi no ben sabi san no wan man;
Fa yu ben lobi mi so te,
En fa mi lobi yu ete.

Mi ben de kari yu mooi skrifiman,
Yu puru mi na nenne Anan;
Fa yu ben lobi mi so te,
En fa mi lobi yu ete.

Te yu ben bosi yu Jaba,
Mi ben taki: kaba, kaba!
Da falsi lobi, yu no ke,
Ho fassi yu du so tidey?[20]

Pardon Meneri! Pardon! Pardon!
Yu ben lobi da skin wan tron.
Mi begi yu! Mi begi: ke!
Meneri a no nofo ete?

Meneri, meneri, memre na pikin,
da sori yu mi lobi krin.
Mi begi yu, mi begi: ke!
Basia a no nofo ete?

Hoe fassi? Mi taki fon!
A wentje mek mi ati bron!
Mi taki fon! Fon en so te,
Al wassi a fadon dede.

[Master, master, forgiveness, the child,

Think of the time, think of the time,
How you loved me then
And how I love you still.

Overseer whip her, overseer whip her,
The wench fills my heart with ire.

When you came to this land to keep the books
I had not yet been near a man
How you loved me then.
And how I love you still.

My handsome bookkeeper I called you,
didn't you snatch me from my mother's breast;
How you loved me then,
And how I love you still.

When you kissed your Jaba,
Lay off, I cried!
This love is false, you don't care,
Why this behavior today?

Forgiveness, my Lord! forgiveness please!
You loved this body once
I pray! Oh I pray to thee!
Master, isn't it enough?

Master, master, please think of the child,
It shows you that my love is pure.

I pray, Oh I pray to thee.
Overseer, isn't it enough?

What? Whip her, I say!
The wench fills my heart with ire!
Whip her, I say! Whip her so hard,
Till down she drops dead on the ground.]

The last four-line verse is the voice of the master. Apparently after Jaba has asked the overseer if it isn't enough yet, the basia has slowed down his whipping and is now called to task by the master to resume in a more forceful fashion. The song is heartbreaking in its simplicity.

Although what I have described so far takes place in a heterosexual context, there is no reason to assume that homosexual encounters were exempt from the colonial sexual dynamic of omnipotence, hubris, cruelty, and distance.[21] In my earlier work, I argued that same-sex and opposite-sex sexualities within one particular sexual system diverge as to the gendered objects of desire, but that they resemble each other in many other respects. They share a worldview and practices (Wekker 2006). One might look upon a sexual system as a network, sharing and exchanging ideas, values, practices, and sometimes people, irrespective of the gender of one's object of passion.

Finally, let us return to the here and now of gay life, while I continue to construct a map of a complex, colonial sexual inheritance. I offer some miscellaneous observations from interviews with black gay men, with black women, and from a novel. In the course of the past years, I have, whenever a chance presented itself, interviewed black men and women in the Netherlands about their sexual experiences. This is not a finished project, nor do I claim representativeness for its findings, but a number of interesting patterns have come to the fore. Many gay black Dutch men have had relationships with men of various colors, but they actually often prefer white partners. Some black men from abroad observe that they are surprised by the number of black-white couples, while all-black couples are rare. Whenever they enter a bar, the black men do not make eye contact with them. Black men report that they often were the less economically vital partner in those mixed relationships, and they thought that their attraction for their white partners consisted precisely of their skin color, their vitality, and their supposed sexual endowments.

This same colonial economy of desire for the racial/ethnic other can be found in a heterosexual context. Young black women speak of their experiences with young white men in bars and at dances, who see a sexual experience with a black woman as a rite of passage, a manner of coming of age. These black women, in contrast, are usually not who they would consider for a steady relationship, however. It is many a white man's ultimate dream to be with an intelligent black woman, who has the sexual capital of wildness and abandon at her disposal that has traditionally been associated with black women (Bijnaar 2007).

This is also the dream that the protagonist of the wildly popular and awarded debut novel *Alleen maar nette mensen* (Only decent people) entertains. Published in 2008 by author Robert Vuijsje, it was made into a film in 2010. The novel reaped extraordinary critical praise from juries, which distinguished it as a breath of fresh air. The sexual part of the cultural archive is on abundant display in the novel. The protagonist, David, a twenty-one-year-old Jewish man from upscale South Amsterdam, looks like a Moroccan and is sexually obsessed with big black women from the southeastern part of the city. When David says to his friend that he would like a black woman with at least a 95 F cup in bra size (in United States' terms 42DDD/E) and with brains for a steady girlfriend, the friend is annoyed and aghast. In no uncertain terms, he makes it clear that black women are "lower in the hierarchy. We can all get them" (Vuijsje 2008, 91). Black women are for temporary sexual pleasure only, not for starting a serious relationship with or bringing home to introduce to your family.

In "Eating the Other," bell hooks (1992a, 24) maintains that there is continuity in the fact that the body of the other, both in colonial times and now, is seen instrumentally as only having raison d'être to satisfy the sexual desire of white men. It is not so much about possessing the other as about having a transgressive experience. After all, that other body is terra incognita, a symbolic border that is fertile ground for constructing a new masculine norm, to position oneself as a transgressive, desiring subject—a rite of passage in which sex with an ethnic/racial other is seen as more exciting, more vital, and more sensual. With the coat of color-blindness, these are not issues we are frequently concerned with in the Netherlands. A benevolent and widespread reading of such a long-term connection with a black woman or man is that it proves one's credentials in the realm of antiracism, beyond the shadow of a doubt.

I certainly do not claim representativeness for the different insights and artifacts that I have accessed for this chapter, especially the volatile mixture of disgust and desire toward young Muslim and black men. While the expression of disgust towards Muslim men is widely socially accepted in the current political climate, desire is taken to be part of one's most intimate, private sphere of life. Interracial preferences, however often they occur, aren't part of a public discussion or reflection; they are bracketed. Fortuyn's verbal transgressions, in which he clearly took great delight, were exceptional and inadvertently allow a glance into the racialized building blocks of white Dutch self-image. I see the frequency of interracial attractions as a present-day, only partially repressed expression of the unexamined Dutch cultural archive, in which race is deeply informed by gendered and sexualized patterns.

I have been arguing that the affective economies toward racialized/ethnicized others, based on almost four centuries of empire, have produced a sexual map with typical sensibilities, responses, and structures of feeling and thought. These patterns have silently been transmitted to us in the twenty-first century and continue to structure white sexual responses whenever a racialized/ethnicized other, whether Muslim or black, comes into play. The place of Muslims and other others on this map will require more study than is possible here.

As opposed to the usual, self-flattering gay reading of Fortuyn's statements as undercutting racism—how can he be a racist when he is fucking Moroccan men?—I propose a different, postcolonial reading that considers tenacious continuities in the cultural archive. Part of this complex sexual inheritance is also present in the case study of the three white women who claimed to possess Hottentot nymphae (chapter 3). By claiming a particular gendered and sexual positioning through the grammar of race, they showed the depth of race in the cultural archive and how race enabled them, through projection and displacement, to create an unorthodox female subjectivity for themselves. The complex sexual map, embedded in the cultural archive and conjugated through race, represents black people and other others by foregrounding a construction of their sexuality as one that needs to be controlled. Black people and Muslims are often still attributed more sexual aliveness, vitality, and libido than white partners. Cross-racial sexual partnerships are imagined as affording huge power differences, which enhance eroticism. An emotional detachment, in which the aim is not to possess the other but to experience a rite of sexual passage, and the combination of disgust and attraction that characterized interracial sexual relationships in colonial times may also be part of the sexual codes that have been transmitted. Some of the same motifs that played out in a colonial context are still present in a context that claims innocence.

CHAPTER 5

"... For Even Though I Am Black as Soot, My Intentions Are Good"

The Case of Zwarte Piet/Black Pete

> The value of blackness resided in its metaphorical
> aptitude, whether literally understood as the fungibility
> of the commodity or understood as the imaginative
> surface upon which the master and the nation
> came to understand themselves.
>
> Saidiya Hartman, *Scenes of Subjection*

By far the most beloved folkloric figure in the Netherlands is Zwarte Piet/ Black Pete.[1] This figure is a blackened man—a white man, but also often a white woman (Bal 1999) with a blackened face; the blacker the better—with thick red lips, golden earrings, an Afro wig, clad in a colorful Moor's costume, and, until recently, wielding a quite deplorable grammar, "dumbspeak" (figure 5.1). Zwarte Piet is imagined to be a Moorish servant of a white bishop, Sinterklaas or Saint Nicolas, who hails from Spain and, in alternative versions, from Turkey.[2]

The yearly festivities, culminating on December 5, are driven by powerful commercial interests, which are made manifest through the overwhelming presence of (images of) the two in stores, restaurants, and offices, from October on. There are ubiquitous advertisements on TV, in newspapers, and in stores of this year's recommended presents;[3] the production of festive wrapping paper is another major player in the commercial circuit. Weeks in advance, children put out a shoe at night with a carrot in it for Sinterklaas's horse and wait for it to be filled with sweets by Zwarte Piet, who supposedly comes down through the chimney. This is the widely em-

Figure 5.1 Black Pete/Zwarte Piet. Photo by Gon Buurman.

braced reason why he or she is black. The festivities are heightened by *de intocht* (their entry), which takes place in every major city, sometimes by steamboat, and every year the entry is televised from a different city in the Netherlands, in the middle of November. Every night, the children and their parents watch the Sinterklaas news, keeping them up to date on everything pertaining to the pair. The festivity culminates in a merry evening on December 5, when presents are given to children, but also exchanged by adults, accompanied by original critical and often funny poems. It is a moment when mild personal criticism and mockery are encouraged, and it is celebrated in the sphere of family and friends.

The contrasts between the wise old white bishop Sinterklaas, with his huge white beard, and his childlike, silly black servants are underlined by the fact that Sint (singular) rides on his white horse, while the Petes (plural) walk, some on stilts, frolicking, having fun. It is still quite common for Pete to have an unabashedly quasi-Surinamese accent, and sometimes nowadays, as fancy takes people, a Moroccan accent. Black Pete embodies what Stuart Hall (1997, 245) has called "ritualized degradation," a representation that is so natural that it requires no explanation or justification. Zwarte

Piet belongs to the idealized and sentimentalized "happy black" type, who neither has a worry in the world nor a brain in his head, but who sings, dances, and cracks jokes all day long and whose greatest joy it is to please white folks and their children (Hall 1997; Morrison 1992a).[4] Hall (1997, 258) also reminds us that stereotyping tends to occur when there are gross inequalities of power; we are dealing with a violent hierarchy here.

Excursion

In April 2014, I gave a presentation for the College for Human Rights, the former Committee for Equal Treatment, at the fateful site of Media Park in Hilversum.[5] While my talk is on the Dutch cultural archive and especially on the depth and layeredness of stereotyped images about blacks and Muslims, the section that incites the liveliest discussion are my remarks, which are made in passing, on Black Pete. My audience consists predominantly of white men and women, with a sprinkling of black women. I am wondering why the protests against Zwarte Piet, which have entered a new, unprecedented round since October 2011, elicit such vehement and aggressive reactions in whites. What is at stake here? Which precious good or cherished feelings are felt to be under attack and need to be so forcefully defended? Several white women in the audience want to speak to the issue. One woman introduces herself as a sociocultural worker and says that black people do not realize how much pain it causes whites to hear that Black Pete is a racist figuration. Blacks do not realize how hurtful it is to have to give up a figure that you have grown up with and who has given you so much joy, and it also hurts that her children will not be able to enjoy him in the same way that she has. All of that she is willing to sacrifice, but the only thing she wants is for a black person to say to her, "I know you are hurting, but you are doing the right thing." I am getting angry and, although I know better, still surprised at her innocence; the openness with which she speaks about what is being taken away from her, the displacement evident in her self-presentation as a victim, and then, on top of that, that it is black people, who have been talking about and acting against the racism of the figuration for at least four decades, who need to give her a pat on the back. Her utterance may be read as one instance of what Philomena Essed and Isabel Hoving call "entitlement racism": "Entitlement racism is a sign of the times we live in, where it is believed that you should be able to express yourself publicly in whatever way you feel like. Freedom of expression, though an individual right, is quintessentially a relational phenomenon. The expresser wants his or her opinion to be heard or seen" (2014b, 14). Essed and Hoving place this form of racism in the evolution from a "carefully fabricated image of tolerance in the twentieth century to the "right to offend in the twenty-first" (13). This is certainly part of a reading of the aggressive and defensive reactions that protests against Zwarte Piet elicit these days. The woman in my example certainly wanted her opinion to be heard, probably without having the slightest idea that her opinion was offensive to me.

This chapter engages with Dutch popular culture, with folklore, and especially with the meaning of the figuration of Zwarte Piet in the white Dutch imagination. Zwarte Piet is considered by many white Dutch people to be at the heart of Dutch culture, an innocent and thoroughly pleasant traditional festivity. As yearly surveys show, only 1 percent of the population—and in some surveys 3 percent at most—thinks that there might be a racist problem with Zwarte Piet. I agree, as others have pointed out, that events around Zwarte Piet "expose a prevalent anxiety around momentous changes in the make-up of the Dutch population at the end of twentieth and the beginning of the twenty-first century" (Smith 2014, 229; see also Jordan 2014; Van der Pijl and Goulordava 2014).

I first give a brief overview of the different protests against this figure, starting at the end of the 1960s, but concentrating on unprecedented recent events. It is not my ambition to be complete or exhaustive here, just to convey a sense of the feverish, shrill pitch of the debate, which in no small part is due to the looming question whether the Netherlands is or is not a country where racism is a fact of life, and the incommensurability of the standpoints: a gridlock. The protests against Zwarte Piet are not an isolated phenomenon: In the past decade, heated debates about the royal "golden carriage" with its colonial imagery (Legêne 2010) and about a five-part series on the history of Dutch slavery, broadcast in the fall of 2011, have all brought parallel readings of history and culture to the fore. At their core is the question of whether the history of blacks should be part and parcel of metropolitan history (Jones 2012).

During the current movement, several events have been noteworthy, opening up the Sinterklaas celebration to international scrutiny and criticism, but also to a lawsuit in different installments. The protest against Zwarte Piet since 2011 is the first issue so clearly and massively to divide white and black Dutch, although it needs to be stressed that there are some white protesters and some blacks defending Zwarte Piet. Research by the city of Amsterdam, at the end of 2012, showed that 27 percent of the Surinamese, 18 percent of the Antillean, and 14 percent of the Ghanaian population felt discriminated against by the appearance and speech of Zwarte Piet, compared to 1 percent of white Amsterdammers (Bosveld and Greven 2012). Amsterdam is clearly the motor of change for the rest of the country. It also bears pointing out that my attention to Zwarte Piet does not mean that I put more weight on cultural issues than on socioeconomic ones, such as the unemployment rate of blacks, migrants, and refugees, especially youths, which is three times as high as among white youths; or housing and education, where equally pernicious conditions pertain. It is that Zwarte Piet has become the focal point, the symbolic spearhead of a now year-round debate on fundamental racial inequalities in Dutch society. In the main body of this chapter, I analyze the voluminous hate mail bombardment by members of the Dutch public against two artists, to the Van Abbemuseum in Eindhoven, and to Doorbraak, an activist group supporting the anti–Zwarte Piet activities of the artists, in 2008. German and Swedish artists Annette Krauss and Petra Bauer initiated a project, Read the Masks: Tradition Is Not Given, which critically interrogated the phenomenon of Zwarte Piet.[6] The e-mail bombardment that ensued was so fierce and threatening that the museum decided, unilaterally, that the protest march, scheduled as a part of Read the Masks, had to be canceled. There are more recent discussions on popular websites about Zwarte Piet, but the themes that I distill from the 2008 data are still applicable to these later exchanges. I investigate the nature of the ten themes that the correspondents bring up. Collectively, I argue that these e-mail messages paint a thick picture of the white Dutch self in the first decade of the twenty-first century. Innocence, in manifold senses, turns out to be central. In the final part, I explore the role that Zwarte Piet has played historically, and to this day, in constructing a white "we" versus a black "they." In my reading of the vehemence of the Zwarte Piet defense, which at times borders on the hysterical, I foreground an anxiety that is what Paul Gilroy (2005) has identified for Britain as "postcolonial melancholia." This intricate and often contradictory conglomerate of affects is, as I show, strongly connected in the Dutch context to a differential chain of associations, in which the memory of empire is divided for the eastern (the Indies) and western (Suriname and the Dutch Antilles) parts, and where innocence, smallness, and defenselessness, as pertaining to children, to us, the Dutch, and to the country itself, plays a central, organizing part.

(Inter)National Skirmishes around Zwarte Piet

At the end of the 1960s, anti–Zwarte Piet protests took off in Dutch society. The earliest protests were initiated by white people, and later on predominantly black people became more active (Helsloot 2005).[7] Since 2008, the year of the Van Abbemuseum exhibition, anti– and pro–Black Pete activism has grown. The current round of protests was initiated by the abuse of two young black men, Quinsy Gario and Kno'ledge Cesare, who were wearing black T-shirts with the text "Zwarte Piet is racisme" (Black Pete is racism), by the police at the festive entry of Sinterklaas and Zwarte Piet into Dordrecht in November 2011. The abuse galvanized many in the black community and garnered a lot of media attention. Since then, the Labor Party mayor of Amsterdam, Eberhard van der Laan, has initiated a behind-closed-doors roundtable with several involved parties—activists and the Netherlands Centre for Popular Culture and Immaterial Heritage (V.I.E.)—to come up, in Dutch polder fashion, with a compromise, a new form of Black Pete, that would be acceptable to everyone. At the first presentation of this compromise, in the summer of 2014, his earrings already having been shed in 2013, Black Pete had become brown, his dark hair straight. The idea was that he would become progressively less "negroid" in incremental steps of four years. It is noteworthy about Dutch pragmatism, here as in other domains, that the fundamental issue, racism, is obfuscated and instead practical measures are proposed, which may take away some of the sharpest edges of a problem, but certainly do not go to the heart of it.

A noteworthy event, kicking off 2013, was a letter sent to the Dutch government by the Working Group of Experts of People of African Descent, a human rights group under the umbrella of the United Nations, in the person of Jamaican professor Verene Sheperd. In the letter, the working group asked for clarification about the Dutch Sinterklaas festivity, having received information "that Zwarte Piet supports a stereotypical image of African people and people of African descent as second-class citizens, feeds underlying ideas about inferiority within Dutch society and gives rise to racial feelings and racism."[8] As could be expected, the letter was overwhelmingly met with dismissal and ridicule, threats and insults, both from the general public and from officials, who exhibited a great degree of intolerance. In early July 2014, the working group visited the Netherlands, speaking with different constituencies and stressing that the government needs to facilitate a national debate. A little earlier, in 2013, a report of the European Commission against Racism and Intolerance was published which stated that racism is a fact of life in the Netherlands, chastising the country for its lukewarm reaction to racism in the public sphere. Noteworthy in all these events was the nonreaction or the dismissal of the international charge of racism by the majority of politicians. Their response appeared to be, "We cannot be bothered by this totally unimportant issue and what do these foreigners know about us, anyway?" In the fall of 2013, two white Dutch men started a page on Facebook under the name Pietitie, calling on people to sign a petition to hold on to Zwarte Piet, this most cherished of Dutch traditions. Within weeks, the page was liked over two million times, an all-time record for any Internet petition in the Netherlands.

For the first time in November 2013, a court case was brought before an administrative judge, after a notice of objection against the presence of Zwarte Piet in the yearly entry parade was dismissed by the city of Amsterdam. The case was brought by twenty-one black and white Amsterdam plaintiffs who wanted to prohibit his presence in the entry parade of 2013, on the grounds that the permit to hold the Sinterklaas parade constituted an infringement on the plaintiffs' right to respect for their private and family life, since Zwarte Piet is a negative stereotype of black people. The mayor, Eberhard van der Laan, did grant the permit, however, so the plaintiffs went on to file their complaint with an administrative court. On July 3, 2014, the administrative judge, building on a statement by the College of Human Rights that Zwarte Piet is racist, ruled that the mayor of Amsterdam had taken the feelings of black Amsterdammers into sufficient account, but the judge dismissed the complaints of the white plaintiffs. The ruling was that the mayor of Amsterdam had to reconsider Zwarte Piet's presence. Although the ruling has been welcomed as a victory by the anti–Zwarte Piet camp, as Egbert Alejandro Martina has insightfully remarked, "treating racist oppression as a feeling of hurt, avoids addressing it as a structural problem." Furthermore, remaining within a discourse of distress leaves no room for white plaintiffs to lodge complaints against racism, because they supposedly are not personally affected by a racial stereotype of a black person.[9] In the ruling, we recognize the preferred and reflex position that is taken up by whites and that has been described by Markus Balkenhol (2014) as "the politics of compassion"; whites as the rescuers, saviors of blacks, driven by pity and compassion.

The mayor decided to appeal this verdict, in August 2014, although not on the grounds just outlined. The mayor took the position that the question whether Zwarte Piet is racist is not a political decision but a social one that should be decided upon in the social arena. In the next installment of the legal battle, the highest administrative court, De Raad van State (Council of State), held a session on October 16, 2014, in the case of the plaintiffs against the mayor of Amsterdam and the Black Pete Guild, on whether the mayor had been right in admitting Black Pete to the entry parade of 2013. The verdict of course would have consequences for the entry parade of 2014 and for the rest of the country. The verdict was given on November 12, 2014, in favor of the mayor of Amsterdam, that is, that he had been right in using criteria of public order and safety in deciding on the presence of Zwarte Piet in the entry parade, and not on whether the figure is racist. Such a question also should not be brought before the Raad van State, the council itself judged, but to a civil court.[10] The plaintiffs also saw possibilities in the decision of the council to continue the legal battle. Zwarte Piet was thus again part of the parade in 2014 and was ubiquitously present.

Since 2008, the year of the particular batch of Internet communications on Zwarte Piet I analyze, and now, attitudes have hardened and become more polarized. In light of the Dutch postcolonial desire to play a marked role internationally, the critical international attention to Zwarte Piet in the past few years has hurt considerably, also exposing the Dutch sensitivity to outside criticism.

An Excursion into Academic Space

At the end of 2011, while I am on a sabbatical leave at NIAS, the Netherlands Institute for Advanced Studies, employees start to decorate the main buildings with images of Sinterklaas and Zwarte Piet. This is about the same time that activists against Zwarte Piet frequently emerged in the national news. This organizing apparently has totally escaped the employees at NIAS, who are trying to make the buildings cozier in the festive season, in their own version of white innocence. Among the fellows this year is a group of Africans, but it is mainly the white Americans who, at the communal lunch, are aghast and vocal about the Dutch version of blackface, wanting more information on what is going on. Since, earlier in the year, I announced that I am working on race in the Dutch cultural archive, I have started to receive mail from fellow white Dutch scholars at NIAS, including a copy of David Sedaris's (2008) funny short story "Six to Eight Black Men," which I take as an intellectual reminder to lighten up, to show a sense of humor, and to go along with the dominant consensus that Zwarte Piet is harmless. I decline that implicit invitation and ask for speaking time at the next seminar to explain to the scholars and the employees at NIAS why Zwarte Piet is untenable and cannot possibly be maintained in his current form. I am aware of the double bind before me: "If you do not go along with the dominant consensus that Zwarte Piet is harmless and innocent, you cannot be one of us." In subscript, and in a lower key: "Yet, even if you do accept him, you still are not one of us."[11] Between "Black Pete is not racist" and the fallback position "We do not mean it to be racist," not much space is left for critical self-reflection on the cultural archive.

The Place That Black Pete Occupies in White Dutch Self-Representation

In 2008, the Van Abbemuseum of modern art in Eindhoven organized a multifaceted exhibition, Be(com)ing Dutch, in which the participating artists were asked to reflect on the question what it means to be or to become Dutch. German artist Annette Krauss, living in the Netherlands, and her Swedish colleague Petra Bauer initiated a project, Read the Masks: Tradition Is Not Given, in which they critically interrogated the phenomenon of Zwarte Piet, wanting to reopen a decades-long debate on the possible presence of racism and the colonial past in this time-honored tradition. The artists were aware beforehand that the tradition "has been depoliticized, neutralized and incorporated in the collective consciousness of contemporary society."[12] The project consisted of four parts: an installation, a protest march to be performed on August 30, 2008, a debate, and a film, which debuted on March 8, 2010 (Smith 2014, 230).[13] The protest march, planned in summer, was publicized by the right-wing daily De Telegraaf, which, having the largest readership in the country, led to an avalanche of overwhelmingly negative reactions. In my analysis of the voluminous hate mail from members of the Dutch public, I am interested in the nature of these reactions, the themes that the correspondents bring up, and which arguments they use to convey their malaise. On the one hand, we are confronted with an undiluted aggressiveness and hatefulness in the majority of the hate mails, while, on the other, in an interesting gesture of displacement, a cluster of thoughts and affects—innocence, smallness, defenselessness, being under siege, victimhood—turns out to be central. What does all of this tell us about the cultural archive and current Dutch self-perception?

I distinguish ten themes in the about 1,500 messages in the massive e-mail bombardment of August 28 and 29, 2008. Typically, the messages are anonymous, only signed with a first name or with "een Nederlander" (a Dutchman), or with pseudonyms. The messages are very short, at the most six or seven lines, and often shorter. Most messages contain several themes, and I have coded them all. The thickest messages contain four or five themes and thus codes. As the themes overlap and flow into each other, I argue that together they present a thick tapestry of current Dutch self-representation, beset by enemies within and outside the nation. I list the themes in order of their thickness, that is, how often they are mentioned, and I reflect most elaborately on the themes of "this is our culture, our tradition" and "childhood/innocence," which encapsulate the most important characteristics of the Dutch postcolonial melancholia syndrome I want to describe. Subsequently, I compare an analysis by Teun van Dijk, of a similar collection of statements from the public addressing criticism of Zwarte Piet, dating from 1998. Finally, I lay out my reading of Zwarte Piet, in light of these themes.

These are the ten themes that came to the fore in 2008:

1. THIS IS OUR CULTURE, OUR TRADITION
Starting out with "this is our culture, our tradition," a thick conglomerate of meanings comes together. This is a strong theme in terms of thickness, that is, the number of times it is invoked and the connectedness it shows with other themes. Partly a self-positioning—"Who are we, in this first decade of the twenty-first century?"—this theme overwhelmingly covers a range of forces against which we need to defend ourselves. In terms of self-positioning, the following topoi come to the fore: The sense of having been too tolerant; we are taken advantage of; our country is being destroyed; they are taking all our celebrations from us; and the "get rid of us" mentality.

A good amount of malaise is expressed about who we are: "Ridiculous!! This is Dutch culture now. This is not allowed anymore? We are masters at putting foreign cultures on a pedestal and lowering our own culture. Black Pete has nothing to do with discrimination. The people who say this often discriminate against other people the most."[14] An abyss of negative affect, almost a feeling of self-loathing, of everyone being allowed to trample on the Dutch, of a "we" that, to a ridiculous extent, is turning the other cheek, rises from the pages: We have been too soft, too tolerant. So much dissent in the country; we have become a scary country!! "Let's do away with us, because we are slave traders (blah blah blah). When will this self-hatred stop?" It is easy to see the connections with the body of thought propagated at the time by the xenophobic populist political parties Partij voor de Vrijheid (Party for Freedom, PVV) of Geert Wilders and Rita Verdonk's Trots op Nederland (TON, Proud of the Netherlands). The latter had made the defense of Zwarte Piet part of her political program, when she stated that we should not allow "them" to take him away from "us." Especially PVV, with its nine seats in parliament at the time, though it was headed for a much larger share of twenty-seven in 2010, spoke to a significant part of the electorate.

This sentiment means that Dutch culture should be defended, against many different forces, enemies within and outside the nation. A mother in Zeist notes: "Every day, it is getting crazier at school. Pupils are free to celebrate the offering feast (Id al-Adha, 70 days after Ramadan) and the sugar feast (Id-al-Fitr, the end of Ramadan) and all those other celebrations of theirs and those of our own as well and now they are ruining our festivities. . . . Such bullshit!! I want to give my son the same traditions that I also had in my youth, so that includes Black Pete." Another big hit is the loss of the names of typically Dutch food items: "First it was negerzoenen [Negro kisses]. What is going to happen to Jodenkoeken [Jew cakes] and blanke vla [white flan]? Now they want to take Zwarte Piet from us."[15] This is repeated, in many different variations, again and again. Put together, these statements convey the anger that writers experience at everything being taken away from them, often presented in the form of irony. Overwhelmingly then, in this first strong theme, the part of white self-representation on display is one that experiences a sense of deep loss, that things aren't the way they used to be anymore for the Dutch people; we are being questioned in our own home by ungrateful guests, whom we have received as gracious hosts. The guests have overstayed their welcome and are pointing out everything that is wrong with us. Jointly this intricate and contradictory complex has been well understood by Paul Gilroy (2005) in the British context as postcolonial melancholia. With it he points to "the guilt-ridden loathing and depression that have come to characterize Britain's xenophobic responses to the strangers who have intruded upon it . . . recently" (90). This volatile mixture of sadness, melancholia, loss, displacement, and anger in the Netherlands takes center stage in the last section of this chapter.

2. A CHILDREN'S CELEBRATION

A majority of writers refer to Sinterklaas and Zwarte Piet as a children's celebration that is thoroughly innocent. Lian from Amsterdam opines, "Whatever does this have to do with discrimination? It is a traditional children's festivity. And do you think that those kiddies think that Pete is a black person, who is abused? We live in 2008!! Pete is sweet and you can laugh with him. With whites, there is nothing to laugh about." This last statement inadvertently offers a glimpse of how Lian perceives blackness and whiteness—sweetness and being funny, versus nothingness. It is reminiscent of the assessment of scholars like Ruth Frankenberg (1993) for U.S. whiteness and Richard Dyer (1997) for British whiteness, that whiteness is perceived as invisible, normal, without characteristics, nothingness, which of course points to the all-encompassing presence of whiteness as the unmarked norm. The invisibility of whiteness is a white delusion, as Frankenberg remarks, but it does position blacks as the marked category, irrational, overly emotional, childish, and contented. Lian's statement also brings up the connection made by Saidiya Hartman (1997) in her aptly named chapter "Innocent Amusements" in *Scenes of Subjection*, where she argues that blacks during slavery were subjected to white power by having to show pleasure and enjoyment under the violent treatment that was meted out to them. "Ironically," as she shows, "the maintenance of racial boundaries occurred through the donning of the blackface mask or the display of tragically bifurcated racial bodies" (27). She points to the inextricable entanglement of pleasure and terror, violence and entertainment, which also is so clearly present in the Zwarte Piet spectacle.

"Children do not see color" is a frequently invoked refrain. In a variation on that theme, the intent is ascribed to the protesters to deny sweet childhood memories to the children, but also retroactively take them away from the adults. People are both at a loss and furious at the thought of having to tell their children and grandchildren that there will be no more Black Pete. This is another strong theme, both in terms of how often it is mentioned, because of the strong feelings one senses behind it, and also because of the richness of associations that are called up. Here a white self-image is presented that insists on seeing itself and children as innocent, small, inherently good, color-blind, and antiracist. It is also a self that is under siege; it is a small child that is invoked, defenseless, that is plagued by an onslaught of bigger, leftist, and foreign bullies who want to take away its pleasures and spoil its fun. There are plenty of killjoys around, as Sara Ahmed would term them. It is hard not to see an analogy between this small child and the Netherlands as a small nation, which is threatened by an onslaught of foreigners, who want "to take our culture away."

The theme of smallness resonates richly in a number of other (self-) descriptions: our little country, our little festivity, our little fairy tale, a little color. The diminutive both expresses a feeling of endearment and underlines the harmlessness of the things under consideration. Both of these aspects lead to a heightened affect of being under siege. With regard to the Dutch tendency to describe people of color as having a tinge of color, or a little color, Hondius (2014a, 277; 2014b), along the same lines, remarks upon the intention to "disarm" color difference.

A final remark here about the links between childhood and innocence:[16] As I have noted elsewhere (Wekker 2006), different cultures have different conceptualizations of the nature of childhood. In Western cultures, childhood is set aside as a special period, in which the child is not seen as a full member of society yet, and society adjusts to the child, for instance, through special furniture for children, protection caps on electricity sockets, or little gates at the top of the stairs so the child does not fall down. In other societies, childhood is something to be overcome as fast as possible, and the model is "the child needs to adjust to society." It strikes me as significant that the Netherlands is firmly located within the first model, which gives an almost sacrosanct position to the child, elevating its joy and pleasures above virtually all else. Thus to symbolically attack children is not only perceived as an infrahuman act, it also attacks the operative principle that "the child, like us, is good and innocent." I argue that it is this benevolent, self-flattering self-representation as inherently good, tolerant, and nonracist that, as the most cherished cultural good, is felt to be under attack, giving rise to a neurotic form of aggressiveness.[17]

3. ARE THOSE FOREIGNERS GOING TO TELL US HOW TO DO THINGS HERE?

There was an extremely aggressive reaction to the artists, German Annette Krauss and Swedish Petra Bauer, as foreigners, as allochtones,[18] who do not know anything about our tradition and who have come to the Netherlands to criticize us and tell us how to properly do things. Wim5050 from Amersfoort remarks: "Are those foreigners going to tell us how we have to do things here? We should try that in another country. They should try to demonstrate in Russia or in Africa or in the Middle East. Against important things. But they do not dare to do that. Immediate expulsion." The artists are represented as lazy, as shirking true work, "unlike all of us," and a connection is made with the supposedly overly liberal art subsidy policies of the city of Eindhoven and the Labor Party in the national government, the so-called Left church. This is the derogatory term, introduced by Pim Fortuyn and generally used by the Right, to chastise the cultural-political, socialist elite that the Right has had enough of being told what the only correct way of seeing and doing things is.[19]

Time and again, the nationalities of the artists are singled out to mark the utter inappropriateness of their project. This strand infuriates the writers and is ubiquitously present in the e-mails. It speaks to a hypersensitivity to foreign criticism of the way we do things here, in our little country.

4. LET'S CUT THE MUSEUM SUBSIDY IMMEDIATELY!!

A good amount of hate mail is directed against the Van Abbemuseum, which, together with the artists, is positioned as belonging to the Left church, using our hard-earned tax money to stage such a hateful exhibition. Jolanda from The Hague states, "That museum should be ashamed of itself. To accept money from the community. And then use it against the Dutch." Many e-mails stress that the city of Eindhoven and the government should immediately end the subsidies to the museum. The workers at the museum are seen as traitors and zakkenvullers (lining their pockets). Gerard from Haarlem is one of the hundreds of people wanting to take strong measures: "So a museum gives a platform to foreigners to call us racists. Museum needs to be shut down and the foreigners should get lost."

The project is characterized as *links getreiter* (bullying by the Left). All in all, the museum is strongly identified with a leftist position and with having too much foreign personnel, which apparently is not very popular with the writers.

5. BOTTOM LINE: ZWARTE PIET IS NOT RACIST

In many messages it is stated without any qualification that Zwarte Piet is not racist. No discussion is possible or desirable. A variety of strategies are used to bring the fundamental nonracist point across: humor, inversion, hyperbole. "It does not have anything to do with racism" is the bottom line, with the powerful conclusion: "If you want to live here, you have to adjust to us. Otherwise just leave!! Nobody asked you to come!!" A. from Spijkenisse uses inversion: "The most remarkable thing is that organizations that are so strongly opposed to Black Pete are actually saying, in covert ways, that it is bad to be black, and thus they are striving toward a white society. I find absolutely nothing scandalous, racist, or bad about Black Pete." This inverted argument is quite a find, displacing the problem to black people, who supposedly find it bad to be black, wanting to be white. This is the default understanding, appearing frequently, that black people who have problems with Zwarte Piet in reality have a problem with being black and should seek psychological help.

This is a persistent way of looking at blacks. To name but one example, in a TV talk show aired in the summer of 2014, Quinsy Gario, one of the initiators of the anti–Black Pete protest in 2011, explained why he decided to withdraw from the roundtable negotiations with the mayor of Amsterdam, on the grounds that once racism has been established, it makes no sense to further tinker with it by finding a compromise. Opposite him, a white singer, Antje Monteiro, was flabbergasted at his charge of racism at the phenomenon of Zwarte Piet, but immediately displaced her puzzlement by telling him that she could not understand why he was saying such things, when he was such a handsome, attractive black man. While ostensibly complimenting him and, in passing, demonstrating her nonracialism, she was implying that he had a psychological problem for which he should seek help. Her reaction fits well into the mold described by Markus Balkenhol (2014) as the "politics of compassion," that is, that whites can only interact with blacks on the basis of pity and compassion, not on the basis of egalitarianism.

The basic point under this heading simply is that there is no racism in the Netherlands. Nonracism is taken as axiomatic. The certainty is derived from the idea "this is our culture," so how can it be racist?

6. THE LEFT CHURCH/NATIONAL POLITICS

In many of the contributions, ministers of the coalition in power in 2008, Balkenende IV, with the political parties Christian Democrats, the Labor Party, and the Christian Union are mentioned. The Labor ministers Cramer, Koenders, and Vogelaar are especially singled out as examples of handing out money too freely to sorry causes that "we" have not asked for. The city government of Eindhoven, with its Labor mayor and national leftist parties, specifically Labor and the Green Left, are chastised for being politically correct, for subsidizing projects that destroy us; for spreading hate among the population; in inverted logic, again, inciting racism.

Many people announce, "Now for sure I am going to vote for Geert and Rita Verdonk. Geert for president!!" All of this is in line with the new realist discourse (Prins 2002) I outlined earlier: Finally the person in the street has found a voice, and it is directed against the Left. And many of the writers probably did vote for Wilders, who, with his twenty-seven seats in the following political period, became one of the supporting pillars of the government Rutte-I.

7. PIET'S GENEALOGY

Many of the e-mail writers berate the artists and everyone else who is opposed to Zwarte Piet, on their stupidity for not knowing anything about the history of the figures. This is the consensus: "Stupid stuff!! Pete became Black Pete because he had to pass through the chimney." And realist, from Amersfoort: "Let me explain it one more time. Black Pete is not a Negro, but a Moor, and a Moor comes from North Africa, and so Black Pete simply is a Moroccan."

It has become a national pastime to speculate about the origins of the Sinterklaas tradition, when his servant Zwarte Piet joined him and they both made their historic entry into the Netherlands. According to Blakely (1993), the lineage of the pair dates back as far as the Middle Ages, with the medieval St. Nicholas, patron saint of sailors and children, as the main inspiration for Sinterklaas. He sees both Christian and pagan influences in the figure, and the convergence of these influences also explains the dark complexion of the saint's companion. In many western European countries, comparable dark-complexioned figures, their faces covered with soot or ashes and impersonating the devil, have been noted. Zwarte Piet joined Sinterklaas as a servant, carrying a sack in which he would take bad children away.

The heated exchange of arguments often serves to deflect attention away from what is really at stake: whether Zwarte Piet is a racist figuration and/or incites racism. The reasoning seems to be that if it can be proven that there are figures comparable to Zwarte Piet in other parts of Europe, or if he can be shown to have Norse or Germanic origins, then there is no possibility that he can be associated with racism.[20] Meanwhile, the debate from both sides remains firmly couched within a positivistic framework: "If only we can get the facts right," while no attention is paid to power/knowledge. This theme is basically a variation on theme 1, "this is our culture, our tradition."

8. ANTI-MUSLIM SENTIMENTS

Among the enemies within, one would expect blacks to be the main culprits, but on the contrary, Muslims feature most prominently in the e-mails. "This protest is meant to make the Netherlands a bit more Muslim again. In a while, the muzzelmen will be in power here." There is a tension in the fact that most protesters against Black Pete are black, yet it is overwhelmingly Muslims who get blamed for everything that is wrong in the Netherlands in the e-mail bombardment. That it defies logic seems not to bother the writers. In light of the populist ideas propagated by the xenophobic parties PVV and TON, lighter versions of which have spread across the political spectrum, Muslims are consistently singled out as the main culprits of social dissent, and the problems of multicultural convivial living are laid at their doorstep. Muslims are constantly constructed as unwelcome, unassimilable, the disposable of the disposable. Regularly measures are proposed by PVV but also by such respectable parties as Labor about what to do with Muslims, especially young Moroccan men:[21] put them in camps to be resocialized; take away their dual citizenship or strip them of Dutch nationality;[22] downsize the subsidies (e.g., child allowances and subsidies to widows and orphans) sent to people in the countries of origin; "humiliate them before their friends."[23] These measures are either against the Dutch constitution or against international law and thus serve no other purpose than to further stack the cards against Moroccans. At various moments in the past decades, different groups like Moluccans and Surinamese have, in gendered forms, occupied that space of unassimilability and abjection. An imagined cohesion among large groups of the population only seems possible at the expense of one recognizable group that is abjected.

9. MY SURINAMESE, ANTILLEAN, AND AFRICAN FRIENDS
AND NEIGHBORS THEMSELVES LIKE ZWARTE PIET

One foolproof way of disarming dissent against Zwarte Piet is to mobilize black people for the cause: "I know so many Surinamese and Antilleans, people with *een kleurtje*, a tinge of color, who celebrate it too and who don't see anything wrong with it."[24] Surinamese, Antilleans, and Africans are mobilized and deployed as allies: They, too, do not see anything wrong with the Zwarte Piet tradition. Prime Minister Rutte of the Conservative Democrats exhibited the same state of mind when he opined, in the heat of the discussions in the spring of 2014, "Black Pete is black, after all; there is nothing that I can do about it." Calling on his "Antillean friends," who also celebrate the festivity with abandon, he regretted the hard work that he had to do to scrub the black paste from his face afterward, while the friends did not have to do anything.

Whereas it may very well be the case that Surinamese, Antilleans, and Africans do not see a problem with the tradition, the mobilizing of blacks for the dominant cause leaves out of consideration the power relations that are operative: That is, the dominant discourse holds that the figuration is not racist. Concomitantly, a strong cost is attached to coming out (of the closet) and protesting against Black Pete: ridicule, ostracism, abjection, and aggressive and dismissive reactions. Especially when there are only a handful of black families in a white neighborhood, village, or town, it is not a very popular position to take. Going to one's children's school, talking with the teachers, and explaining to them why your child is not going to participate in the Sinterklaas activities takes significant civil courage (Raalte 1998; Schor 2013). It bears pointing out that there is a gendered division of labor in the protests against Zwarte Piet: While it is (mostly black) men who are in the public eye, it is black and white mothers of mixed-race or black children who make the day-to-day low-key protests at school, protecting their children, speaking to the mostly all-white school boards and teachers.[25]

Moreover, the appropriating of blacks as allies also leaves unacknowledged that since racism is hardly talked about in school or at university, that there are few (e.g., familial) sites where one learns to become antiracist. Among the approximately 1,500 e-mails, some six or seven came from blacks, also anonymous, who, sometimes tentatively, spoke up against the racist character of Zwarte Piet. They were the only ones who dared to break through the avalanche of defenders. Finally, the most insidious aspect of this positioning of blacks as allies is that it calls up the silent rule in the Dutch citizenship contract: "If you want to be one of us, you, too, have to deny that there is such a phenomenon as racism in operation." The positioning of blacks as allies also speaks to an imaginary in which Muslims are beyond the pale and blacks have reached a place of more familiarity.

10. GENDER

Gender also comes up in the e-mail bombardment, but not very often. It is mentioned about seven times and then directed at the artists, as in, "Just go and take care of your household and do the dishes." Gender is also invoked when the artists are urged to use their time in a more useful way, such as fighting the stoning of women in Afghanistan or when they are asked, "When are you going to do something about the headscarves that are so hostile to women"? Thus gender comes up in assigning the artists a traditional place and in gendering the hostile and despicable other. In this gesture, Muslim women serve as the undesirably positioned counterpart of "our" women, who are fully emancipated.

Together, these ten themes call up an image of a Dutch white self, at the end of the first decade of the new millenium. Experiencing the protests against Black Pete, white Dutch citizens express how something is being taken away from an innocent "us" and from our innocent children; a strong notion of victimhood; a massive resistance against change; a feeling of being under siege, both as individuals and as a nation, and the threats coming from inside and outside the nation; a threat from an overwhelmingly Left church and from Muslims, while Surinamese, Antilleans, and Africans, who have in reality been at the forefront of the protest, are deployed to underwrite the lack of racism in Zwarte Piet. The tone of the messages is generally hateful, ugly, injured, aggrieved—a host of defensive mechanisms put on display. The discourse is the discourse of neorealism (Prins 2002), where the common man or woman has found his or her voice and is "telling it like it is," fulminating from a right-wing position against a perceived leftist elite that has protected foreigners, allochthones, Muslims, and has not defended and protected white Dutch culture. Let me finally say, on a more personal note, that it was hard to read these e-mails: It is like taking an undiluted dose of poison. The hatred is a firm reminder of the risk that presents itself when one breaks through the unspoken dominant consensus that race is a nonissue in the Netherlands.

A Comparison with 1998

In the heat of the most recent controversies about Zwarte Piet, it is easy to forget that we are going through some of the same motions again. Activism against Zwarte Piet has been ongoing since the late 1960s, as well as his defense. Interestingly, Teun van Dijk analyzed a collection of letters to the editor in big daily newspapers in 1998, also pertaining to the protest against Zwarte Piet. His analysis allows an assessment of what changed between 1998 and 2008, in terms of themes brought to the fore by defenders, but also, and importantly, in terms of the political climate. Van Dijk distinguishes eleven arguments defending the festivity:

1. Children are innocent and do not discriminate.
2. All children like it.
3. Minorities themselves like it.
4. Denial.
5. Historical denial: Zwarte Piet was not a slave.
6. Absurd comparison ("Suppose we abolished the queen's birthday?").
7. The festivity of Sinterklaas is already changing.
8. We need to maintain our cultural traditions.
9. Do not moan or exaggerate!
10. Irony and ridicule.
11. The Sinterklaas festivity is a metaphor for the inequality in society.

While there is a lot of overlap in the arguments and themes in 1998 and 2008 (the innocence of children; minorities themselves like it; we need to maintain our cultural traditions) and in the style of arguing (ridicule, irony, absurd comparisons, admonitions to adjust or leave) there are two terrains where I see differences. First is the tone of the communications. More recently, that tone has changed to a downright aggressive and hateful timbre, seeking to humiliate and wound, to extirpate those who do not belong here from the nation. This marked change in tone can be connected to the anonymity of the Internet as opposed to letters to the editor, where one must at least sign one's name, although the name might have been made up. Moreover, we also recognize in the communications from 2008 the characteristics of what Baukje Prins (2002) has termed the "new realist discourse." The different, far harsher political climate in 2008 is evident from the second difference I note: that is, the ubiquitous presence of Muslims as the culprits in the correspondence. Inscribing Muslims into the Zwarte Piet problematic points to the roller-coaster decade in which right-wing politicians like Pim Fortuyn, Rita Verdonk, and Geert Wilders came to the fore with their anti-Muslim rhetoric. It also points to the shifting circumstances in Dutch society in which, even though Dutch people of Surinamese, Antillean, and African backgrounds have taken leadership positions in the protest against Zwarte Piet, it is mostly Muslims who get blamed. But it is congruent with the new realist discourse in which Muslims are depicted as the most unassimilable minority, who have taken advantage of our hospitality and are now, like bad guests, even criticizing us. The harshness of the tone in the debate has even grown shriller, and the discussion has become year-round.

Dutch Postcolonial Melancholia

I now want to turn to Gilroy's (2005) Postcolonial Melancholia and investigate how the Dutch configuration is a variation on this concept. Gilroy departs from the psychoanalytical insight that the loss of the colonial empires and the accompanying prestige and stature have not been faced, much less mourned, in many Western European nations. Neither the shame and discomfort connected to the atrocities and the very nature of empire, which regularly flare up and then, by common consent, die down again, nor the more pleasurable aspects of empire, from which everyone in the metropole benefited, have been worked through. Those imperial benefits included psychological capital, in the sense of moral and cultural superiority, and infrastructural goods—many houses, impressive buildings, roads and railways, museums, and the success of enterprises were financed by the possession of colonies. The obfuscation of these benefits has left no impetus and no ways to come up with viable, western European multicultural societies in the present (Wekker 2001; Gilroy 2005; Lentin and Titley 2011). Rather than collectively working through the feelings of loss, the empire was conveniently forgotten. Gilroy argues incisively that rather than working through the colonial past, "a chain of defensive argumentation" is triggered, "that seeks firstly to minimize the extent of the empire, then to deny or justify its brutal character, and finally, to present the British themselves as the ultimate tragic victims of their extraordinary imperial successes" (2005, 94). To possess an empire means to be caught up as a nation in narcissistic structures, in a "fantasy of omnipotence" (99), which, when confronted with irreparable loss, results in melancholia, guilt, and depression. Then, in the unsustainability of that conglomeration of affects, the nation turns around and rejects the newcomers, blacks and other immigrants, extending a less than hearty welcome to them, and in a baffling turn of displacement blames them for the loss of a homogeneous identity and the disappointments of multicultural society, meanwhile firmly prescribing how they should behave.

A variation on this complex configuration is also uncannily applicable to the reaction patterns with regard to Zwarte Piet in the Netherlands. I use "uncanny" here in the sense of "that which ought to have remained secret and hidden but has come to light," "that which ought to have remained repressed and unconscious but which has frighteningly surfaced into (pre)-conscious perception" (Wright 1992, 436).

Let me try to sketch out how the postcolonial melancholia syndrome operates in the Netherlands, which necessitates a brief excursion into the nature of Dutch imperialism. Preliminarily, I should note two things: First, the general and comparative observations about Dutch imperialism that I make below are not very usual in a Dutch context. Historians and journalists are predominantly concerned with either the East Indies or the West Indies, not with the two parts of empire at the same time. The main scholarly and media preoccupation is with the East Indies, or the memory of it, as will become apparent. My other main observation with regard to the Netherlands is that guilt is not one of the main driving forces of the national postcolonial syndrome, even if in repressed form, but a division of affect is operative with regard to imperialism in the East, where a discourse of regret reigns. Differently, with regard to Suriname, feelings of relief are dominant. And toward the Dutch Antilles, still part of the kingdom, indifference and criminalization are the main affects.

The Dutch imperial period is usually defined from the first exploratory sea journeys, around 1600, until the transfer of sovereignty to Indonesia (1945/1949) and Suriname (1975).[26] During the heyday of imperialism, the Dutch ventured as far as South Africa, through Persia, Tonkin, the coasts of India, Ceylon, and the Indonesian Archipelago to Malacca, Taiwan, and Japan. They established trade posts and slave forts on the West African coast and occupied territory in the New World, parts of the Caribbean, Brazil, and North America (van Goor 1993). For a small nation, the empire spanned vast territory, and it elevated the Netherlands to a stature in the world that it otherwise would not have possessed. Yet, ironically, the term "reluctant imperialism" has, conveniently, been used to describe the Dutch variety of imperialism: a mixture of innocent, unplanned actions that forced the Dutch, almost against their wish, to become colonizers, coupled with strong moral overtones of superiority and of a sacred mission. Yet when we consider the vastness of the Dutch empire and the fact that the Dutch were in Indonesia and Suriname for almost four centuries, it is hard to maintain that reluctant imperialist position.

Second, the empire expanded and then crumbled and eventually was downsized to the Indies as the East, and Suriname and the Dutch Antilles as the West. It is entirely clear that the possession of the Indies always tugged much more at the heartstrings of the Dutch nation than the West. Repeatedly, over the centuries, it has been said that without its Indonesian possessions, the Netherlands would be no more than a third-rate nation: "Indië Verloren, Rampspoed Geboren" (When the Indies are lost, disaster is born). The West, however, was and, as far as the former Antilles are concerned, still is regarded as a perennial financial burden. Indeed, the first and main characteristic of Dutch imperialism was (and is) that the eastern part of empire was much more valued than the western part. One author in 1937 remarks, in self-congratulation: "It is the quietest peoples of Asia who, through history, have been brought together with the quietest people of Europe" (Meyer Ranneft, cited in Breman 1993, 18). The privileged position of the Indies not only is connected to the vastness of the Indonesian Archipelago, its beauty, and the number of its inhabitants, but is also a function of the number of Dutch people who went to settle there as public servants, as owners of tea, tobacco, and rubber plantations, and thus, of the thickness of familial networks that were established.[27] Furthermore, the appreciation for Indies cultures as old, venerable ways that should be respected and not interfered with was, from the start, radically different from the devaluation of the pagan black cultures in the West, which were considered void of meaning, the people as tabulae rasae, in bad need of education and raising up by the Dutch. Finally, the revenues from the Indies financed the industrialization of the metropole. Moreover, and ironically, when slavery was abolished in the western part of the empire in 1863, it was the revenues from the East that financed restitution to slave owners in the West—three hundred guilders per adult slave. Of course, the enslaved themselves did not get any restitution.

The privileged position of the Indies in the Dutch imaginary is evident, for example, in the number of articles devoted to the East and to the West in the renowned journal *De Gids*, the journal of the educated middle class where discussions about the imperial possessions took place. Published in the Netherlands, the journal was also read in the colonies. Until 1945, the West was the subject of discussion about twenty-five times, while the Indies were featured 170 times. After the war, the ratio was ten to thirty-four, with five contributions devoted to New Guinea (Breman 1993, 7, 8).

The special position that the Indies occupy in the Dutch imaginary is illustrated by the fact that affairs calling up ghosts from the past invariably involve the Indies, hardly ever the western colonies: war crimes, massacres, defecting Dutch soldiers flare up in the media and then quickly disappear from view. The combination of affects toward the Indies is complex and convoluted: The loss of the Indies is regretted, and there is a widespread nostalgia for *tempoe doeloe*, the good old times. A sizeable amount of literature, photo albums, and films recalls life in the Indies (Pattynama 2014). There is also guilt, which is mostly quickly covered up; there is belligerence about court cases, where widows and children of massacred Indonesian citizens seek redress, such as the widows of the village of Rawagede, whose husbands and sons were killed; and about the long disregard for the fate of the Indo population, who were interned by the Japanese during World War II. This kaleidoscope of feelings has not been worked through in any systematic way, but the collective memory of the Indies, not limited to the many contemporary Dutch people—an estimated one million—who reckon their descent through the Indies, is multifaceted and varied: pride, joy, nostalgia, regret, anger.

On the other hand, I am arguing that the memory of the western part of empire is less varied and complex. An overriding experience that first-generation Surinamese and Antillean migrants expressed, between the 1950s and the 1980s, was their surprise and dismay at the asymmetry in what they knew about the Netherlands—"The river Rhine enters our country at Lobith," as many migrants could recite—that is, they were pointing to the imperial education in geography that they had received in their native countries, which was almost exclusively focused on the Netherlands. They soon found out how little Dutch people knew about them and their countries of origin (Marchetti 2014), accompanied by the subtext that not much was deemed to be lost by that either. There is a vast canvas, punctuated by negative affect and relief at Suriname's independence. Nostalgia toward the West is not the overriding sentiment among the white Dutch public; neither do wonderful memories nor knowledge about the endless atrocities during colonialism circulate widely. The construction of the West as a perennial financial burden on the Netherlands has taken firm hold. The tone that was historically set toward the western part of the empire was captured painfully well by PVV parliamentarian Hero Brinkman, when he proposed in 2007 that the Antilles, still part of the kingdom, be sold on Marketplace, a prominent selling and buying site on the Internet for mainly used and second-hand goods. In comparable fashion, Prime Minister Rutte said in 2013 that if the Antilles wanted out of the kingdom today, he would arrange it tomorrow. Not much love, nostalgia, or melancholia has been lost between the Netherlands and the western part of its empire.

In comparing the memories of the East and the West, I am not engaging in a zero-sum game, in a logic of scarcity, in what Michael Rothberg (2009) calls "competitive memory," whereby the first category would usurp all the memories of the latter. I underline his concept of "multidirectional memory," in which the memories of a particular event or place are not cast in iron, but are much more fluid, with "dynamic transfers taking place between diverse places and times during the act of remembrance" (11), for instance, when he brings the genealogy of the memory of the Holocaust in connection with contemporaneous processes of decolonization. Inspired by Rothberg's understandings, I argue that while both the memories of the East and the West are overshadowed by memories of the Holocaust (Hondius 2014b), the memory of the East may, in Freudian fashion, function as a "screen memory," more palatable and more comfortable than memories of the West. Similarly, in the United States, the memory of the Holocaust as the mother of all traumas functions as a screen memory for the foundational genocide of Native Americans (or the enslavement of African Americans), those displaced from consciousness because they are more disturbing or painful. Thus it might be the case that memories of the West are suppressed in the Netherlands.

I am arguing that one important way in which the West has come to occupy a position in Dutch memory and culture is through the figuration of Zwarte Piet. The overriding affect is enjoyment of blackness, which was already briefly evident in Lian's earlier statement, under theme 2: "Pete is sweet and you can laugh with him. With whites, there is nothing to laugh about." Inspired by Saidiya Hartman's *Scenes of Subjection*, I am trying to imagine what the meanings of Zwarte Piet might have been for the white metropolitan audiences for whom he (or she) was supposed to perform, when he made his appearance.[28] While Hartman's study is an in-depth look at the everyday routines of racial subjugation in the United States—for example, "forcing the enslaved to witness the beating, torture and execution of slaves, changing the names of slave children on a whim . . . and requiring slaves to sing and dance for the owners' entertainment and feign their contentment" (1997, 8)[29]—I want to consider the power mechanisms that play out when an overseas white population is brought into contact with a rare, blackened figure, whose antics, on the most superficial level, are meant to amuse and frighten children into obedience. I want to peer beneath that surface level, at the ways in which relations of domination between white and black were maintained or inculcated in the metropolitan audience "by demonstrations and enactments of power" (James Scott, quoted in Hartman 1997, 7).

It is in 1850—thirteen years before the abolition of slavery, while debates are going on in society and in parliament about the sustainability of slavery—that the Dutch teacher Jan Schenkman introduced the figure of Zwarte Piet as the obedient servant of Sinterklaas, in an illustrated children's book. Moreover, at around the same time, 1852, Beecher Stowe's *Uncle Tom's Cabin* came out and became an immediate best seller in the Netherlands, going through numerous reprints. The images of black people in the book—"lying, loafing, stealing, gifted with great love and loyalty towards whites, childish, dancing, having fun and frolicking" (Hartman 1997, 28)—must have influenced the already present representations of Dutch Zwarte Piet, his character and way of being in the world. The relations of domination evident in the stark inequality of the pair, and what I earlier, after Stuart Hall, called the ritualized degradation of Piet, infused the phantasmatic spectacle put on for the benefit, education, and enjoyment of a metropolitan audience. With the spectacle of Sinterklaas and Zwarte Piet, several aims were accomplished: First, there is continuity between Zwarte Piet and earlier sooty bogeymen in other parts of Europe, who scared children (Zwarte Piet threatened to take bad children with him to Spain). That Zwarte Piet has medieval ancestors, black or sooty figures who originate in Norse, Germanic, and other European mythologies, insulates him in no way from the later influences of racism, when Jan Schenkman draws him. Elmer Kolfin (2013), art historian at the University of Amsterdam, confirms the likeness between the dress of black servants or pages in regents' paintings in the nineteenth century and the dress that Black Pete wears in the course of the twentieth century: "colorful knickerbockers, tights, often a millstone collar, it is the same."

Second, the Dutch audience needed to be convinced of the happiness of the black character; that blacks were naturally funny, carefree, frolicking, without a worry in the world, having no objections to their status and only a limited capacity for suffering, wonderfully suited to their roles of the enslaved. The happy-go-lucky character of Zwarte Piet justified the continuation of slavery and convinced whites that there was nothing to worry about. In Hartman's words, "The constitution of blackness as an abject and degraded condition and the fascination with the other's enjoyment went hand in hand. Moreover, blacks were envisioned fundamentally as vehicles for white enjoyment . . . ; this was . . . the consequence of . . . the excess enjoyment imputed to the other, for those forced to dance on the decks of slave ships crossing the Middle Passage, step it up lively on the auction block, and amuse the master and his friends were seen as the purveyors of pleasure" (1997, 22, 23). When Lian remarked in 2008, "Pete is sweet and you can laugh with him. With whites, there is nothing to laugh about," she showed that that message had come across. Just as whites in the colonial United States had no interest in knowing about the extreme violence of the institution of slavery, it was even less the case for metropolitan Dutch whites. The violence that was visited on black people overseas went unregistered, was obfuscated and disavowed.

Third, the spectacle conveyed and inculcated what it took to be a member of a metropolitan, colonial citizenry: "they" surely could not be "us," and vice versa. Among the qualities setting white and black apart was the attribution to the black figuration of "childishness, primitiveness, content-edness and endowment with great mimetic capacities" (Hartman 1997, 23) and the counterparts of these characteristics to whites. These different amalgams inexorably fed into already existing feelings of superiority, while inferiority was always already imputed to blacks. The spectacle of Zwarte Piet was an education on what it meant to be a member of a metropoli-tan, imperial citizenry and a symbol of the violent inequality envisioned for blacks.

Note that Zwarte Piet has for decades been the first black(-ened) person that small children in Dutch society are exposed to, and this may very well still be the case in environments outside the big cities in the west of the country. It is this figure that sketches for them, before they can even walk or talk, the contours of how and what a black person is; he maintains and perpetuates this imagery in white adults and exposes black people, in an intensified way, to it in the months from October to December. Research from the United States and the United Kingdom shows that little children by the age of three or four are already aware of what skin color they have and which advantages being white carries (Williams 1998). The phenome-non of Black Pete is the Dutch equivalent of the cowboys and Indians game in the United States, where a black child is very quickly taught that he can only be Zwarte Piet or an Indian, never Sinterklaas or a cowboy.

To oppose Zwarte Piet has become an increasingly sensitive gesture, one that provokes ever more negative—blatantly angry, aggressive, threatening, condescending, evasive, disavowing—affect in a society that has managed to convince itself that nearly four hundred years of colonialism have, mi-raculously, not left any traces of racism, either in culture, history, language, representations of the self and the other, or in institutions. "We are a small nation, innocent; we are inherently antiracist; moreover, we do not have bad intentions" is a shorthand to sum up this white sense of self. That these defensive mechanisms have become increasingly strong over the past years, in step with the growing protests, points to the importance of preserving this ideal image of ourselves as deeply tolerant, ethically elevated and justi-fied, color-blind, and antiracist, seemingly at all costs. Ultimately, the pres-ervation of that precious innocent sense of self is the most repressed as well as the most driving reason for the vehemence of the debate. Questioning this most dearly held core of the Dutch sense of self not only is felt as a direct attack, it also means that the nonbeliever, the antiracist killjoy, is putting himself or herself above "us," which in itself again runs deeply counter to another strand in the Dutch sense of self: "gelijke monnikken, gelijke kappen" (literally, equal monks, equal cowls), which invokes the deep egalitarian strand in Dutch self-representation. Critical self-reflection, moreover and ironically, is a scarce commodity in a culture that delights in imagining itself as "nothing," "just normal" (Ramdas 1998), without specific characteristics, much less infused with deep racializations. The point of not knowing, racial ignorance, and innocence has long passed.

"But What about the Captain?"

Slavery had established a measure of man and a
ranking of life and worth that has yet to be undone.
If slavery persists as an issue in the political life of black
America, it is not because of an antiquarian obsession
with bygone days or the burden of a too-long memory,
but because black lives are still imperiled and devalued
by a racial calculus and a political arithmetic that
were entrenched centuries ago. This is the afterlife of
slavery—skewed life chances, limited access to health
and education, premature death, incarceration, and
impoverishment. I, too, am the afterlife of slavery.

Saidiya Hartman, *Lose Your Mother*, 2007

One of the most memorable events surrounding the 150th anniversary celebration of the abolition of slavery in the Dutch empire, at the end of June
2013, is a reading by Professor Saidiya Hartman at Imagine IC, a lively center for cultural heritage in southeast Amsterdam. It is memorable because
of the content of her reading, but also because of how it unfolds. The room
is packed, a mixed audience of black and white women and men. Hartman
(2007) reads from her book *Lose Your Mother*, a heartbreaking counterhistory
about an enslaved girl aboard a transatlantic slaver, the *Recovery*, who is severely abused, physically and sexually, by the captain.[1] Hartman attempts
to write "at the limit of the unspeakable and the unknown," miming "the
violence of the archive and attempts to redress it by describing as fully as

possible the conditions that determine the appearance of Venus and that dictate her silence" (2008, 1). The girl is flogged to death, on the deck. In the court case that ensues, the captain is acquitted for the murder.

The reading is personal, brittle as glass, poetic, intensely moving. "It would not be too far-fetched to consider stories as a form of compensation or even as reparation, perhaps the only kind we will ever receive" (Hartman 2008, 4). After her reading, a thick silence settles in the room. Everyone, I imagine, is trying to find his or her bearings and to come back from a place of horror to this sweltering room. Before the silence can become uncomfortable, it is broken by a white middle-aged man, who straightforwardly asks, "But what about the captain?" Several people in the room gasp, looking at each other, rolling their eyes. Jennifer Tosch, a Surinamese African American ex-student and founder of Black Heritage Tours in Amsterdam, who is sitting close to me, whispers, "This is not good." I am livid and start explaining to Saidiya why I find the question highly inappropriate and that she now gets a firsthand exposure to what we are up against here.

"But what about the captain?" Indeed, what about the captain? From which frame of mind does such a question emerge? The question encapsulates much of what I have been trying to say here about white Dutch self-representation and entitlement. The question is not asked by someone who did not care about the predicament of blacks, either during slavery or now. On the contrary, the questioner is a prominent politician of the Labor Party, very active in Amsterdam on behalf of "ethnic minorities," an ally who is, according to reports of people who know him well, always exerting himself to find funding for new initiatives, supporting them, and generally one of the last warriors left standing who believe in multicultural society. Let's call him N. N.

Let me therefore make an effort to understand what he is asking, why, and where it is coming from. After the story that focuses on the enslaved girl, I imagine that he wants to know, on the first level, whether additional information on the captain is available. For instance, he might want to know: What more do we know about him, his experiences? Did he have prior or later difficulties on his transatlantic journeys? How did his life go on? Did he remain a captain on slave ships? But why does N. N. want to know those things? In which way would this information, which is not available, help him to understand the way in which the captain acted? I obviously do not know the answers to these last two questions. I surmise that what he is reaching for, underneath it all, is some kind of shared humanity with the captain, some circumstances that will help N. N. to understand why he acted the way he did. But maybe, in addition and in contradistinction to Hartman's personal narrative, he is steering toward some kind of objectivity in the tale, something measurable, verifiable, detached: logbooks or bills of carriage, for example. He juxtaposes his "godlike" way of knowing (Haraway 1991) to Hartman's situated way of knowing; these modalities are hierarchically ordered in themselves and associated with gendered stances. As in other pernicious binaries, the implied subtext is that his way of knowing is superior to hers.

As a second observation, I offer the following. While it is clear that many of us in the room, black and white alike, are identifying with the girl, he is identifying with the captain, another white man. This is a rather common phenomenon I have started to note. White men, particularly older men, watching or reading narratives of slavery identify with other white men in the movie or the narrative. Thus, on public TV, the host of the late-night talk show *Pauw en Witteman*, Paul Witteman, admitted, after seeing the movie 12 *Years a Slave* (McQueen 2013), that he had to look away, because he could not stomach the sight of the white masters and their behavior.[2] Why is it that Witteman or N. N. cannot bring themselves to identify with Solomon Northup, the black protagonist of the film or with the black girls aboard the *Recovery*? Is what we were witnessing that afternoon at Imagine IC simply an expression of worn-out patterns of identification—"lazy identification patterns" to paraphrase Toni Morrison (1992a)—which take place "automatically" and below the level of consciousness? My points are precisely, first, that we cannot afford to leave those identifications below the level of consciousness and, second, that we need to change our understanding of the unconscious from the "privatized, individualized and claustrophobic Freudian conception" to one that sees the unconscious as "the life of others and other things within us" (Gordon 2008). One of the tasks ahead, if we want to move beyond the present stalemate, move beyond "aggressive ignorance" (Mills 2007) and fearful avoidance, is to become conscious of those patterns and then to be able to choose whom we want to identify with. We can, as Martha Nussbaum (2010) suggests, benefit from the enlarged and varied imagination that literature, films, and other cultural products afford us to start to occupy different positionings than we usually occupy. In that way, we will no longer be automatically complicit with the unearned benefits of whiteness, held up within the racial contract. The good news is that one can unlearn those lazy identification patterns, see Bram de Swaan's (2013) self-reflection in his presentation "The Pains of Victimhood." De Swaan recounts how he catches himself when he is confronted with the resident physician in the hospital, a black man with an Afro, when in the first milliseconds of the encounter, he wants to see a "real" doctor. It takes courage to become aware of and own up to these Pavlovian reactions.

Third, the configuration, again, brings innocence to the fore. There is innocence in the way that N. N. unwittingly, unblushingly, speaks out first in a setting that asks for some sensitivity in who gets to speak and in what order. His move is not only reflective of current power arrangements, it also reinstalls notions of who gets to speak authoritatively in public space about race. I often wish for an interracial etiquette in which everyone would know what appropriate behavior is, much like before, during the height of the feminist movement, men of whatever hue would know better than to have the first or the final word during meetings on sexism. It is of course not etiquette in a narrow sense that concerns me; it is a consciousness of one's positioning along lines of race and gender. But more importantly, the entitlement to speak first in such a setting is a reflection of who has socially and culturally been empowered to think that their thoughts are always already enriching and highly pertinent to whatever the issue at hand might be. This means that the authority to speak about race and racism is, as N. N. has learned, assigned to white men.

This brings me to my fourth observation: entitlement. Power relationships have not been left at the door but are on full display. In line with the former point, this concerns gender and power. It happens regularly that in public meetings about race and racism, it is white men who speak out first and authoritatively, invariably maintaining that there is no racism either in the academy, in society, or in the figure of Zwarte Piet. At a meeting at the Free University in Amsterdam, organized in the framework of anti-racism in the academy,[3] a twenty-something white male student tells me self-assuredly that there is no racism in the Netherlands. He, an inhabitant of Volendam, a small, overwhelmingly white town by the borders of the Ijsselmeer, has not noticed it at all. The epistemological question about who has knowledge about what and on what grounds does not seem to enter his picture. This is militant, aggressive ignorance, posing as knowledge, that will not go away quietly. No sensitivity is evident, neither a questioning attitude, nor the slightest hint of an awareness that he might learn something here, merely the aggressive rejection and denial that is often characteristic of white men, even when they see themselves as politically progressive. It strikes me as significant, as I have laid out in chapter 2, that white progressive women display anxiety, fear, and avoidance about broaching the topics of race and racism. Thus, we see widely diverging, gendered reactions when race is brought up as a fundamental axis of personal, symbolic, and institutional signification, and neither reaction is very helpful, I must add. Coming back to N. N. and his intervention, my impression is that he, accustomed to being the center of society, of history, of the world, finds that too much attention is being paid to the victims. In the painstaking rewriting of history that Hartman is presenting, the captain is marginalized in the narrative, and that means marginalizing N. N., and that surely cannot be allowed to stand.

Fifth, in the different layers that embed innocence, there is also the distortion that is inherent in a particular kind of social cognition: an inability to see the atrocities committed by white people, which simultaneously says something about a persistent feeling that the enslaved women must have done something to bring the treatment they received upon themselves. Was it their nakedness, their powerlessness, their skin color that eroticized them and brought out that fatal combination of pleasure and danger in the colonial libidinal economy? This is the heart of sexual racism; the unspeakable horror of sexual transgressions against enslaved women, who as property had no way of defending themselves. It is not the predicament of the enslaved women that speaks most forcefully to N. N.; it is the predicament of the captain and how he can be salvaged from being labeled a ruthless rapist, how he can be maintained as a decent fellow, who did everything he could to perform his dangerous and thankless job. Here we do not even have the "politics of compassion" (Balkenhol 2014) or paternalism (Hondius 2014b) directed at the women. It is directed at the captain. All of this remains below the level of consciousness in someone who is an ally.

Sixth, all of this has consequences for education, at all levels. In teaching about sensitive topics like colonialism and slavery—sensitive in different ways to different students—multiple perspectives need to be shown. In an environment in which the seventeenth century, the Golden Century, has always been looked upon with pride in the Netherlands, and where we have been taught to see trade and prosperity as something neutral, we need another "embarrassment of riches." The time is more than ripe for other narratives; otherwise we will forever remain stuck with the perspective of the captain. Multiple perspectives first necessitate multiple stories from the perspective of the enslaved and the colonized.[4]

"What about the captain?" has become a running gag among some of the audience members who were there that afternoon, and there are far too many occasions when it is appropriate to use the expression. It is a shorthand for racially insensitive speech and behavioral acts, in short, racially inappropriate behavior, that bespeaks white innocence of the Dutch variety.

NOTES

Introduction

1 While I use the terms "postcolonial" and "decolonial," I find that "postcolonial" is increasingly used in a manner that is subject to inflation and is uncritical; that is, one can do postcolonial studies very well without ever critically addressing race. In that sense, it has come to resemble an old-fashioned type of anthropology, in that the other is unblushingly studied without questioning one's own position, while anthropologists have, since the late 1960s, sternly interrogated their own discipline for its racializing power moves. Decoloniality, decolonial studies, or the decolonial option is the more cutting-edge approach, which starts from the realization of the nexus of modernity and coloniality.

2 But also see Flax (2010).

3 Some exceptions have manifested. For example, in southeast Amsterdam, where I live and where the majority of the population is black, the working group Committee 4–5 May organizes an inclusive memorial and the yearly George Maduro lecture, which I had the honor to deliver in 2013. George Maduro was an Antillean student, active in the Dutch resistance, who was killed during the war. Madurodam, the miniature city in The Hague, is named after him and was originally financed by his family. Things may be less progressive outside of the four big cities, however. In the early 2000s, my father, active in a Tilburg committee that wanted to organize an exhibition on World War II in the West, met with outright hostility from parts of the Tilburg population who maintained that they had no interest whatsoever in whatever happened in Suriname and the Antilles during the war.

4 This part is based on an earlier publication (Wekker 2001).

5 Ons Indië, "Our Indies," is the old, nostalgic way of referring to the colony, which freed itself from the Dutch in 1945, although most Dutch believe Indonesian independence only happened in 1949.

6 Between 1945 and the early 1950s, about 300,000 white Dutch and Indos, descendants of white men and indigenous women, settled in the Netherlands. In the same period, about 3,500 Moluccan soldiers, having fought on the Dutch side in the Indonesian war of independence, and their families, 12,500 people altogether, were demobilized in The Netherlands. They were housed in separate barracks and camps, many of which had been used for prisoners and Jews during World War II, symbolizing the temporary nature of their stay in the Netherlands and their desire to return to Indonesia, which never materialized. The consequences of this housing policy, which meant segregation, are still palpable to this day, as Moluccans have lower educational attainments than the rest of the population. Shortly before the independence of Suriname in 1975, huge numbers of Surinamese, of many different ethnic groups, found their way to the Netherlands, due to lack of trust in the new political situation in their country of birth. As of January 1, 2014, 348,000 people are of Surinamese descent, in addition to 147,000 from the Antilles and Aruba (CBS 2014, 26). On October 10, 2010, the six islands forming the Dutch Antilles were dissolved into Saba, St. Eustacius, and Bonaire, which became municipalities of the Netherlands, while Curacao and St. Martin became autonomous territories. Aruba resembles the latter two, with its *status aparte*.

7 Circum-Mediterranean labor migrants started to arrive in the early 1960s, having been requested to add their labor power to the unfolding economic boom. They were expected to go back to their countries of origin, the so-called myth of return, and many of them did, but at the end of the day Turks (396,000 persons) and Moroccans (375,000) are now the largest migrant groups, including second and third generations (CBS 2014, 26).

8 Thanks to Alex van Stipriaan, personal communication, who notes, partially based on Lucassen and Penninx (1993): "Until the 19th century citizenship was regulated by local, municipal governments. This changed with the founding of the Dutch Kingdom after the Napoleonic wars in 1814, and tendencies towards a homogenizing nation state came into being. This meant that more and more regulations were made differentiating who belonged to the national 'we' and who did not, or who did so only partially. According to the Constitution of 1815, for example, every one born in the Dutch empire or its foreign possessions was by law considered Dutch, including all political and other rights that went with it. This did not apply to the enslaved populations in the empire, because they were legally not considered humans. This all changed with the new democratic constitution of 1848, when the indigenous population of the colonies were excluded of the political rights that were part of Dutch citizenship. In 1893 the territorial nationality by birth, was replaced by nationality by blood, or rather descendancy."

9 Later, in 1959, my youngest brother Paul was born; he died unexpectedly in his sleep in December 2011, while I was on sabbatical at NIAS and starting to write this book. I dedicate this book, among others, to him, trusted critic and

great supporter, precisely because he did not always agree with me. I miss him dearly.

10 Hirsi Ali was a highly controversial politician, first because, in an unprecedented move, she abandoned the Labor Party, the traditional home of groups and individuals seeking emancipation, for the more right-wing VVD, the party of neoliberal entrepreneurs. In her view, the socialists were simply not up to the task of moving multicultural society forward by setting clear standards for Muslims, especially men who were oppressing women. Significantly, Hirsi Ali was not appreciated by the constituency whose interests she said she was representing, that is, Muslim women, nor was she liked by significant numbers of feminists, of whatever hue.

11 Literally translated, "equal monks, equal cowls."

12 Verdonk's decision was soon overturned by parliament, but Hirsi Ali decided to move to the United States, where she works for a conservative think tank in Washington, DC, the New Enterprise Institute. The Balkenende II government fell a little later, on June 29, 2006, as a result of the debate outlined in this section.

13 But interestingly, fights have had to be waged to expand the memory of World War II, as it was experienced in both parts of the colonial empire, the East and the West. For a long time, only metropolitan grief counted and at that, a limited conception of metropolitan grief, since, for example, gays, blacks, Roma, and Sinti who were residing in the Netherlands at the time and were also persecuted were overlooked. This also was true for Surinamese Jews, like my great-uncle Cosman Abraham Gomperts, brother of my grandmother Eva Gomperts, my father's mother. Cos had studied medicine in Groningen in the 1930s and was a general practitioner in upscale Amsterdam South, when he was abducted by the Germans. He was killed in Auschwitz in 1943.

14 Except for the rare colonial monuments, such as the General van Heutz monument in Amsterdam, which honors his "heroic" deeds in the Aceh war in Indonesia.

15 I am, together with Alex van Stipriaan, Dienke Hondius, Guno Jones, Kwame Nimako, and Francio Guadeloupe, a member of the Scientific Council of NiNsee.

16 These are words of the poet Lucebert, in the poem "De zeer oude zingt" (The very old sings): "everything of value, is defenseless."

17 Essed and Hoving (2014, 24, 25) distinguish three characteristic patterns of Dutch racism: (1) the Dutch sense of moral and cultural superiority, based on moral righteousness and ideological repression; (2) the anxious claim of innocence, merging into smug ignorance; and (3) the strong sense of Dutch entitlement.

18 Thanks to Siep Stuurman for his insights on religion, shared at the presentation of Dienke Hondius's (2014b) *Blackness in Western Europe*, Free University, Amsterdam, October 21, 2014.

19 For instance, by being an unquestioning ally of the United States and want-
    ing to be among the first nations to be asked to participate in its wars and
    airstrikes. Whenever one of the Dutch prime ministers visits the president of
    the United States, whether Bush or Obama, the entire nation watches breath-
    lessly. Are we being taken seriously as an ally? And does the prime minister's
    English pass muster? Prime Minister Balkenende, especially, stuck out like a
    sore thumb in the White House, standing around like the boy who gets picked
    last on the soccer team. Obama's visit to the Netherlands on March 24, 2014,
    preceding the Nuclear Security Summit in the Hague, arriving by helicopter
    and spending a full fifty minutes in the Rijksmuseum, easily was one of the
    news highlights of the year.

20 Examples abound. In November 2013, white TV personality Jack Spijkerman
    said to his black colleague Humberto Tan, talk show host of RTL Late Night,
    "Good grief!! Not only black, but also dumb," when Tan incorrectly answered
    a question about soccer. Spijkerman claimed a privileged long-standing
    nonracist positioning—after all, he claimed to be friends with Tan, which
    supposedly undid the racist nature of his remark. I analyze more, comparable
    examples in chapter 1.

21 Sending death threats to someone who points to the racism in Dutch society
    is not new. When I was working as a civil servant for the city of Amsterdam in
    1984 (see chapter 2) and was responsible for drafting the first antiracism pol-
    icy paper, I regularly received death threats, by anonymous telephone calls.

22 Thanks to Mikki Stelder, PhD candidate in cultural studies at the University
    of Amsterdam and member of Queeristan, for her remarks and questions at
    a first presentation of chapter 3, and for our subsequent conversation in the
    summer of 2014.

23 For an excellent new addition to this blossoming field of archival research, see
    Heather Hermant's (2016) PhD dissertation on the eighteenth-century multi-
    ple crosser Esther Brandeau/Jacques La Fargue, the first Jewess to set foot in
    New France, Canada. Esther/ Jacques was not only crossing in terms
    of gender, but also in terms of religion, claiming Christianity.

24 "We" in this book is a shifting pronoun, sometimes including me, as I cannot
    and do not want to deny being Dutch. I claim Dutchness, while at other times,
    which I will indicate, I exclude myself. The position that fits me best is that of
    the "outsider within" (Hill Collins 1986; Wekker 2006).

25 Polder is the Dutch word for a piece of land that is reclaimed from the water.
    This endeavor took a lot of negotiating, discussing back and forth to finally
    reach a compromise that everyone could agree to. Thus the verb "polderen" is
    still used nowadays to indicate the endless back and forth to reach consensus
    on an issue.

26 At other history departments, for example at the Free University, Amsterdam,
    and at Erasmus University, Rotterdam, non-Western history was introduced
    in the 1970s, and all students had to take compulsory courses in that field.

The idea was that these courses would in time become part of the regular curriculum. Currently, there is a move toward separation between world or global history and European and national history, while at the same time thematic history (religion, migration, media, cultural encounters), is growing. Thanks to Alex van Stipriaan for these insights.

Chapter 1. Case Studies of Everyday Racism

1 As far as psychoanalysis is concerned, I seek my inspiration in the many theorists who, since the 1930s, have explored the potential of the problematic field of psychoanalysis for the exploration of colonialism and racism. The master project of psychoanalysis has been the theorization of sexual difference, which was taken to be the foundational psychological and social drama of our culture, and in its early years it did not problematize whiteness, but rather universalized and naturalized it. From the late 1930s and 1940s onward, however, and especially in the 1950s, important (though not always uncontested) psychoanalytical studies of colonization began to appear by scholars, many of whom lived in the Caribbean, in Africa, or in the black European diaspora, including Wulf Sachs (1937), Jean-Paul Sartre ([1948] 1976), Lillian Smith (1948), Dominique-Octave Mannoni ([1950] 1991), Aimé Césaire (1972), Suzanne Césaire (2009), Frantz Fanon ([1952] 1967), and Albert Memmi (1965). After the 1980s, when Fanon's work also became a source of inspiration for booming Anglophone postcolonial scholarship, psychoanalysis was no longer seen as necessarily in support of colonialism, as Christopher Lane argues. Psychoanalysis could even serve as an important analytical contribution to the critique of colonial discourse and racism—though not without thorough revision. Psychoanalysis, according to Doane, "unshaken in its premises, cannot be applied to issues of racial difference but must be radically destabilized by them" (1991, 216).

2 Indos, the descendants of white Dutch and indigenous people from the East Indies, during the four hundred years of Dutch colonial rule of Indonesia formed a separate stratified layer in the population (see Pattynama 1997, 2014). Around and after the independence of Indonesia (1945/1949), they were forced to relocate to the Netherlands (see Captain 2014). On Indos, see further chapters 3 and 5.

3 Another topic that has not been investigated in depth yet, which I have not done either, is the difference in the kinds of racism that black and (supposedly) Islamic women encounter. My colleague Halleh Ghorashi (2014) points to the gratitude that she, as a former Iranian refugee, needs to display toward her benefactors, whereas the main affect that I am confronted with professionally is a disbelief that I am a member of the academic community. This observation is based on a very limited sample, but definitely needs more study.

4 There are enough other novels that foreground the representation of black women, such as Joost Zwagerman's *De Buitenvrouw* (The outside wife, 1994) and Robert Vuijsje's *Alleen maar nette Mensen* (Only decent folks, 2008), later also made into a film with the same title. These novels are written by white men and they are numbing in their display of the racist cultural archive. I am more interested in exploring how a black female author deals with the representation of black women. Interestingly, while Vuijsje initially was rather obdurate in defending his book as a product of the imagination, having nothing to do with racism, he has more recently, as a convert in the Zwarte Piet debate, also acknowledged the racism of his book (Vuijsje, R., 2014 in *De Volkskrant*, October 15), www.biebtobieb.nl/system/files/berichten/bijlages /interview_volkskrant_15–10–2014_robert_vuijsje_over_kinderboek_alleen _maar_stoute_pieten.pdf.

5 *De Wereld Draait Door* is a play on words. Literally, it means, "The world keeps on turning," while metaphorically it indicates that the world is going crazy. In an interview Bril later gave, he stated that his daughter now had a boyfriend, a Russian, who was much less scary than the big Negro, whom, he added, he was wary of because "he might hurt his daughter" (Dagelet 2007). Martin Bril, who was much beloved, died in April 2009. Not surprisingly, in none of his obituaries was there any mention of this episode.

6 Later installments of his show confirm van Nieuwkerk's habitus: never at a loss for words on any subject, he is perpetually perplexed about how to react when it comes to racism and never personally calls anyone on racist statements. The message is either that racism is not important or that he does not recognize it, or both. For example, in the edition of May 13, 2015, a white male guest, a former tennis player of Czech descent Martin Simek called boat refugees from Africa *zwartjes*, little blacks, claiming his being married to a black woman as the ultimate proof of his fondness of blacks. Another guest on the show, Surinamese Dutch dancer/ presenter Silvana Simons, is visibly shocked at Simek's utterance and asks him for clarification. Van Nieuwkerk sits back and lets things unfold. However, the next evening, he offered Simons an opportunity to explain her position. Subsequently Simons was inundated with hate mail on social media. She was especially chastised for interrupting Simek's "interesting and important narrative with her moaning."

7 I do not know of research in the Dutch context that establishes at which age children start to notice race differences, although experiential evidence suggests it to be between four and six years. In an American context, Patricia Williams (1998, 1–14) movingly describes the process by which her four-year-old black son was introduced to race difference in kindergarten, where he never gets to be a cowboy, but always has to be an Indian. The equivalent in a Dutch setting is the impossibility of a black child playing the role of white Sinterklaas, but always being assigned to the role of Black Pete.

8 From an interview with Sandrine van der Molen, pseudonym, in August 2009.

9 In a Dutch context, the title professor is assigned only to full professors and is thus rare. It carries more weight than in a U.S. setting, where "doctor" is the most respectful term of address.

10 In the process of writing this book, a definite change has come about, whereby a young generation of black men and women, are refusing to put up with racism any longer. After a short moment in the early 1980s, now a second anti–racist movement is underway, which started with the protest against Black Pete, led by Quincy Gario and Kno'ledge Cesare in the fall of 2011.

11 The statement by Prime Minster Jan Peter Balkenende in November 2006 that "we should return to the VOC mentality"—pertaining to the mentality of the United East India Company, the body governing the East Indies during colonial times, is exemplary in this regard (see Jordan 2014).

12 Possibly the first such debate in the Netherlands took place on May 20, 2011, at the noteworthy symposium "Shared Cultural Heritage: Theory and Practice in Mirror Image" at the Moluccan Museum in Utrecht, organized by Nancy Jouwe of Kosmopolis Utrecht. Not only did academics, curators, and artists focused on postcoloniality lecture at this symposium, but Dutch national history and the histories of the Dutch East Indies, Suriname, and the Antilles were also brought into one analytical plane, seeking to map the traces that Dutch colonial history has left both in the Netherlands and in the former colonies.

13 "Animus revertendi" is the desire to leave the colony as fast as possible, once one had amassed enough riches.

14 In the Placard Books (1667–1816), the colonial government tried to regulate the behavior of the various groups in Surinamese society, including native Surinamese, Christian and Jewish settlers, the enslaved, and freedmen and freedwomen, also laying down the punishments for transgressions.

15 Readers of *Gay Krant* choose the PVV as the most popular party, http: www .gk.nl/index//.php?id=9&a=bericht&bericht=8446&markeer=pvv. Accessed May 31, 2011. The old Gaykrant does not exist anymore, nor is it online any longer. It has merged into Winq|Gaykrant.

Chapter 2. The House That Race Built

1 I worked for seven years on behalf of the emancipation of blacks, migrants, and refugees for the national government and later for the local government, the Bureau for Ethnic Minority Affairs in the city of Amsterdam, where I was responsible for drafting an antiracism policy paper in 1984, after the famous Princenhof conference on antiracism, earlier that same year. I subsequently worked for more than twenty years in anthropology, African American studies, and gender studies in the academy, at UCLA, at Oberlin College, Ohio, and at Utrecht University, where I was strongly invested in sexuality studies, antiracism, and intersectionality.

2   As elsewhere in the book, I use the terms blacks, migrants, and refugees when I speak in my own voice about the groups that are called allochtonen in the dominant, official language. I have discussed the pitfalls of each of these terms in the introduction.

3   I alternatively use the terms women's studies and gender studies for the discipline.

4   See the ATHENA series "The Making of European Women's Studies: A Work in Progress Report on Curriculum Development and Related Issues in Gender Education and Research," for an overview of developments with regard to intersectionality in different European countries, see among other issues: Braidotti and Vonk, eds. 2000; Braidotti, Vonk, and van Wichelen, eds. 2000; Braidotti, Lazaroms and Vonk, eds. 2001; Braidotti, Hirs and Nieboer, eds. 2002; Braidotti and Just, eds. 2004; Braidotti and van Baren, eds. 2005; Braidotti and Waaldijk, eds. 2006., Also, the ATGENDER Series (e.g., Hipfl and Loftsdóttir 2012); also see Lykke 2011; Lutz, Vivar, and Supik 2011; Cho, Crenshaw, and McCall eds., 2013.

5   In Dutch: Het Ministerie van Welzijn, Volksgezondheid en Cultuur. It carried this name between 1982 and 1994.

6   It is quite common to continue calling migrant populations that have been settled in the Netherlands for decades by the names of their countries of origin: for example, Surinamese, instead of Surinamese Dutch.

7   On November 30, 2013, a report by Ana van Es on the train hijacking from 1977, written by a civil servant at the Ministry of Justice, Ernst Hirsch Ballin, who was later to become minister of justice himself, was made public. The report, which had been kept under wraps for all those years, stated that the hijackers had been killed by a rain of bullets (144 bullets killing six of the eight young Moluccans, several of whom were unarmed) and that, contrary to what then Minister of Justice van Agt had stated, the marines' actions were meant to kill the hijackers. http://www.volkskrant.nl/binnenland/geheime-nota -molukse-treinkapers-door-kogelregen-gedood~a3553851/.

8   In Dutch: Ministerie van Sociale Zaken en Werkgelegenheid.

9   Ministerie van Sociale Zaken en Werkgelegenheid. "Kamerbrief Agenda Integratie," February 2013, ref. no. 2013–0000015514, https://www.rijksoverheid.nl /documenten/beleidsnotas/2013/02/19/agenda-integratie. Accessed September 15, 2015. Emphasis added.

10 For an excellent critique of the assumptions underlying the Integration Agenda and the Inburgeringsprogramma, the program designed for newcomers to integrate into society, see de Leeuw and van Wichelen (2014).

11 ECRI mentions: locking up children of asylum seekers in prison, whose parents are already detained, having exhausted their legal possibilities to stay; the ever increasing demands and costs of the inburgeringsexams (acculturation exams) that newcomers need to take in order to participate in Dutch society; not taking racist motives into account in the punishment of crimes; the un-

equal treatment of Eastern Europeans on the labor market; and the discriminatory discourse by parliamentarians and media against Muslims and the lack of sturdy antiracism measures (ECRI 2013).

12 This chapter is partly based on earlier work (Wekker 1996a, 1998, 2002, 2009b, 2013; Wekker and Lutz 2001).

13 It is noteworthy that the most prevalent term to harass us and put us, brown children, in our place in the 1950s refers to Chinese, a group that has been present in the Netherlands as seamen, peanut vendors, and later restaurant workers and owners, since the 1930s (see Mak 2000; Huang 2015). Chinese do not belong, nor have they ever belonged, to the target groups of government ethnic minority policy.

14 These years mark the first time a policy paper indicating the aims and measures of women's and ethnic minority policy was issued by different ministries. The year 1970 marks the publication of the "Nota Buitenlandse Werknemers" (Policy paper on foreign workers), or Nota Roolvink, named after the minister, which departs from the notion that guest workers will return to their countries of origin.

15 Dutch Organization for Scientific Research, NWO, and Royal Dutch Academy of Sciences, KNAW.

16 The knowledge infrastructure still subsidized by the national government in 2015 on behalf of women's and LGBT emancipation consists of the following organizations: Atria, Women Inc., the Organization for the Integration of LGBT people, COC NL, the LGBT-Heritage Foundation IHLIA, National Women's Council NVR, and Transgender Network TNN. Atria is the institute for emancipation and women's history, a fusion of the IIAV—the former archives and information center of the women's movement in Amsterdam— and E-Quality, the expertise center on emancipation in The Hague. Women Inc., a national women's organization in Amsterdam, organizes debates in the cultural and literary field and is increasingly concerned with initiatives to guide low-income women into the labor market and help with women's pensions.

17 In Dutch, the ministry is called OC&W, Onderwijs, Cultuur en Wetenschap (Education, Culture and Science). Since 2007, LGBT policy is also housed in this ministry.

18 Organized every year by the George Mosse Foundation at the University of Amsterdam, on a topic related to gay and lesbian liberation. I gave the lecture, titled "Van Homo Nostalgie en Betere Tijden" in September 2009.

19 Letter of minister of OC&W to parliament, May 10, 2013. Parliament no. 30420.

20 The five instances: (1) Antillean and Moroccan boys and men who are causing problems of social nuisance and criminality (Ministerie van OC&W, 2013, 9); (2) the miserable educational results of non-Western allochthonous boys are mentioned (13); (3) Turkish and Moroccan youth who have a negative attitude toward homosexuality (20); (4) acceptance of homosexuality within groups of

migrants and within religious groups needs to be promoted and made into a topic of discussion (24); and (5) that the gender-stereotypical choices of boys and girls in secondary education (girls, the care sector; and boys, technical skills) are not only gender related but also connected to ethnic backgrounds, where allochthonous boys often choose commerce and economy. The minister wants to pay special attention to opening up other professional avenues for "girls" and "allochthonous boys" in the direction of math, science, and technology (24–25).

21   In the course of the forty-some years that I have been active in the women's movement, numerous black, migrant, and refugee women and also white women have tried, ad nauseam, to explain to the Directorate for the Coordination of Emancipation Affairs why its reasoning is faulty. Thus far, to no avail. In the last session at the ministry in which I participated, in October 2012, which was meant to consult experts on what emancipation still could and should mean in this day and age, I was finally invited to a general meeting. My invitation did not come directly from the ministry, however, but through Dr. Renee Römkens, director of Atria, who asked me to replace her.

22   One-third of all women in the Netherlands have ever been victims of sexual violence and 12 percent have ever been raped (Bijleveld and Mans 2009).

23   See my unpublished paper (Wekker 2008).

24   This analysis does not take into account some disciplines, such as medicine, economics, and movement/life sciences, where significant efforts have been undertaken to develop gendered perspectives on their subject matter.

25   There are other sites where ethnic relations are studied in the Dutch academy, mostly in sociology departments; these, however, are the main centers.

26   IMES (UvA) stands for Institute for Migration and Ethnic Studies; it focuses on the social anthropology and political science of ethnic minority populations. ERCOMER (UU) is the European Research Center on Migration and Ethnic Relations; the social psychology of ethnic relations and modes of exclusion. ISEO (EUR) is the Institute for Sociological and Economic Research, which is engaged with the sociology and economics of ethnic minority disadvantage, mobility, and integration (see their respective websites).

27   Essed, P. 1982. "Racisme en Feminisme," in *Femsoc Teksten*.

28   The opposite situation, in which black students, often for the first time too, experience having a black professor, leads to complex affect, too.

29   Jonathan Jansen (2002), "The Curriculum from Hell." I responded with "A Response to the Curriculum from Hell" (Wekker 2002c).

30   The one-year MA program at Utrecht University is now called "Sustainable Perspectives in Emancipation Policies, Diversity Management, Cultural Initiatives and Political Activism."

1 A much earlier version of this chapter in a different form appeared as "Intimate Truths about Subjectivity and Sexuality: A Psychoanalytical and a Postcolonial Approach," in Buikema, Griffin, and Lykke (2011b). While Moore claimed that we simply do not have enough information to really understand what was happening with these women, but instead must focus on the racial and gendered images circulating in the analytic context and in cultural productions, I want to deepen my own analysis here, starting from the assumption that with the term "Hottentot nymphae," meaningful statements are being made about gender, race, sexuality, and subjectivity.

2 But also see the work of Siep Stuurman (2009), van Stipriaan et al. (2007), and Waaldijk and Grever (2004).

3 I quote from the reprinted version in Ruitenbeek (1966).

4 This is the same patient that was discussed during van Ophuijsen's presentation at the second meeting of the Dutch Association of Psychoanalysis in 1917. There is a remarkable similarity between van Ophuijsen's Patient H. and the first of two patients described by Jeanne Lampl de Groot in her 1928 (1966) article, "The Evolution of the Oedipus Complex in Women" (cf. Hamon 1992). The patient had been handed over to Lampl de Groot by a male colleague due to "unresolved, ambivalent transference," and her analysis with Lampl de Groot was also cut short because of her unmistakable desire to woo her analyst, to win her love. Harry Stroeken (2009, 9) even suggests that a more careful comparison of the data might show that Patient H. is the famous psychoanalyst Jeanne Lampl de Groot herself.

5 The myth of the dark continent, as Brantlinger (1985) usefully reminds us, masks the fact that Africa was not dark to start with, but became dark during the process of European expansion.

6 In this chapter, I cannot possibly provide an overview of the prolific debates between male and female psychoanalysts of the period, nor of the later, for example Lacanian, rewritings of the Freudian paradigm, with its postulates of Having or Being the Phallus (cf. Butler 1990). It is striking to me, however, how few early psychoanalysts threw doubt on the basic Freudian assumption of the enormous psychic significance of the lack of a penis and of penis envy in the erotic life of women (but see, Horney [1933] 1966; Thompson [1950] 1966).

7 The fantasy "a child is being beaten," according to Jeanne Lampl de Groot ([1928] 1966: 44), refers to the masturbation of the little girl in the phallic phase: "The child which is beaten or caressed is at bottom the clitoris (i.e. the penis)."

8 This section is based on the description of Van Ophuijsen's life, which Harry Stroeken (2009, 7–44) has painstakingly and usefully put together.

9 The dataset from the Central Bureau of Statistics pertaining to the presence

of people from the colonies is to be found under: https://easy.dans.knaw.nl/ui/datasets/id/easy-dataset:38767, last accessed May 25, 2014.

10 I would also surmise that the few migrants from the west at the time, 1917, would be more inclined to go to Amsterdam and Rotterdam, where the population coming from the West Indian part of the empire found niches as laborers in the harbors and in the music and entertainment sectors.

11 I will resist my desire to offer a psychological/psychoanalytical reading of van Ophuijsen, but were I to do that, certainly identity issues would come to the fore. Some of the issues I would be interested in: Did he have a native *babu*, nanny, in the Indies? Why did he choose psychoanalysis as his medical specialization? Didn't his tendency to fall in love with his patients, highly frowned upon nowadays, signal a preference for a dominant, authoritarian position in his intimate relationships? Is there a correlation between his chronic financial problems/gambling debts and identity issues? (With thanks to the Transcultural Therapy Collective, Amsterdam: Anna de Voogd, Dirck van Bekkum, Glenn Helberg, Urmy McNack, Kitlyn Tjin A Djie, Hermine Klok, Fatima Rhmaty, and Pui Fan Yip.)

12 *Tweehonderd Jaar Statistiek in Tijdreeksen.* http://www.cbs.nl/NR/rdonlyres/7934A2DE-B87C-4CDF-8BC7-D34F02225620/0/200jaarstattijdreeksen.pdf, accessed March 15, 2014.

13 Art, here, is meant in a very broad sense and includes so-called emblemata (Blakely, 1993, 78)—a kind of illustrated fables worked in stained glass, jewelry, tapestry, needlework, and architecture—genre and portrait painting, the plastic arts, and commercial advertisements.

14 South African poet Diana Ferrus, a visiting student at the Department of Gender Studies in Utrecht, wrote the poem "I Have Come to Take You Home" while in Utrecht, which provided the impetus for the chain of events leading to Sarah Baartman's return to South Africa.

15 E.g., Gilman (1985), Schiebinger (1990), Stepan (1993), Harding (1993), Stepan and Gilman (1993), Somerville (2000), Markowitz (2001), Rossiter (1982, 1998, 2012).

16 But see Noordman (1989) on the history of eugenics; Harmsen, van Leeuwen, and van Rijen (1988) on scientific racism; Piet de Rooy (1996, 2015); also Stefan Dudink (2011), and the work of Amade M'Charek (2005, 2015).

17 In, for instance, the work of British sexologist Havelock Ellis (1905), thought to be second only to Freud in shaping modern conceptions of sexuality and gender. Ellis's work has also been central to the modern sexualization of African women (Gilman 1985; Markowitz 2001).

18 The Dutch version of the book was published in Amsterdam by Scheltema and Holkema, a prestigious publisher.

19 For an interesting reading on the inner lives of hermaphrodites, the contemporary term used for physical sexes that raised doubt, see Mak (2012). The term "hermaphrodite" was abandoned in the 1920s.

1 Gaykrant, www.gk.nl, last accessed October 2010. Website no longer active.
2 Geert Wilders is the only member of his party. He is also the chairman and the party leader, in addition to being the chair of the parliamentary delegation. This concentration of functions is highly unusual and antidemocratic.
3 The literal translation of "kopvoddentax" is "tax on head rags."
4 The trial against Wilders has been postponed until 2016 at the request of the prosecution, due to full agendas of all parties involved and to a number of investigations which Wilders' defense has requested. http://www.joop.nl /politiek/detail/artikel/33624_proces_wilders_om_minder_marokkanen _uitspraak_uitgesteld/. Accessed September 17, 2015.
5 *Verkiezingsprogramma* (Electoral program), PVV 2012—*Hún Brussel, Óns Nederland*, 35.
6 See Botman, Jouwe, and Wekker (2001) for a history of the black, migrant, and refugee women's movement.
7 The information about Audre's reflection on this Saturday morning talk with me is thanks to archival research by Stella Bolaki (see Ellerbe-Dueck and Wekker 2015; on the beautiful Joanna see further Wekker 1984a, Sharpe 2003; Hartman 2008).
8 See Wekker et al. (2007) for a critical treatise on interracial adoption practices by heterosexual couples in the Netherlands. The same patterns posited for these families, such as profound color-blindness, will also be operative in gay families.
9 I base this passage on unpublished presentations I gave at conferences on STI/AIDS in The Hague (October 2010) and on Uitsluitend Emancipatie, in Amsterdam, de Balie (October 2011).
10 Habibi Ana means "my darling" in Arab.
11 I came across supi in my own neighborhood in the southeast of Amsterdam, when talking with the few female *snorders*, illegal cab drivers, when I was telling them about my research on mati. They volunteered that a comparable phenomenon exists in Ghana.
12 But see Hermans and Wekker (2009) for a first inventory.
13 The Immigration and Naturalization Service, part of the Ministry of Justice, is responsible for the first decision on the status of foreigners and asylum seekers in the Netherlands.
14 This drivenness by what are perceived as concrete, social problems is of a more general nature in Dutch society and leads to an entanglement of policy and academic concerns. This tendency is only becoming stronger under present neoliberal conditions (see chapter 2). It is true not only in the social sciences but also in the interdisciplinary fields of ethnic and migration studies and for gender studies (cf. Wekker 1996a; Essed and Nimako 2006). Another consequence is the lack of funds for fundamental research, for instance into the diversity of sexual cultures that are present in the Netherlands.

15 But see Mepschen, Duyvendak, and Tonkens (2010) for an analysis of the sexualized order.

16 An edition of the diary is Douglas Hall (1980), In Miserable Slavery: Thomas Thistlewood in Jamaica, 1750–1786.

17 I have no information on who wrote the song.

18 I have left out the refrain that follows each verse.

19 From Creole Drum (Lichtveld and Voorhoeve 1975). I have transliterated their already transliterated version of Sranan Tongo, the Surinamese Creole, into a more modern version.

20 I know this verse as: "Memre taki yu / ben kari mi / mi moi Jaba / mi swit' lobi (Remember that you / used to call me / my beautiful Jaba / my sweet love).

21 From Surinamese court records, there are two known historical cases of male homosexuality, in the 1730s, one involving the son of Governor de Goijer, Matthijs de Goijer, and the other, Dirk Swart, the captain of a ship (Schellekes and Hoogbergen 2001).

Chapter 5. The Case of Black Pete

1 I alternate use of Black Pete and Zwarte Piet in this chapter.

2 I do not pay much attention to this particular stream of the discussions about Sinterklaas and Zwarte Piet, that is, their genealogy, except insofar as it is a theme in the e-mail communication (theme no. 7). From a Germanic and Norse origin, via Morocco, Turkey, and Spain, both figurations are imagined as transnational (see Blakely 1993; Helsloot 2005).

3 On August 26, 2014, the news was that HEMA, one of the biggest department stores in the Netherlands, intended to ban Pete, which means that they will not sell chocolate figures of Pete nor use packing paper displaying the figure in 2015 (de Valk, E., 2014). A month later, in September 2014, HEMA is equivocating, because a boycott has been proclaimed against the store on social media for going along with the anti-Pete protest (Baas, B., 2014). Other megastores like Albert Heijn (groceries) and Bart Smit (toys) say they do not want to get caught up in the social discussion about Black Pete. Bijenkorf, a big, upscale department store, announced that it will continue its time-honored tradition of Black Petes climbing up and down in the store. In the summer of 2015, however, Bijenkorf announced that the climbing Black Petes would henceforth be golden Petes.

4 See Toni Morisson's (1992a) masterly analysis of Willa Cather's novel Sapphira and the Slave Girl in Playing in the Dark.

5 Fateful, because this is where Pim Fortuyn was murdered in May 2002 by activist Volkert van der G., who was released from prison in June 2014.

6 I want to thank Annette Krauss and Petra Bauer for giving me access to the hate mail they, the Van Abbemuseum, and Doorbraak received in the summer

of 2008. Thanks also to Annette and Patricia Schor for their comments on this chapter.

7 See, for more elaborate framings of the history of anti–Black Pete protests, Helsloot (2005); van der Pijl and Golourdova (2015); Smith (2014); van Stipriaan (2014) en Wekker (2014b).

8 Althuisius, "Een VN-Resolutie tegen Zwarte Piet?," 2013.

9 See Martina, "My Thoughts on the Ruling," 2014.

10 On October 15, 2014, one day before the session of the Council of State, the Center for Cultural Heritage, one of the parties attempting to come up with a compromise regarding Zwarte Piet, announced that it had decided to propose to UNESCO to place Pete on the World Immaterial Heritage List.

11 "Not being one of us" is made clear to me anyway, for instance, when, in the first weeks at NIAS, I am consistently addressed in English by Dutch fellows and personnel alike. It happens in a most friendly manner, but apparently it is hard to wrap one's head around the fact that one can be a black academic woman and Dutch at the same time.

12 Personal communication from Annette Kraus, November 2013.

13 The debate was held in the Van Abbemuseum in November 2008. The name of the documentary is *Read the Masks*, http://vimeo.com/53495267.

14 All quotes are my translation.

15 The "Negro kiss," a chocolate-covered cream puff, was renamed "kisses" through the protest actions of Roy Groenberg, a.k.a. Kaikusi.

16 Another domain in which this link between innocence and childhood is often invoked is the hysterical protests against pedophilia, which even for a moral panic has taken on excessive forms during the past decade.

17 The best example of this was at a pro-Pete demonstration in the Hague, on October 27, 2013. A lone Papua woman was demonstrating for the freedom of her country of origin, West Papua, which has been annexed by Indonesia. She was holding the West Papuan flag, which is forbidden both in Papua and increasingly also in the Netherlands, under pressure of the Indonesian embassy (personal communication Nancy Jouwe, September 18, 2015). The woman was attacked by a bloodthirsty crowd, who saw her, obviously on the basis of her skin color, as anti–Black Pete, and she had to be removed "for her own safety" by the police.

18 The artists are formally Western allochthones, according to the definition of CBS, the Central Bureau of Statistics.

19 The term "Left church" implies that just as religious parties once had the monopoly on how to see and be in the world, socialists now claim that monopoly.

20 Professor Alex van Stipriaan and I submitted anti–Zwarte Piet statements for the session of the Raad van State in The Hague, on October 16, 2014. Both van Stipriaan (2014) and I (Wekker 2014b) deconstruct the widely held notion

that because Zwarte Piet has a pre-Christian origin, he cannot possibly be racist.

21 Certain derogatory expressions that have become widespread originated with the Labor Party: "kut Marokkanen" (cunt Moroccans) was whispered by Rob Oudkerk in 2002 to the Labor mayor of Amsterdam, Job Cohen, unaware that a microphone was still on. The term has become a nom de guerre adopted by young Moroccans, who use it on the Internet.

22 In the summer of 2014, this measure was again proposed, this time by the Conservative Democrat-Labor government, in the person of the Labor minister of social affairs, L. Asscher, to be used against jihadis who have engaged in combat in the Middle East, on the side of the Islamic State.

23 Thus spoke the chairperson of the Labor Party, Hans Spekman.

24 Note again: "een kleurtje," a little color. The diminutive is used to underline how unimportant and inconsequential being of color in the Netherlands is.

25 Thanks to Patricia Schor, Brazilian Dutch activist, mother, and academic, who pointed this out to me. This is an aspect that has not been noted yet and that became clear as she told me of numerous examples of mothers of mixed-race or black children who in their protests are severely condescended to, humiliated, and disciplined by school directors, teachers, and school boards. On September 17, 2015, De Volkskrant reports that The Hague, as the first of the big Cities, has decided that its 150 primary schools cannot maintain Pete in his traditional form. The schools have three years to present a "neutral" Pete, and for 2015 it means doing away with at least one of his five derogatory characteristics: red lips, kinky hair, golden earrings, black skin and stupidity in his presentation (ANP 2015).

26 From an Indonesian perspective, 1945 is the date when independence was proclaimed; from a Dutch perspective it was 1949, after the two "police actions."

27 During World War II, 300,000 Dutch people ruled 70 million East Indies people (van Goor 1993).

28 For a gendered approach to Zwarte Piet, see Bal (1999). I cannot engage with that aspect here, except to say two things. First, generally Piet is overwhelmingly thought of as masculine, and part of the fun and the challenge in performing him as a woman is in making the transgender crossing go undetected. Second, I am struck by the fact that while there are gendered versions of Zwarte Piet, such variety is unthinkable for Sinterklaas, who only comes in white, masculine form. I understand this phenomenon as connected to the fact that there is only one Sinterklaas and multiple Petes, and how both of these aspects relate to power. That is, while Zwarte Piet may be tinkered and played with in form, this is not the case for the more powerful figure. As far as sexuality is concerned, I have not found any aspects of Zwarte Piet that refer to sexuality, which stands to reason if we imagine him or her as a figuration for innocent children.

29 This routine brings to mind the degrading routine in the Surinamese context of taking slaves' own names away and giving them new, ridiculous names like Coffee, Chocolate, Caesar, and so on (see Van Stipriaan 1990).

Coda. "But What about the Captain?"

1 Also see Hartman's (2008) essay "Venus in Two Acts."
2 Thanks to Ineke Mok for pointing out this episode to me.
3 Meeting at the Free University in Amsterdam, "I, Too, Am vu/UvA," organized by Mitchell Esajas, Jessica de Abreu, and Black Urban Collective, March 2014.
4 Thanks to Dineke Stam for this insight.

REFERENCES

Abel, E., B. Christian, and H. Moglen, eds. 1997. *Female Subjects in Black and White: Race, Psychoanalysis, Feminism.* Berkeley: University of California Press.

Ahmed, S. 2010. "Feminist Killjoys (and Other Willful Subjects)." *The Scholar and Feminist Online* 8, no. 30. Accessed September 3, 2014. http://sfonline.barnard .edu/polyphonic/print_ahmed.htm.

Ahmed, S. 2012. *On Being Included: Racism and Diversity in Institutional Life.* Durham, NC: Duke University Press.

Akkermans, A. 2011. "Nationalisme Onder Homosekuelen." *Nieuw Amsterdams Peil*, January 28. Accessed September 23, 2014. http://www.napnieuws.nl /2011/01/28/nationalisme-onder-homoseksuelen.

Alexander, M. J. 2005. *Pedagogies of Crossing: Meditations on Feminism, Sexual Politics, Memory, and the Sacred.* Durham, NC: Duke University Press.

Altena, M. 2008. "Acceptatie door Confrontatie: het 'zwart-witte Huwelijk' van Joseph Sylvester en Marie Borchert 1928–1955." In *Tijdschrift voor Geschiedenis*, vol. 121, 22–39.

Althuisius, J. 2013. "Een vn- Resolutie tegen Zwarte Piet?" In *De Volkskrant*, October 23. Accessed August 21, 2014. http://www.volkskrant.nl/archief/een -vn-resolutie-tegen-zwarte-piet~a3531716/.

ANP. 2015. "Haagse Basischolen schaffen Zwarte Piet af." In *De Volkskrant*, September, 17. http://www.volkskrant.nl/binnenland/haagse-basischolen -schaffen-zwarte-piet-af~a4143981/.

Arndt, S., M. M. Eggers, G. Kilomba and P. Piesche, eds. 2009. *Mythen, Masken und Subjekte. Kritische Weissseinsforschung in Deutschland.* Munster: UNRAST Verlag.

Baas, B. 2014. "HEMA moet steviger positie kiezen in pietendiscussie." In: *Trouw*, September 24. Accessed September 9, 2015. http://www.trouw.nl/tr/n14324 /Nieuws/detail/3754462/2014/09/24.

Bal, M. 1999. "Zwarte Piet's Bal Maské." In A. Fox, *Zwarte Piet.* London: Black Dog.

Balkenhol, M. 2014. *Tracing Slavery: An Ethnography of Diaspora, Affect and Cultural Heritage in Amsterdam.* Amsterdam: Vrije Universiteit.

Bannerji, H., L. Carty, K. Dehli, S. Heald, and K. McKenna. 1992. *Unsettling Relations: The University as a Site of Feminist Struggles.* Boston: South End.

Beckles, H. 1999. *Centering Woman: Gender Discourses in Caribbean Slave Society.* Kingston: Ian Randle.

Beecher Stowe, H. (1852) 2005. *Uncle Tom's Cabin.* Mineola, NY: Dover.

Bijleveld, L., and L. Mans. 2009. *Women's Rights—Some Progress, Many Gaps.* Utrecht: Aim for Human Rights.

Bijnaar, A. 2007. "Black Magic Woman: 'De Driften der Negerinnen' en Andere Denkbeelden Over Zwarte Vrouwen." In *Grenzeloos Niewsgierig: Opstellen voor en over Abram de Swaan.* Amsterdam: Bert Bakker.

Blakely, A. 1993. *Blacks in the Dutch World: The Evolution of Racial Imagery in a Modern Society.* Bloomington: Indiana University Press.

Bloembergen, M. 2002. *De Koloniale Vertoning: Nederland en Indië op de Wereldtentoonstellingen (1880–1931).* Amsterdam: Wereldbibliotheek.

Blom, P. 2009. *De Duizelingwekkende Jaren, Europa 1900–1914.* Amsterdam: De Bezige Bij.

Bos, H., and J. Ehrhardt. 2010. "Ervaringen van Lesbische en Bisexuele Vrouwen." In *Steeds Gewoner, Nooit Gewoon: Acceptatie van Homoseksualiteit in Nederland,* edited by S. Keuzenkamp. The Hague: Sociaal en Cultureel Planbureau.

Bosch, M. 1994. *Het Geslacht van de Wetenschap. Vrouwen en Hoger Onderwijs in Nederland, 1878–1948.* Amsterdam: Sua.

Bosch, M. 2004. *Aletta Jacobs 1854–1929. Een Onwrikbaar Geloof in Rechtvaardigheid.* Amsterdam: Uitgeverij Balans.

Bosveld, W., and J. Greven. 2012. "Hoe Denken Amsterdammers over Zwarte Piet?" Gemeente Amsterdam Bureau Onderzoek en Statistiek, December. Accessed October 15, 2014. http://www.os.amsterdam.nl//pdf/2013_zwarte%20piet.pdf.

Botman, M., N. Jouwe, and G. D. Wekker, eds. 2001. *Caleidoscopische visies: De Zwarte, migranten en vluchtelingen-vrouwenbeweging in Nederland.* Amsterdam: Koninklijk Instituut voor de Tropen.

Bouras, N. 2012. "Het Land van Herkomst: Perspectieven op Verbondenheid met Marokko, 1960–2010." PhD diss., Leiden University. Hilversum: Uitgeverij Verloren BV.

Bourdieu, P. 1977. *Outline of a Theory of Practice.* Cambridge: Cambridge University Press.

Bourdieu, P., and L. Wacquant. 1999. "On the Cunning of Imperialist Reason." *Theory, Culture and Society* 16 (1): 41–58.

Brah, A. 1996. *Cartographies of Diaspora: Contesting Identities (Gender, Racism, Ethnicity).* London: Routledge.

Braidotti, R., E. Charkiewicz, S. Hausler, and S. Wieringa, eds. 1994. *Women, the Environment and Sustainable Development: Towards a Theoretical Synthesis.* London: Zed.

Braidotti, R., and E. Vonk, eds. 2000. *The Making of European Women's Studies. A Work in Progress Report on Curriculum Development and Related Issues*. Utrecht: ATHENA/Utrecht University.

Braidotti, R., E. Vonk, E. and S. van Wichelen, eds. 2000. *The Making of European Women's Studies, Volume II: A Work in Progress Report on Curriculum Development and Related Issues in Gender Education and Research*. Utrecht: ATHENA/Utrecht University.

Braidotti, R., I. Lazaroms and E. Vonk, eds. 2001. *The Making of European Women's Studies, Volume III. A Work in Progress Report on Curriculum Development and Related Issues in Gender Education and Research*. Utrecht: ATHENA/Utrecht University.

Braidotti, R., S. Hirs and J. Nieboer, eds. 2002. *The Making of European Women's Studies, Volume IV*. Utrecht: ATHENA/Utrecht University.

Braidotti, R. and E. Just, eds. 2004. *The Making of European Women's Studies, Volume V*. Utrecht: ATHENA/Utrecht University.

Braidotti, R. and A. van Baren, eds. 2005. *The Making of European Women's Studies. A Work in Progress Report on Curriculum Development and Related Issues, Volume VI*. Utrecht: ATHENA/Utrecht University.

Braidotti, R. and B. Waaldijk, eds. 2006. "The Making of European Women's Studies: a Work in Progress Report on Curriculum Development and Related Issues in Gender Education and Research, Volume 7." In *Advanced Thematic Network in Activities in Women's Studies in Europe*. Utrecht: ATHENA/Utrecht University.

Brantlinger, P. 1985. "Victorians and Africans: The Genealogy of the Myth of the Dark Continent." In *"Race," Writing, and Difference*, edited by H. L. Gates Jr., 185–222. Chicago: University of Chicago Press.

Braun, M. 1985. "Gelijk Recht voor Allen! Feministische Strijd tegen de maritale Macht." In *De eerste Feministische Golf. Zesde Jaarboek voor Vrouwengeschiedenis*. 138–161. Nijmegen: SUN.

Breman, J. 1993. "Ten Geleide." In *Een Ereschuld: Hoofdstukken Uit Onze Koloniale Geschiedenis*, by R. Fruin et al., 7–21. Amsterdam: Meulenhoff.

Brinkgreve, C. 1984. *Psychoanalyse in Nederland: Een vestigingsstrijd*. Amsterdam: Uitgeverij De Arbeiderspers.

Buijs, L., J. W. Duyvendak, and G. Hekma. 2008. *Als Ze Maar Van Me Afblijven: Een Onderzoek Naar Antihomoseksueel Geweld in Amsterdam*. Amsterdam: Amsterdam University Press.

Buikema, R. 2009. "The Arena of Imaginings: Sarah Baartman and the Ethics of Representation." In *Doing Gender in Media, Art and Culture*, edited by R. Buikema and I. van der Tuin, 78–93. New York: Routledge.

Buikema, R., G. Griffin, and N. Lykke. 2011a. "Editorial Introduction: Researching Differently." In *Theories and Methodologies in Postgraduate Feminist Research: Researching Differently*, edited by R. Buikema, G. Griffin, and N. Lykke, 1–15. New York: Routledge.

Buikema, R., G. Griffin, and N. Lykke, eds. 2011b. *Theories and Methodologies in Postgraduate Feminist Research: Researching Differently*. New York: Routledge.

Buitelaar, M. 2006. "'I Am the Ultimate Challenge': Accounts of Intersectionality in the Life-Story of a Well-Known Daughter of Moroccan Migrant Workers in the Netherlands." *European Journal of Women's Studies* 13 (3): 259–276.

Bulhof, I. N. 1983. *Freud en Nederland: De Interpretatie en Invloed van zijn Ideeën.* Baarn: Uitgeverij Ambo.

Buruma, I. 2006. *Murder in Amsterdam: The Death of Theo van Gogh and the Limits of Tolerance.* New York: Penguin.

Bussemaker, J. 2013. "De Grenzen van Emancipatiebeleid." S&D *Jaargang* 70 (6): 52–57.

Butler, J. 1990. *Gender Trouble: Feminism and Subversion of Identity.* London: Routledge.

Campbell, J. 2000. *Arguing with the Phallus: Feminist, Queer and Postcolonial Theory. A Psychoanalytic Contribution.* London: Zed.

Captain, E. 2014. "Harmless Identities: Representations of Racial Consciousness among Three Generations of Indo-Europeans." In *Dutch Racism,* edited by P. Essed and I. Hoving, 53–69. Amsterdam: Rodopi.

Carby, H. V. 1987. *Reconstructing Womanhood: The Emergence of the Afro-American Woman Novelist.* New York: Oxford University Press.

CBS, Central Bureau of Statistics. *Tweehonderd Jaar Statistiek in Tijdreeksen.* http://www.cbs.nl/NR/rdonlyres/7934A2DE-B87C-4CDF-8BC7-D34F02225620/0/200jaarstattijdreeksen.pdf. Accessed September 2, 2015.

CBS, Central Bureau of Statistics, *Census 1920.* https://easy.dans.knaw.nl/ui/datasets/id/easy-dataset:38767. Accessed September 2, 2015.

CBS, Central Bureau of Statistics, 2014. *Jaarrapport Integratie.* Den Haag/ Heerlen, 26, and www.cbs.nl/NR/rdonlyres/E6878ED8–0347–4EDO-8A8D-360 AB790–22B2/0/jaarrapportintegratie2014.pub.pdf. Accessed September 2, 2015.

Césaire, A. 1972. *Discourse on Colonialism.* New York: Monthly Review Press.

Césaire, S. 2009. *Le grand Camouflage: Ecrits de Dissidence (1941–1945).* Paris: Seuil.

Cho, S., K. Crenshaw, and L. McCall, eds. 2013. "Intersectionality: Theorizing Power, Empowering Theory." *Signs: Journal of Women in Culture and Society* 38 (4): 785–810.

Clemencia, J. 1996. "Women Who Love Women in Curaçao: From Capuchera to Open Throats. A Commentary in Collage." *Feminist Studies* 22 (1).

Cliff, M. 1980. *Claiming an Identity They Taught Me to Despise.* Watertown, MA: Persephone Press.

Corbey, R. 1989. *Wildheid en Beschaving. De Europese Verbeelding van Afrika.* Baarn: Ambo.

Crenshaw, K. 1989. *Demarginalizing the Intersection of Race and Sex: A Black Feminist Critique of Antidiscrimination Doctrine, Feminist Theory, and Antiracist Politics.* Chicago: University of Chicago Legal Forum 140: 139–167.

Crenshaw, K. 1991. "Mapping the Margins: Intersectionality, Identity Politics, and Violence against Women of Color." *Stanford Law Review* 43 (6): 1241–1299.

Dagelet, T. 2007. "In Bed met Tatum," *Viva,* June 22.

Davis, A. Y. 1981. *Women, Race and Class*. New York: Random House.

Davis, K. 2008. "Intersectionality as Buzzword: A Sociology of Science Perspective on What Makes a Feminist Theory Successful." *Feminist Theory* 9 (1): 67–85.

Deekman, A., and M. Hermans. 2001. "Heilig Vuur: Bezieling en Kracht in de Organisatie-Vorming van de zmv-vrouwenbeweging in Nederland." In *Caleidoscopische Visies*, edited by M. Botman, N. Jouwe, and G. D. Wekker, 81–115. Amsterdam: KIT Publishers.

de Lauretis, T. 1994. *The Practice of Love: Lesbian Sexuality and Perverse Desire*. Bloomington: Indiana University Press.

De Leon, Mos. Pa., et al. (1788) 1968. *Essai Historique sur la Colonie de Suriname*. Amsterdam: S. Emmering. Reprint of the original edition, Paramaribo.

Derrida, J. 1998. "Geopsychoanalysis: ". . . and the rest of the world." In *The Psychoanalysis of Race*, edited by C. Lane, 65–90. New York: Columbia University Press

Van Dijk, T. 1993. *Elite Discourse and Racism*. Newbury Park, CA: Sage.

Van Dijk, T. 1998. "Sinterklaasje en Zwarte Piet: Is het Racisme of is het 't Niet?" In *Sinterklaasje, kom maar binnen zonder knecht*, edited by S. Gravenberch and L. Helder, 118–135. Berchem: EPO.

Doane, M. A. 1991. *Femmes Fatales: Feminism, Film Theory, Psychoanalysis*. New York: Routledge.

Du Bois, W. E. B. 1903. *The Souls of Black Folk: Essays and Sketches*. Chicago: A. C. McClurg.

DuCille, A. 1997. "The Occult of True Black Womanhood: Critical Demeanor and Black Feminist Studies." In *Female Subjects in Black and White: Race, Psychoanalysis, Feminism*, edited by E. Abel et al., 21–56. Berkeley: University of California Press.

Dudink, S. P. 2011. "Homosexuality, Race, and the Rhetoric of Nationalism." *History of the Present: A Journal of Critical History* 1 (2): 259–264.

Duyvendak, J. W. 1996. "The Depoliticization of the Dutch Gay Identity, or, Why Dutch Gays Aren't Queer." In *Queer Theory/Sociology*, edited by S. Seidman. Malden, MA: Blackwell.

Dyer, R. 1997. *White*. London: Routledge.

ECRI (European Commission against Racism and Intolerance). 2013. "ECRI Report on the Netherlands." October, Ref. CRI (2013): 39. Accessed July 30, 2014. https://www.coe.int/t/dghl/monitoring/ecri/country-by-country/netherlands /NLD-CbC-IV-2013–039-ENG.pdf.

Eijberts, M. 2013. *Migrant Women Shout Out Loud: The Integration/Participation Strategies and Sense of Home of First- and Second-Generation Women of Moroccan and Turkish Descent*. Amsterdam: VU University Press.

Ellerbe-Dueck, C., and G. D. Wekker. 2015. "Naming Ourselves as Black Women in Europe: An African American-German and Afro-Dutch Conversation on the Significance of Audre Lorde." In *Audre Lorde's Transnational Legacies*, edited by S. Bolaki and S. Broeck. Amherst: University of Massachusetts Press.

Ellis, H. Havelock. 1905. *Sexual Selection in Man. Studies in the Psychology of Sex*, Volume 4. Philadelphia: F.A. Davis.

El-Tayeb, F. 2011. *European Others: Queering Ethnicity in Postnational Europe*. Minneapolis: University of Minnesota Press.

Van Es, A. 2013. "Geheime Nota: Molukse Treinkapers door Kogelregen gedood." In *De Volkskrant*. Accessed November 13, 2013. http://www.volkskrant.nl /binnenland/geheime-nota-molukse-treinkapers-door-kogelregen-gedood ~a3553851/.

Essed, P. 1982. "Racisme en Feminisme." *Socialisties-Feministiese Teksten* 7: 9–41.

Essed, P. 1984. *Alledaags Racisme*. Amsterdam: Feministische Uitgeverij Sara.

Essed, P. 1987. *Academic Racism: Common Sense in the Social Sciences*. Amsterdam: Center for Race and Ethnic Studies Publication Series. Working paper no. 5.

Essed, P. 1990. *Everyday Racism: Reports from Women of Two Cultures*. Claremont: Hunter House.

Essed, P. 1994. *Diversiteit*. Amsterdam: Ambo/Baarn.

Essed, P. 2002. "Everyday Racism: A New Approach to the Study of Racism." In *Race Critical Theories*, edited by P. Essed and D. T. Goldberg, 176–194. Malden, MA: Blackwell.

Essed, P., and D. T. Goldberg, eds. 2002. *Race Critical Theories*. Malden: Blackwell.

Essed, P., and I. Hoving, eds. 2014a. *Dutch Racism*. Amsterdam: Rodopi.

Essed, P., and I. Hoving. 2014b. "Innocence, Smug Ignorance, Resentment: An Introduction to Dutch Racism." In *Dutch Racism*, edited by P. Essed and I. Hoving, 9–29. Amsterdam: Rodopi.

Essed, P., and K. Nimako. 2006. "Designs and (Co)Incidents: Cultures of Scholarship and Public Policy on Immigrants/Minorities in the Netherlands." *International Journal of Comparative Sociology* 47: 281–312.

Van Essen, M. 1990. *Opvoeden met een Dubbel Doel. Twee Eeuwen Meisjesonderwijs in Nederland*. Amsterdam: SUA.

Ewing, K. P. 2008. *Stolen Honor: Stigmatizing Muslim Men in Berlin*. Stanford, CA: Stanford University Press.

Fabian, J. 1983. *Time and the Other: How Anthropology Makes Its Object*. New York: Columbia University Press.

Fanon, F. (1952) 1967. *Black Skin, White Masks*. New York: Grove. Originally published as *Peau Noire, Masques Blancs*. Paris: Seuil.

Ferrus, D. (1998) 2010. "I Have Come To Take You Home." In *I Have Come To Take You Home*, 15–16. Kuils Rivier, South Africa: Diana Ferrus.

Flax, J. 2010. *Resonances of Slavery in Race/Gender Relations: Shadow at the Heart of American Politics*. New York: Palgrave Macmillan.

Fortuyn, P. 1997. *Tegen de Islamisering van Onze Cultuur: Nederlandse Identiteit als Fundament*. Amsterdam: A. W. Bruna.

Fortuyn, P. 2002. "De islam is een achterlijke cultuur." *De Volkskrant*, February 9.

Foucault, M. 1964. *Madness and Civilization: A History of Insanity in the Age of Reason*. New York: Pantheon.

Foucault, M. (1976) 1990. *The History of Sexuality. Vol. 1, An Introduction*. New York: Penguin.

Frankenberg, R. 1993. *White Women, Race Matters: The Social Construction of Whiteness*. Minneapolis: University of Minnesota Press.

Freud, S. (1908) 1977. "On the Sexual Theories of Children." In *On Sexuality*, vol. 7. Harmondsworth: Penguin.

Freud, S. (1919) 1993. "A Child Is Being Beaten." In *On Psychopathology*, vol. 10, edited by A. Richard, 159–194. Penguin Freud Library. London: Penguin.

Freud, S. 1924. "The Infantile Genital Organization of the Libido: A Supplement to the Theory of Sexuality." *International Journal of Psycho-Analysis* 5: 125–129.

Freud, S. (1926) 1990. *The Question of Lay Analysis*. London: W. W. Norton.

Fruin, R., et al. 1993. *Een Ereschuld: Hoofdstukken Uit Onze Koloniale Geschiedenis*. Amsterdam: Meulenhoff.

Gans, E. 2014. "'They Have Forgotten to Gas You': Post-1945 Antisemitism in the Netherlands." In *Dutch Racism*, edited by P. Essed and I. Hoving, 71–100. Amsterdam: Rodopi.

Gates, H. L., Jr., ed. 1985. *"Race," Writing, and Difference*. Chicago: University of Chicago Press.

Gay, J. 1986. "'Mummies and Babies' and Friends and Lovers in Lesotho." In *The Many Faces of Homosexuality: Anthropological Approaches to Homosexual Behavior*, edited by E. Blackwood. New York: Harrington Park Press.

Ghorashi, H. 2003. "Ayaan Hirsi Ali: Daring or Dogmatic? Debates on Multiculturalism and Emancipation in the Netherlands." In *Focaal: European Journal of Anthropology* no. 42, 163–173.

Ghorashi, H. 2006. *Paradoxen van Culturele Erkening: Management van Diversiteit in Nieuw Nederland* (Oratie). Amsterdam: Vrije Universiteit, Faculteit der Sociale Wetenschappen.

Ghorashi, H. 2014. Racism and "the Ungrateful Other" in the Netherlands. In *Dutch Racism*, edited by P. Essed and I. Hoving, 101–116. Amsterdam: Rodopi,

Gilman, S. 1985. "Black Bodies, White Bodies: Toward an Iconography of Female Sexuality in Late Nineteenth-Century Art, Medicine and Literature." In *"Race," Writing, and Difference*, edited by H. L. Gates Jr., 223–261. Chicago: University of Chicago Press.

Gilman, S. 1993. *Freud, Race, and Gender*. Princeton, NJ: Princeton University Press.

Gilroy, P. 1993. *Small Acts: Thoughts on the Politics of Black Cultures*. London: Serpent's Tail.

Gilroy, P. 2005. *Postcolonial Melancholia*. New York: Columbia University Press.

Van Ginkel, R. 1997. "Gespiegeld in de Caleidoscoop: Vreemde blikken op Nederlandse eigenaardigheden." In *Notities over Nederlanders*. Meppel: Boom.

Gobardhan-Rambocus, L. 2001. *Onderwijs als sleutel tot maatschappelijke vooruitgang: Een Taal- en onderwijsgeschiedenis van Suriname, 1651–1975*. Zutphen: Walburg Pers.

Goonatilake, S. 1993. "Modern Science and the Periphery: The Characteristics of

Dependent Knowledge." In The "Racial" Economy of Science: Toward a Democratic Future, edited by S. Harding, 259–274. Bloomington: Indiana University Press.

Van Goor, J. 1993. De Nederlandse Koloniën: Geschiedenis van de Nederlandse Expansie 1600–1975. The Hague: Velotekst (B. L. van Popering).

Gordon, A. F. 2008. Ghostly Matters: Haunting and the Sociological Imagination. Minneapolis: University of Minnesota Press.

Gravenberch, S., and L. Helder, eds. 1998. Sinterklaasje, kom maar binnen zonder knecht. Berchem: EPO.

Grever, M., and B. Waaldijk. 1998. Feministische Openbaarheid: De Nationale Tentoonstelling van Vrouwenarbeid in 1898. Amsterdam: IISG/IIAV.

Griffin, G., with R. Braidotti. 2002. "Whiteness and European Situatedness." In Thinking Differently: A Reader in European Women's Studies, edited by G. Griffin and R. Braidotti. London: Zed.

Grigg, R., D. Hecq, and C. Smith, eds. 1999. Female Sexuality: The Early Psychoanalytical Controversies. London: Rebus.

Groen-Prakken, H. 1993. "The Psychoanalytical Society and the Analyst, with Special Reference to the History of the Dutch Psychoanalytical Society 1917–1947." In The Dutch Annual of Psychoanalysis, edited by H. Groen-Prakken and A. Ladan, 13–37. Amsterdam: Swets and Zeitlinger BV.

Groen-Prakken, H., and A. Ladan, eds. 1993. The Dutch Annual of Psychoanalysis. Amsterdam: Swets and Zeitlinger BV.

Habel, Y. 2012. "Challenging Swedish Exceptionalism? Teaching while Black." In Education in the Black Diaspora: Perspectives, Challenges, and Prospects, edited by K. Freeman and E. Johnson, 99–122. London: Routledge.

Halberstam, J. 1998. Female Masculinity. Durham, NC: Duke University Press.

Hall, D. 1998. In Miserable Slavery: Thomas Thistlewood in Jamaica, 1750–1786. Kingston: University of West Indies Press.

Hall, S. 1992. "What Is This Black in Black Popular Culture?" In Black Popular Culture, edited by G. Dent, 21–36. Seattle: Bay Press.

Hall, S., ed. 1997. Representation: Cultural Representations and Signifying Practices. London: Sage.

Hall, S. 2000. "Conclusion: The Multi-cultural Question." In Un/Settled Multiculturalisms: Diasporas, Entanglements, Transruptions, edited by B. Hesse, 209–241. London: Routledge.

Halperin, D. 1990. One Hundred Years of Homosexuality: and other Essays on Greek Love. London: Routledge.

Ham, M., and J. van der Meer. 2012. De Etnische Bril: Categorisering in het Integratiebeleid. Amsterdam: Amsterdam University Press.

Hamon, M. C. 1992. Pourquoi Les Femmes Aiment-Elles Les Hommes? Paris: Seuil.

Haraway, D. 1991. "Situated Knowledges: The Science Question in Feminism and the Privilege of Partial Perspective." In Simians, Cyborgs, and Women: The Invention of Nature. London: Free Association.

Harding, S. 1993. *The "Racial" Economy of Science: Toward a Democratic Future*. Bloomington: Indiana University Press.

Haritaworn, J. 2008. "Loyal Repetitions of the Nation: Gay Assimilation and the 'War On Terror.'" *Darkmatter* 3. Accessed September 24, 2014. http://www.darkmatter101.org/site/category/issues/3-post-colonial-sexuality/.

Haritaworn, J. 2012. "Women's Rights, Gay Rights and Anti-Muslim Racism in Europe." *European Journal of Women's Studies* 19 (1/2), 73–80.

Harmsen, P., F. van Leeuwen, and M. van Rijen. 1988. "Wettenschappelijk Racisme: Vergeten Aspecten in de Nederlandse Geschiedenis 1870–1940." In *Een Bleek Bolwerk: Racisme en Politieke Strategie*, edited by M. Hisschemöller, 99–117. Amsterdam: Pegasus.

Hartman, S. 1997. *Scenes of Subjection: Terror, Slavery, and Self-Making in Nineteenth-Century America*. Oxford: Oxford University Press.

Hartman, S. 2007. *Lose Your Mother: A Journey along the Atlantic Slave Trade*. New York: Farrar, Straus and Giroux.

Hartman, S. 2008. "Venus in Two Acts." *Small Axe* 12 (2): 1–14.

Helsloot, J. I. A. 2005. "Het feest: De strijd om Zwarte Piet." In *Veranderingen van het alledaagse 1950–2000*, edited by I. Hoving, H. Dibbits, and M. Schrover, 249–271. The Hague: Sdu.

Hermans, M. 2002. "Zwart, lesbisch en strijdbaar: Herinneringen aan Sister Outsider." LOVER no. 2: 17.

Hermans, M., and G. D. Wekker. 2009. "Zmv-vrouwen: Aicha Is Cool, Black Orchid en Kroesje." In *Lesbo-Encyclopedie*, edited by M. Hemker and L. Huijsmans, 231–244. Amsterdam: Ambo/Anthos.

Hermant, Heather. 2016. "Esther Brandeau/Jacques La Fargue: Performing a Reading of an 18th Century Multicrosser." PhD diss., University of Utrecht.

Hill Collins, P. 1986. "Learning from the Outsider Within: The Sociological Significance of Black Feminist Thought." *Social Problems* 33 (6).

Hill Collins, P. 2004. *Black Sexual Politics: African Americans, Gender, and New Racism*. New York: Routledge.

Hine, D. C., T. D. Keaton, and S. Small, eds. 2009. *Black Europe and the African Diaspora*. Urbana: University of Illinois Press.

Hipfl, B., and K. Loftsdótir, eds. 2012. *Teaching Race with a Gendered Edge*. Budapest: Central European University Press.

Hira, S. 2011. *Verboden Liefde: Familie en Homoseksualiteit in de Surinaamse Gemeenschap*. The Hague: Amrit.

Hondius, D. 2003. *Return: Holocaust Survivors and Dutch Anti-Semitism*. Westport, CT: Praeger/Greenwood.

Hondius, D. 2014a. "Black Dutch Voices: Reports from a Country That Leaves Racism Unchallenged." In *Dutch Racism*, edited by P. Essed and I. Hoving, 273–294. Amsterdam: Rodopi.

Hondius, D. 2014b. *Blackness in Western Europe: Racial Patterns of Paternalism and Exclusion*. New Brunswick, NJ: Transaction.

Hondius, D., N. Jouwe, D. Stam, J. Tosch, and A. de Wildt. 2014. *Gids Slavernijverleden Amsterdam: Slavery Heritage Guide.* Arnhem: LM Publishers.

hooks, b. 1984. *Feminist Theory from Margin to Center.* Boston: South End Press.

hooks, b. 1992a. *Black Looks: Race and Representation.* Boston: South End Press.

hooks, b. 1992b. "Eating the Other." In *Black Looks: Race and Representation.* Boston: South End Press, 21–40.

Horney, K. 1924. "On the Genesis of the Castration Complex in Women." In *International Journal of Psycho-Analysis* 5: 50–65.

Horney, K. (1933) 1966. "The Denial of the Vagina." In *Psychoanalysis and Female Sexuality: Classic and Contemporary Essays on the Impact of Psychoanalysis on Female Sexuality*, edited by H. M. Ruitenbeek, 73–87. New Haven, CT: College and University Press.

Van der Horst, L. 2004. *Wereldoorlog in de West: Suriname, de Nederlandse Antillen en Aruba 1940–1945.* Hilversum: Uitgeverij Verloren BV.

Hoving, I. 1996. "Het Plezier van de Koprol." In *Praten in het Donker: Multiculturalisme en Anti-racisme in Feministisch Perspectief*, edited by G. D. Wekker and R. Braidotti. Kampen: Kok Agora.

Huang, S. 2015. *Being a Mother in a Strange Land: Motherhood Practices of First-Generation Chinese Migrant Women in the Netherlands.* PhD diss. Utrecht: Utrecht University.

Hutcheon, L. 1994. *Irony's Edge: The Theory and Politics of Irony.* New York: Routledge.

Israel, J. I. 1998. *The Dutch Republic: Its Rise, Greatness, and Fall, 1477–1806.* The Oxford History of Early Modern Europe. Oxford: Clarendon.

Jansen, J. 2002. "Curriculum from Hell: Values in Education in South Africa and the Netherlands. Challenges for a Multicultural Society." Presentation at Utrecht University, February 19.

Jones, G. 2012. "De Slavernij is Onze Geschiedenis (niet): Over de Discursieve Strijd om de Betekenis van de NTR-televisieserie De Slavernij." *BMGN—Low Countries Historical Review* 127 (4): 56–82.

De Jong, L. 1969–1991. *The Kingdom of the Netherlands during World War II.* Amsterdam: NIOD.

Jordan, J. D. 2014. "The Enunciation of the Nation: Notes on Colonial Refractions in the Netherlands." In *Dutch Racism*, edited by P. Essed and I. Hoving, 201–218. Amsterdam: Rodopi.

Keuzenkamp, S., ed. 2010. *Steeds Gewoner, Nooit Gewoon: Acceptatie van Homoseksualiteit in Nederland.* The Hague: Sociaal en Cultureel Planbureau.

Khanna, R. 2003. *Dark Continents: Psychoanalysis and Colonialism.* Durham, NC: Duke University Press.

Kilomba, G. 2010. *Plantation Memories. Episodes of Everyday Racism.* 2nd edition. Munster: UNRAST Verlag.

Klinkers, E. 2011. *De Geschiedenis van de Politie in Suriname, 1863–1975: Van Koloniale tot Nationale Ordehandhaving.* Amsterdam: Boom.

Kolfin, E. 1997. *Van de Slavenzweep en de Muze*. Leiden: Instituut voor Taal-Land en Volkenunde.

Kolfin, E. 2013. "Geen twijfel: 'Zwarte Piet stamt af van kindslaven.'" Interview by M. Kruijt. *De Volkskrant*, October 23.

Kolfin, E., and E. Schreuder, eds. 2008. *Black Is beautiful: Rubens to Dumas*. Amsterdam: De Nieuwe Kerk, Waanders Uitgeverij.

Koopmans, R. 2003. "Het Nederlandse Integratiebeleid in Internationaal Vergelijkend Perspectief: Etnische Segregatie onder de Multicultureel Oppervlakte." In *Politiek in de multiculturele samenleving (Jaarboek Beleid & Maatschappij)*, edited by H. Pellikaan and M. Trappenburg, 64–100. Meppel: Boom.

Kursun, H., and I. El Kaka. 2002. *Mijn Geloof en Mijn Geluk: Islamitische Meiden en Jongens over Hun Homoseksuele Gevoelens*. Amsterdam: Schorer Boeken.

Lampl de Groot, J. (1928) 1966. "The Evolution of the Oedipus Complex in Women." In *Psychoanalysis and Female Sexuality: Classic and Contemporary Essays on the Impact of Psychoanalysis on Female Sexuality*, edited by H. M. Ruitenbeek, 36–50. New Haven, CT: College and University Press.

Lane, C., ed. 1998. *The Psychoanalysis of Race*. New York: Columbia University Press.

De Leeuw, M., and S. van Wichelen. 2014. "Institutionalizing the Muslim Other: *Naar Nederland* and the Violence of Culturalism." In *Dutch Racism*, edited by P. Essed and I. Hoving, 337–354. Amsterdam: Rodopi.

Van Leeuwen, L. 2008. *Ons Indisch Erfgoed: Zestig Jaar Strijd om Cultuur en Identiteit*. Amsterdam: Uitgeverij Bert Bakker.

Van Leeuwen, L. 2009. "De Politieke Roots van Geert Wilders: Wreker van Zijn Indische Grootouders." *De Groene Amsterdammer*, September 2.

Legêne, S. 2010. *Spiegelreflex: Culturele Sporen van de Koloniale Ervaring*. Amsterdam: Uitgeverij Prometheus, Bert Bakker.

Lentin, A., and G. Titley. 2011. *The Crises of Multiculturalism: Racism in a Neoliberal Age*. London: Zed.

Lewis, G. 2013. "Unsafe Travel: Experiencing Intersectionality and Feminist Displacements." *Signs: Journal of Women in Culture and Society* 38 (4): 869–892.

Leydesdorff, S. 1994. *We Lived with Dignity: The Jewish Proletariat of Amsterdam, 1900–1940*. Detroit: Wayne State University Press.

Lichtveld, U. M., and J. Voorhoeve, eds. 1975. *Creole Drum: An Anthology of Creole Literature in Surinam*. New Haven, CT: Yale University Press.

Van Lier, R. (1949) 1977. *Samenleving in een Grensgebied: Een Sociaal-historische Studie van de Maatschappij in Suriname*. The Hague: Nijhoff.

Loewenthal, T. 1984. "De witte toren van vrouwenstudies." *Tijdschrift voor Gender Studies* 5 (1): 5–17.

Loewenthal, T. 2001. "Er Ontbreekt Altijd een Stuk van de Puzzel: Een Inclusief Curriculum Gewenst." In *Caleidoscopische Visies: Zwarte, Migranten-en Vluchtelingen Vrouwenbeweging in Nederland*, edited by M. Botman, N. Jouwe, and G. D. Wekker, 51–80. Amsterdam: KIT.

Loewenthal, T., and M. Verboom. 1997. *Kleur in het Curriculum: Perspectieven voor Multicultureel Vrouwenstudies-onderwijs.* Utrecht: Nederlands Genootschap Vrouwen Studies.

Lubiano, W., ed. 1998. *The House That Race Built: Original Essays by Toni Morrison, Angela Y. Davis, Cornel West and Others on Black Americans and Politics in America Today.* New York: Vintage.

Lucassen, J., and R. Penninx. 1993. *Nieuwkomers, Nakomelingen, Nederlanders: Immigranten in Nederland 1550–1993.* Amsterdam: Het Spinhuis.

Lugones, M. 2007. "Heterosexualism and the Colonial/ Modern Gender System." In *Hypatia* 22 (1), 186–209.

Lugones, M. 2010. "Toward a Decolonial Feminism." In *Hypatia* 25 (4), 742–759.

Lutz, H. 1991. "Migrant Women of 'Islamic Background': Images and Self-Images." MERA Occasional Paper, no. 11, 1–33. Amsterdam: Middle East Research Associates.

Lutz, H., H. Vivar, and L. Supik, eds. 2011. *Framing Intersectionality: Debates on a Multi-faceted Concept in Gender Studies.* Burlington, VT: Ashgate.

Lykke, N. 2010. *Feminist Studies: A Guide to Intersectional Theory, Methodology and Writing.* New York: Routledge.

Lykke, N. 2011. "Intersectional Analysis: Black Box or Useful Critical Feminist Thinking Technology." In *Framing Intersectionality: Debates on a Multi-faceted Concept in Gender Studies*, edited by H. Lutz, H. Vivar, and L. Supik, 207–221. Burlington, VT: Ashgate.

Mak, G. 2000. *Sporen van verplaatsing: Honderd jaar nieuwkomers in Overijssel.* Kampen: IJsselacademie.

Mak, G. 2005. *Gedoemd tot Kwetsbaarheid.* Amsterdam: Uitgeverij Atlas.

Mak, G. 2012. *Doubting Sex: Inscriptions, Bodies and Selves in Nineteenth-Century Hermaphrodite Case Stories.* Manchester: Manchester University Press.

Mannoni, O. (1950) 1991. *Prospero and Caliban: The Psychology of Colonization.* Ann Arbor: University of Michigan Press.

Marchetti, S. 2014. *Black Girls: Migrant and Domestic Workers and Colonial Legacies.* Leiden: Brill.

Markowitz, S. 2001. "Pelvic Politics: Sexual Dimorphism and Racial Difference." *Signs: Journal of Women in Culture and Society* 26 (2): 389–414.

Martin, K. 1993. "Gender and Sexuality: Medical Opinion on Homosexuality 1900–1950." *Gender and Society* 7 (2): 246–260.

Martina, E. A. 2014. "My Thoughts on the Ruling." Processed Life, July 10. Accessed October 15, 2014. http://processedlives.wordpress.com/2014/07/10/my-thoughts-on-the-ruling/.

McCall, L. 2005. "The Complexity of Intersectionality." *Signs: Journal of Women in Culture and Society* 30 (3): 1771–1800.

McClintock, A. 1995. *Imperial Leather: Race, Gender and Sexuality in the Colonial Context.* London: Routledge.

M'charek, A. 2005. *The Human Genome Diversity Project: An Ethnography of Scientific Practice*. Cambridge: Cambridge University Press.

M'charek, A. 2015. "DNA-Onderzoek en Racialisering. Van Individuele Verdachte tot Verdachte Populatie." In *Diversiteit en Discriminatie: Onderzoek naar Processen van In- en Uitsluiting*, 49–66. Amsterdam: Amsterdam University Press.

McIntosh, P. 1992. "White Privilege and Male Privilege: A Personal Account of Coming to See Correspondence through Work in Women's Studies." In *Race, Class and Gender: An Anthology*, edited by M. L. Andersen and P. Hill Collins, 70–81. Belmont, CA: Wadsworth.

McQueen, S., dir. 2013. *12 Years a Slave* (film). Hollywood: Regency Enterprises.

Memmi, A. 1965. *The Colonizer and the Colonized*. Boston: Beacon.

Mepschen, P. 2009. "Erotics of Persuasion: Media, Aesthetics, and the Sexual Politics of Belonging." Paper presented at ASSR conference, Citizenship, National Canons, and the Issue of Cultural Diversity, University of Amsterdam, January.

Mepschen, P., J. W. Duyvendak, and E. H. Tonkens. 2010. "Sexual Politics, Orientalism and Multicultural Citizenship in the Netherlands." *Sociology* no. 44: 962–979.

Meuwissen, M. 2011. "The Impact of Women Studies." Master's thesis, Department of Women's Studies, Faculty of the Humanities, Utrecht University.

Mills, C. 1997. *The Racial Contract*. Ithaca, NY: Cornell University Press.

Mills, C. 2007. "White Ignorance." In *Race and Epistemologies of Ignorance*, edited by S. Sullivan and N. Tuana, 11–38. Albany: State University of New York Press.

Ministerie van Binnenlandse Zaken. 1981. *Ontwerp Minderheden Nota*. Den Haag.

Ministerie van Binnenlandse Zaken. 1983. *Minderhedennota*. Tweede Kamer, zitting 1982–83, 16102, nrs. 20–21. Den Haag.

Ministerie van Onderwijs, Cultuur en Wetenschap. 2007. *Kabinetsnota Gewoon Homo Zijn. Nota lesbisch en homo-emancipatie beleid 2008–2011*. Den Haag. Accessed September 15, 2015. https://www.rijksoverheid.nl/documenten/beleidsnotas /2007/11/14/nota-lesbisch-en-homo-emancipatiebeleid-2008–2011-gewoon -homo-zijn.

Ministerie van Onderwijs, Cultuur en Wetenschap. 2012–2013. "*Tweede Voortgangsrapportage Emancipatiebeleid*." In Kamerstukken II. Den Haag, 30 420, no. 177.

Ministerie van Onderwijs, Cultuur en Wetenschap. 2013. "*Hoofdlijnenbrief Emancipatiebeleid 2013–2016*." Reference nr. 477641. Den Haag. Accessed September 15, 2015. www.rijksoverheid.nl/.../hoofdlijnenbrief-emancipatiebeleid-2013.

Ministerie van Sociale Zaken en Werkgelegenheid. 2013. "*Kamerbrief Agenda Integratie*." February 19, Ref. 2013–0000015514. Accessed September 15, 2015. https://www.rijksoverheid.nl/documenten/beleidsnotas/2013/02/19/agenda -integratie.

Mintz, S., and R. Price. (1976) 1992. *The Birth of Afro-American Culture: An Anthropological Perspective*. Boston: Beacon.

Mitchell, J. 1981. *Psychoanalyse en Feminisme. Deel 1, Psychoanalyse en Vrouwelijkheid*. Nijmegen: Socialistiese Uitgeverij Nijmegen, Sunschrift 161.

Moglen, H. 1997. "Redeeming History: Toni Morrison's Beloved." In *Female Subjects in Black and White: Race, Psychoanalysis, Feminism*, edited by E. Abel, B. Christian, and H. Moglen, 201–222. Berkeley: University of California Press.

Mok, I. 1999. *In de Ban van het Ras: Aardrijkskunde tussen Wetenschap en Samenleving 1876–1992*. Amsterdam: ASCA Press.

Mok, I. 2011. *Juf, Was dat Écht Zo? Lessen Over Slavernij in het Amsterdamse VO*. Amsterdam: Gemeente Amsterdam.

Moore, H. L. 2007. *The Subject of Anthropology*. Cambridge, MA: Polity.

Moore, H., and G. D. Wekker. 2011. "Intimate Truths about Subjectivity and Sexuality: A Psychoanalytical and a Postcolonial Approach." In *Theories and Methodologies in Post-graduate Feminist Research: Researching Differently*, edited by R. Buikema, G. Griffin, and N. Lykke, 245–257. New York: Routledge.

Morrison, T. 1987. *Beloved*. New York: Penguin.

Morrison, T. 1992a. *Playing in the Dark: Whiteness and the Literary Imagination*. Cambridge, MA: Harvard University Press.

Morrison, T., ed. 1992b. *Race-ing Justice, En-gendering Power: Essays on Anita Hill, Clarence Thomas, and the Construction of Social Reality*. New York: Pantheon.

Morrison, T. 1998. "Home." In *The House That Race Built*, edited by W. Lubiano, 3–12. New York: Vintage.

Nederveen Pieterse, J. 1990. *Wit over Zwart: Beelden van Afrika en Zwarten in de Westerse Populaire Cultuur*. Amsterdam: KIT/Stichting Cosmic Illusion Productions.

Nimako, K. 2012. "About Them, but without Them: Race and Ethnic Relations Studies in Dutch Universities." *Human Architecture: Journal of the Sociology of Self-Knowledge* 10 (1): Article 6.

Nimako, K., and G. Willemsen. 1993. "Multiculturalisme, Verzuilde, Samenleving and Verzorgingsstaat: Naar een Pluralistische Democratie." In *Achter de Coulissen: Gedachten over de Multi-Etnische Samenleving*, edited by G. Pas. Amsterdam: Wetenschappelijk Bureau GroenLinks.

Noordman, J. 1989. *Om de Kwaliteit van het Nageslacht: Eugenetica in Nederland 1900–1950*. Nijmegen: SUN.

Nussbaum, M. 2010. *Not for Profit: Why Democracy Needs the Humanities*. Princeton, NJ: Princeton University Press.

Ombre, E. 2004. *Negerjood in Moederland*. Amsterdam: de Arbeiderspers.

Oostindie, G., and E. Maduro. 1986. *In het Land van de Overheerser II: Antillianen en Surinamers in Nederland 1634/1667–1954*. Dordrecht: Foris.

Oostindie, G. 2010. *Postkoloniaal Nederland; Vijfenzestig jaar Vergeten, Herdenken, Verdringen*. Amsterdam: Bert Bakker.

Van Oostrom, F., et al. 2006. *Entoen.nu De Canon van Nederland*. Rapport van de Commissie Ontwikkeling Nederlandse Canon. Delen A en B. The Hague: Commissie Ontwikkeling Nederlandse Canon.

Van Ophuijsen, J. H. 1916–1917. "Beiträge zum Mannlichkeitskomplex der Frau." *Internat. Zeitschrift Psychoanal*, no. 4, 241–251.

Van Ophuijsen, J. H. (1924) 1966. "Contributions to the Masculinity Complex in Women." In *Psychoanalysis and Female Sexuality: Classic and Contemporary Essays on the Impact of Psychoanalysis on Female Sexuality*, edited by H. M. Ruitenbeek, 61–72. New Haven, CT: College and University Press.

Pateman, C. 1988. *The Sexual Contract*. Stanford, CA: Stanford University Press.

Patterson, O. 1982. *Slavery and Social Death*. Cambridge, MA: Harvard University Press.

Pattynama, P. 1997. "Secrets and Danger: Interracial Sexuality in Louis Couperus' *The Hidden Force* and Dutch Colonial Culture around 1900." In *Domesticating the Empire: Race, Gender and Family Life in French and Dutch Colonialism*, edited by J. Clancy-Smith and F. Gouda, 84–107. Charlottesville: University Press of Virginia.

Pattynama, P. 2014. *Bitterzoet Indie*. Amsterdam: Prometheus Bert Bakker.

Pattynama, P., and M. Verboom. 2000. *Werkboek Kleur in het Curriculum: Interculturalisatie in het Hoger Onderwijs*. Utrecht: NGV.

Pels, T. 1998. *Opvoeding in Marokkaanse Gezinnen in Nederland: De Creatie van een Nieuw Bestaan*. Assen: Van Gorcum.

Pels, T. 2000. *Opvoeding en integratie: Een vergelijkende studie van recente onderzoeken naar gezinsopvoeding en de pedagogische afstemming tussen gezin en school*. Assen: Van Gorcum.

Pessers, D. 2006. *Regels Zijn Regels: Paul Witteman in Gesprek met Dorien Pessers over de Daadkracht van Rita Verdonk*. Amsterdam: Balans/Buitenhof.

Phoenix, A. and P. Pattynama, eds. 2006. Special issue on Intersectionality. *European Journal of Women's Studies* 13 (3).

Phoenix, A., et al. 2010. "Intersectionality, Black British Feminism and Resistance in Education: A Roundtable Discussion." *Gender and Education* 22 (6): 647–660.

Van der Pijl, Y., and K. Goulordova. 2014. "Black Pete, 'Smug Ignorance' and the Value of the Black Body in Post-colonial Netherlands." *New West Indian Guide* 88 (3–4), 262–291.

Politie. 2013. *Anti-Homogeweld in Nederland: Analyse van (dreiging van) Fysiek Antihomogeweld*. Driebergen.

Poorthuis, F. and H. Wansink. 2002. "De Islam is een Achterlijke Cultuur." In *De Volkskrant*, February 9. Accessed March 15, 2014. http://www.volkskrant.nl /binnenland/pim-fortuyn-op-herhaling-de-islam-is-een-achterlijke-cultuur ~a611698/.

Pratt, M. L. 1992. *Imperial Eyes: Travel Writing and Transculturation*. London: Routledge.

Prins, B. 2002. "The Nerve to Break Taboos: New Realism in the Dutch Discourse on Multiculturalism." *Journal of International Migration and Integration* 3 (3–4): 363–379.

Prins, B. 2004. *Voorbij de onschuld: Het Debat Over de Multiculturele Samenleving.* Amsterdam: Van Gennep.

Prins, B. 2006. "Narrative Accounts of Origins: A Blind Spot in the Intersectional Approach?" *European Journal of Women's Studies* 13 (3): 277–290.

Prins, B., and S. Saharso. 1999. *Multicultureel burgerschap.* Bohn Stafleu Van Loghum.

Puar, J. K. 2007. *Terrorist Assemblages: Homonationalism in Queer Times.* Durham, NC: Duke University Press.

Raalte, C. 1998. "Zwarte Piet, wiedewiedewiet." In *Sinterklaasje, kom maar binnen zonder knecht,* edited by S. Gravenberch and L. Helder, 171–183. Berchem: EPO.

Ramdas, A. 1998. "Een Verhaal dat Men Maakt: Interview met de auteur Anil Ramdas." In *Sinterklaasje, kom maar binnen zonder knecht,* edited by S. Gravenberch and L. Helder, 186–193. Berchem: EPO.

Rath, J. 1991. *Minorisering: De Sociale Constructie van Etnische Minderheden.* Amsterdam: Sua.

Regeer Accoord. 2012. "Bruggen slaan: Regeerakkoord VVD—PvdA." October 29. Accessed July 30, 2014. http://www.parlement.com/9291000/d /regeerakkoord2012.pdf.

Reys, J., et al., eds. 1985. *De Eerste Feministische Golf.* 6de Jaarboek voor Vrouwengeschiedenis. Nijmegen: SUN.

Rich, A. 1979. *On Lies, Secrets and Silence: Selected Prose 1966–1978.* London: Virago.

Roemer, A. 1995. *Het Vrolijke Meisje: Verhalen van Vrouwen die Putten uit Meer dan Alleen de Nederlandse Cultuur.* Amsterdam: Arena.

Roggeband, C. 2010. "The Victim-Agent Dilemma: How Migrant Women's Organizations in the Netherlands Deal with a Contradictory Policy Frame." *Signs: Journal of Women in Culture and Society* 35 (4): 943–968.

Roggeband, C., and M. Verloo. 2007. "Dutch Women Are Liberated, Migrant Women Are a Problem: The Evolution of Policy Frames on Gender and Migration in the Netherlands, 1995–2005." *Social Policy and Administration* 41 (3): 271–288.

De Rooy, P. 1996. "De Flessehals van de Wetenschap." *Feit en Fictie* 2 (4): 47–64.

De Rooy, P. 2015. *De Nederlandse Darwin. Bernelot Moens en het Mysterie van Onze Afkomst.* Amsterdam: Wereldbibliotheek.

Rosaldo, R. 1989. *Culture and Truth: The Remaking of Social Analysis.* Boston: Beacon.

Rossiter, M. W. 1982. *Women Scientists in America: Struggles and Strategies to 1940.* Baltimore, MD: JHU Press.

Rossiter, M. W. 1998. *Women Scientists in America: Before Affirmative Action, 1940–1972.* Baltimore, MD: JHU Press.

Rossiter, M. W. 2012. *Women Scientists in America: Forging a New World since 1972.* Baltimore, MD: JHU Press.

Rothberg, M. 2009. *Multidirectional Memory: Remembering the Holocaust in the Age of Decolonization.* Stanford, CA: Stanford University Press.

Ruitenbeek, H. M., ed. 1966. *Psychoanalysis and Female Sexuality: Classic and Contem-*

porary Essays on the Impact of Psychoanalysis on Female Sexuality. New Haven, CT: College and University Press.

Sachs, W. 1937. Black Hamlet: The Mind of an African Negro Revealed by Psychoanalysis. London: Geoffrey Bles.

Said, E. 1993. Culture and Imperialism. London: Vintage.

Said, E. 1995. "Secular Interpretation: The Geographical Element, and the Methodology of Imperialism." In After Colonialism, edited by G. Prakash, 21–39. Princeton, NJ: Princeton University Press.

Sartre, J. P. (1948) 1976. Black Orpheus. Paris: French and European Publications.

Sawyer, L. 2006. "White Laughter and White Academic Space." In Act 5: Denmark, Finland, Norway and Sweden. November 25. Rethinking Nordic Colonialism. Accessed April 29, 2015. www.rethinking-Nordic-colonialism.org/files/pdf/ACT5/MAGAZINES/slut_Sawyer.pdf.

Schama, S. 1987. The Embarrassment of Riches: An Interpretation of Dutch Culture in the Golden Age. New York: First Vintage Books.

Scheffer, P. 2007. Het Land van Aankomst. Amsterdam: De Bezige Bij.

Schellekes, H., and W. Hoogbergen. 2001. "Twee Sodomieprocessen in Suriname, 1731–1733." Oso 20 (2): 254–263.

Schiebinger, L. 1990. "The Anatomy of Difference: Race and Sex in Eighteenth Century Science." Eighteenth-Century Studies 23 (4): 387–405.

Schiltkamp, J. A., and J. T. de Smidt, eds. 1973. Westindisch Plakkaatboek: Plakkaten, Ordonnantiën en Andere Wetten uitgevaardigd in Suriname, delen 1 en 2. Amsterdam: S. Emmering.

Schor, P. 2013. "A Reasonable Alternative to Zwarte Piet." Processed Life, October 14. Accessed September 3, 2014. https://processedlives.wordpress.com/2013/10/14/a-reasonable-alternative-to-zwarte-piet/.

Schreuder, E. 2008. "Mooi Zwart, Hip Zwart en Zwarte Cultuur." In Black Is beautiful: Rubens to Dumas, edited by E. Kolfin, and E. Schreuder, 108–123. Amsterdam: De Nieuwe Kerk, Waanders Uitgeverij.

Schulte Nordholt, H. 2000. Een Staat van Geweld. Rotterdam: Erasmus Universiteit Rotterdam.

Scott, J. 1986. "Gender: A Useful Category of Historical Analysis." American Historical Review 91 (5): 1053–1075.

Scott, J. 2009. "Sexularism: On Secularism and Gender Equality." Lecture, European University Institute, Florence.

Scott, J. 2012. "Emancipation and Equality: A Critical Genealogy." Lecture, University of Utrecht, November 7.

Sedaris, D. 2008. "Six to Eight Black Men." Time Out Amsterdam, December, 62–63.

Sharpe, J. 2003. Ghosts of Slavery: A Literary Archaeology of Black Women's Lives. Minneapolis: University of Minnesota Press.

Shorto, R. 2013. Amsterdam: A History of the World's Most Liberal City. New York: Random House.

Sliggers, B. 2009. De Exotische Mens: Andere Culturen als Amusement. Tiel: Lannoo.

Smith, J. L. 2014. "The Dutch Carnivalesque: Blackface, Play, and Zwarte Piet." In *Dutch Racism*, edited by P. Essed and I. Hoving, 219–238. Amsterdam: Rodopi.

Smith, L. E. 1948. *Strange Fruit*. New York: Signet.

Somerville, S. B. 2000. *Queering the Color Line: Race and the Invention of Homosexuality in American Culture*. Durham, NC: Duke University Press.

Spelman, E. 2007. "Managing Ignorance." In *Race and Epistemologies of Ignorance*, edited by S. Sullivan and N. Tuana, 119–131. Albany: State University of New York Press.

Spivak, G. 1987. *In Other Worlds: Essays in Cultural Politics*. New York: Methuen.

Spivak, G. 1994. "Can the Subaltern Speak?" In *Colonial Discourses and Postcolonial Theory: A Reader*, edited by P. Williams and L. Chisman, 66–111. New York: Columbia University Press.

Stärcke, A. 1918. "Samenvatting van J.W.H. van Ophuijsen's Voordracht 'Het Mannelijkheidscomplex bij de vrouw.'" *Nederlands Tijdschrift voor Geneeskunde*, May 18 (20): 1428.

Stedman, J. G. (1790) 1988. *Narrative of a Five Years Expedition against the Revolted Negroes of Suriname*, edited by Richard Price and Sally Price and transcribed for the first time from the original manuscript. Baltimore, MD: Johns Hopkins University Press.

Stedman, J. G. 1974. *Reize Naar Surinamen en Door de Binnenste Gedeelten van Guiana I–II*. Amsterdam: S. Emmering.

Stepan, N. 1993. "Race and Gender: The Role of Analogy in Science." In *The "Racial" Economy of Science. Towards a Democratic Future*, edited by S. Harding, 359–376. Bloomington: Indiana University Press.

Stepan, N. and S. Gilman, eds. 1993. "Appropriating the Idioms of Science." In *The "Racial" Economy of Science: Toward a Democratic Future*, edited by S. Harding, 170–193. Bloomington: Indiana University Press.

Van Sterkenburg, J. 2011. *Race, Ethnicity and the Sport Media*. Amsterdam: Pallas.

Van Stipriaan, A. 1990. "What's in a Name? Slavernij en Naamgeving in Suriname Tijdens de 18e en 19e Eeuw." *OSO, Tijdschrift voor Surinaamse Taalkunde, Letterkunde, Cultuur en Geschiedenis* 9 (1).

Van Stipriaan, A. 2014. "Repliek op de argumenten van het Pietengilde op de uitspraak over de intocht in Amsterdam van Sinterklaas met Zwarte Pieten," October 22. Accessed October 29, 2014. http://www.ninsee.nl/news/Volledige-repliek-prof-dr-Van -Stipriaan-omtrent-Zwarte-Piet-voor-Raad-van-State.

Van Stipriaan, A., et al. 2007. *Op Zoek Naar De Stilte Sporen Van Het Slavernijverleden In Nederland*. Leiden: Kitlv.

Stoler, A. L. 1995. *Race and the Education of Desire: Foucault's History of Sexuality and the Colonial Order of Things*. Durham, NC: Duke University Press.

Stoler, A. L. 2002. "Carnal Knowledge and Imperial Power: Gender and Morality in the Making of Race." In *Carnal Knowledge and Imperial Power: Race and the Intimate in Colonial Rule*, 41–78. Berkeley: University of California Press.

Stoler, A. L., ed. 2007a. *Haunted by Empire: Geographies of Intimacy in North American History*. Durham, NC: Duke University Press.

Stoler, A. L. 2007b. "Tense and Tender Ties: The Politics of Comparison in North American History and (Post) Colonial Studies." In *Haunted by Empire: Geographies of Intimacy in North American History*, edited by A. L. Stoler, 23–67. Durham, NC: Duke University Press.

Stoler, A. L. 2009. *Along the Archival Grain: Epistemic Anxieties and Colonial Common Sense*. Princeton, NJ: Princeton University Press.

Stratz, C. H. 1897. *Die Frauen auf Java, eine gynäkologische Studie*. German Edition, Kessinger Legacy Reprints. www.amazon.com/Die-Frauen-auf-Java-gynakologische/dp/1168374146. Dutch edition: *De Vrouwen op Java; eene gynaecologische Studie*. 1898. Amsterdam: Scheltema and Holkema.

Stroeken, H. 1993. "The Reception of Psychoanalysis in the Netherlands." In *The Dutch Annual of Psychoanalysis*, edited by H. Groen-Prakken and A. Ladan, 39–53. Amsterdam: Swets & Zeitlinger BV.

Stroeken, H. 2009. "Johan van Ophuijsen, Pandang/Indonesien 1882–New York 1950." *Luzifer-Amor, Zeitschrift zur Geschichte der Psychoanalyse* 2 (44): 2–48.

Stuurman, S. 2009. *De Uitvinding van De Mensheid: Korte Wereldgeschiedenis van het Denken Over Gelijkheid en Cultuurverschil*. Amsterdam: Bert Bakker.

Sullivan, S., and N. Tuana, eds. 2007. *Race and Epistemologies of Ignorance*. Albany: State University of New York Press.

De Swaan, A. 2013. "The Pains of Victimhood and the Gains of Militancy: 150 Years after Slavery." NiNsee Lecture, Amsterdam, June 30. Accessed October 23, 2014. http://cimakefoundation.wordpress.com/ninsee-lezing-2013/.

Thompson, C. (1942) 1966. "'Penis Envy' in Women." In *Psychoanalysis and Female Sexuality: Classic and Contemporary Essays on the Impact of Psychoanalysis on Female Sexuality*, edited by H. M. Ruitenbeek, 246–251. New Haven, CT: College and University Press.

Thompson, C. (1950) 1966. "Some Effects of the Derogatory Attitude toward Female Sexuality." In *Psychoanalysis and Female Sexuality: Classic and Contemporary Essays on the Impact of Psychoanalysis on Female Sexuality*, edited by H. M. Ruitenbeek, 51–60. New Haven, CT: College and University Press.

De Valk, E. 2014. "Hema doet Zwarte Piet in de ban," NRCQ, August 26. Accessed August 27, 2014. https://www.nrcq.nl/2014/08/26/hema-doet-zwarte-piet-in-de-ban.

Van Abbemuseum. 2008. *Becoming Dutch: The Exhibition*. C. Esche and A. Fletcher, curators. Accessed September 3, 2014. http://vanabbemuseum.nl/.

Van der Veer, P. 2006. "Pim Fortuyn, Theo van Gogh, and the Politics of Tolerance in the Netherlands." *Public Culture* 1 (1): 111–124.

Verloo, M. 2006. "Multiple Inequalities, Intersectionality and the European Union." *European Journal of Women's Studies* 13 (3): 211–229.

Verloo, M. 2013. "Intersectional and Cross-Movement Politics and Policies: Reflections on Current Practices and Debates." *Signs: Journal of Women in Culture and Society* 38 (4): 893–915.

Visser, A. 1999. "Ik Ben Nog Altijd Even Mateloos." *Trouw*, April 17. Accessed October 6, 2014. http://www.trouw.nl/tr/nl/5009/Archief/archief/article /detail/2695636/1999/04/17/Ik-ben-nog-altijd-even-mateloos.dhtml.

Vuijsje, R. 2008. *Alleen maar nette mensen.* Amsterdam: Nijgh & Van Ditmar.

Vuijsje, R. 2014. Accessed September 14, 2015. www.biebtobieb.nl/system/files /berichten/bijlages/interview_volkskrant_15–10–2014_robert_vuijsje_over _kinderboek_alleen_maar_stoute_pieten.pdf.

Waaldijk, M. L., and M. Grever. 2004. *Transforming the Public Sphere: The Dutch National Exhibition of Women's Labor in 1898.* Durham, NC: Duke University Press.

Walton, J. 1997. "Re-Placing Race in (White) Psychoanalytic Discourse: Founding Narratives of Feminism." In *Female Subjects in Black and White: Race, Psychoanalysis, Feminism*, edited by E. Abel, B. Christian, and H. Moglen, 223–251. Berkeley: University of California Press.

Weber, M. 1930. *The Protestant Ethic and the Spirit of Capitalism.* New York: Scribner.

Wekker, G. D. 1984a. "De mooie Joanna en haar Huurling." *OSO* 3 (2): 193–203.

Wekker, G. D. 1984b. "Women Migrants from Suriname in the Netherlands." Paper presented at the conference *Colloquy on Women and Migration: Cultural and Educational Aspects.* Council of Europe, Strasbourg.

Wekker, G. D. 1992. "Überlieferinnen: Porträt der Gruppe Sister Outsider." In *Farbe Bekennen: Afro-Deutsche Frauen auf den Spuren ihrer Geschichte*, edited by K. Oguntoye, M. Opitz, and D. Schultz. Frankfurt: Fischer Taschenbuch Verlag.

Wekker, G. D. 1994. *Ik Ben een Gouden Munt: Subjectiviteit en Seksualiteit van Creoolse Volksklasse Vrouwen in Paramaribo.* Amsterdam: Feministische Uitgeverij Vita.

Wekker, G. D. 1995. "Het Beloofde Land." In *Het Vrolijke Meisje*, edited by A. Roemer, 123–129. Amsterdam: Arena.

Wekker, G. D. 1996a. "Praten in het Donker: Reflecties op de Praktijk van het Weten in Nederlandse Vrouwenstudies." In *Praten in het Donker: Multiculturalisme en Anti-Racisme in Feministisch Perspectief*, edited by G. D. Wekker and R. Braidotti, 57–87. Kampen: Kok Agora.

Wekker, G. D. 1996b. "'Wij weigeren uit de Geschiedenis te worden gewist': Introductie van Angela Davis." In *Onderbelicht: Zwarte, migranten, vluchtelingenvrouwen in Nederland. Informatie uitwisseling in Perspectief*, edited by M. Breure and A. Roepman. Amsterdam: IIAV.

Wekker, G. D. 1998. "Gender, Identiteitsvorming en Multiculturalisme: Notities over de Nederlandse Multiculturele Samenleving." In *Multiculturalisme: Werken aan Ontwikkelingsvraagstukken*, edited by C. Geuijen, 39–54. Utrecht: Lemma.

Wekker, G. D. 2001a. "Van Monocultuur naar Caleidoscoop: De Noodzaak van Diversiteit in het Zorgcurriculum." *Tijdschrift voor Humanistiek* 2 (6): 26–33.

Wekker, G. D. 2001b. "Of Mimic Men and Unruly Women. Social Relations in Twentieth Century Suriname." In *Suriname in the Twentieth Century*, edited by

R. Hoefte and P. Meel, 174–197. Leiden/Kingston, Jamaica: KITLV Press and Ian Randle Publishers.

Wekker, G. D. 2002a. "Building Nests in a Windy Place: Thinking about Gender and Ethnicity in the Netherlands." Lecture, Utrecht University, April 19.

Wekker, G. D. 2002b. "Nesten Bouwen op een Winderige Plek: Denken over Gender en Etniciteit in Nederland." *Tijdschrift Voor Genderstudies* 5 (3): 24–33.

Wekker, G. D. 2002c. "'A Response to the Curriculum from Hell': Response to Prof. J. Jansen's Curriculum from Hell." Presented at *Values in Education in South Africa and the Netherlands: Challenges for a Multicultural Society*, Utrecht University, February 19.

Wekker, G. D. 2006. *The Politics of Passion: Women's Sexual Culture in the Afro-Surinamese Diaspora*. New York: Columbia University Press.

Wekker, G. D. 2008. "Like Inanimate Portraits. . . . Re-reading *Essai Historique sur la Colonie de Suriname* (1788): Gender and Citizenship in an 18th Century Jewish Portuguese Text." Presentation, Department of Portuguese Studies, Utrecht University, June.

Wekker, G. D. 2009a. "Another Dream of a Common Language: Imagining Black Europe." In *Black Europe and the African Diaspora*, edited by D. C. Hine, T. D. Keaton, and S. Small, 277–290. Champaign: University of Illinois Press.

Wekker, G. D. 2009b. "Into the Promised Land? The Feminization and Ethnicization of Poverty in the Netherlands." In *Teaching Intersectionality: Putting Gender at the Centre*, edited by M. Franken, A. Woodward, A. Cabó, and B. M. Bagilhole. Utrecht: ZuidamUithof Drukkerijen.

Wekker, G. D. 2009c. "Van Homonostalgie en betere Tijden." George Mosse Lecture, University of Amsterdam, September 16.

Wekker, G. D. 2013. "'What's Homosexuality Got to Do with It?' Some Intersectional Notes on the Current Dutch Sexual Landscape." Keynote lecture, York University, Toronto, March 19.

Wekker, G. D. 2014a. "Diving into the Wreck: Intersections of Gender, Race, Sexuality and Class in the Dutch Cultural Archive." In *Dutch Racism*, edited by P. Essed and I. Hoving, 159–178. Amsterdam: Rodopi.

Wekker, G. D. 2014b. "Zwarte Piet en het Zelf-Feliciterende Zelfbeeld van de Kleurenblinde Nederlander. 8 Wetenschappelijk Onderbouwde Argumenten tegen Zwarte Piet uit de Rechtszaak bij de Raad van State." October, 22. Last accessed October 29, 2014. http://www.joop.nl/opinies/detail/artikel /29146_8_wetenschappelijk_onderbouwde_argumenten_tegen_zwarte _pietargumenten/.

Wekker, G. D., C. Åsberg, I. van der Tuin, and N. Frederiks. 2007. *Je Hebt Een Kleur, Maar Je Bent Nederlands: Identiteitsformaties van Geadopteerden van Kleur*. Utrecht: University of Utrecht.

Wekker, G. D., and R. Braidotti, eds. 1996. *Praten in het Donker: Multiculturalisme en Anti-racisme in Feministisch Perspectief*. Kampen: Kok Agora.

Wekker, G.D. and H. Lutz. 2001. "Een Hoogvlakte met Koude Winden: De Geschiedenis van het Gender-en Etniciteitsdenken in Nederland." In *Caleidoscopische Visies: Zwarte, Migranten-en Vluchtelingen Vrouwenbeweging in Nederland*, edited by M. Botman, N. Jouwe, and G. D. Wekker, 25–49. Amsterdam: KIT.

Wieringa, S., and H. Sivori. 2013. *The Sexual History of the Global South: Sexual Politics in Africa, Asia and Latin America*. London: Zed.

Williams, P. 1998. *Seeing a Colorblind Future: The Paradox of Race*. Reith Lectures. New York: Farrar, Straus and Giroux.

Williams, R. 1998. "Living at the Crossroads: Explorations in Race, Nationality, Sexuality, and Gender." In *The House That Race Built: Original Essays by Toni Morrison, Angela Y. Davis, Cornel West and Others on Black Americans and Politics in America Today*, edited by W. Lubiano, 136–156. New York: Vintage.

De Wit, B. 1993. "Blank in de Bijlmer." *De Volkskrant*, March 15.

Withuis, J. 2002. *Erkenning: Van Oorlogstrauma naar Klaagcultuur*. Amsterdam: De Bezige Bij.

Wright, E., ed. 1992. *Feminism and Psychoanalysis: A Critical Dictionary*. Oxford: Blackwell.

Young, R. 1992. "Colonialism and Humanism." In *"Race," Culture and Difference*, edited by J. Donald and A. Rattansi, 243–251. London: Sage.

Zwagerman, J. 1994. *De Buitenvrouw*. Amsterdam: De Arbeiderspers.

Frankenberg, R., 24
Frankenberg, Ruth, 150
Frauen auf Java, eine gynäkologische Studie, Die (Stratz), 102
Freudian psychology: as dominant paradigm, 185n6; Dutch psychoanalysis and, 84–91; Dutch sexual racism and, 27–28; Fanon and, 34–35; postcolonial melancholia and, 163–166

Gario, Quincy, 144, 153, 181n10
Gay, Judith, 118
gay equality, as Dutch cultural value, 7
gay movement in Netherlands: history of, 111–112; mati couples and, 119–120; politics of, 28, 109–111, 115–120; sexualized racism and, 135–138
Gay Parade event, 117
gelijke monniken, gelijke kappen (equality for all), Dutch policy of, 10
Gemeentelijk Vervoer Bedrijf (GVB) (Dutch municipal transport system), 37–39
gender: academic women's studies and black critique and, 65–70, 184n24; axes of signification in studies of, 70–76; crossgender research and, 178n23; Dutch immigration policy and role of, 9–10; gay politics in Netherlands and, 114–120; Hottentot nymphae case study and role of, 105–107; law enforcement in Netherlands and, 37–39; mixed-race family narratives and, 35–36; Netherlands imperialism and, 305; postcolonial changes and role of, 92–95; psychoanalytic ethnography of Dutch racism and, 32–33; in public policy, 56–65; race and sexuality and, 21–24, 56–65; in scientific context, 98–103; Zwarte Piet controversy and, 156–158, 190n28. *See also* women's issues in Netherlands
gender equality, as Dutch cultural value, 7
geography, postcolonial context for, 93–94
George Maduro lecture, 175n3
Gereformeerden (Christian Reform) movement, 127
German occupation of Netherlands: *Befehl*

ist *Befehl* policy and, 10; ethnic minority persecution during, 177n13; paradox in Dutch self-representation of, 12–13, 176n6
Germany, gender studies in, 72–73
De Geus, 61–62, 115
Gewoon Homo Zijn (Just Being Gay) (government policy paper), 120–126
Ghanese *supi*, 118
Ghostly Matters (Gordon), 108
De Gids, 162
Gilman, Sander L., 81, 102, 104–105
Gilroy, Paul, 3, 29, 143, 150, 159–166
Gomperts, Cosman Abraham, 177n13
Gordon, A. F., 108
government institutions: academia and, 187n14; gay public policy and, 60–65, 120–126, 183n20; public policy toward ethnic minorities and, 52–56, 183nn13–14; support of social movements by, 112–120; women and ethnic minority policies and, 58–65
Green Left, gay women's support for, 109–111

habitus, Dutch cultural archive and, 20
Hague, The, 5: Indo community in, 89–90; Nuclear Security Summit in, 178n19
Halberstam, Judith, 26
Hall, Stuart, 23–24, 140–141, 165
hard work, Dutch self-representation and value placed on, 79
Hartman, Saidiya, 131, 150, 164–166, 168–169, 168–170
Hartnole, John, 131
Hermant, Heather, 178n23
heteronormativity, gay politics in Netherlands and, 114–120
Hirsi Ali, Ayaan, 10–11, 177n10, 177n12
history: Hottentot nymphae case study in context of, 91–98; omission of colonial studies in Dutch historiography, 83–84; sexualized racism and, 39–45; sexualized racism in study of, 39–45
HIV/AIDS conglomerate, 116–120
HIV/AIDS epidemic, gay organizations in Netherlands and, 116–120

digm in Dutch culture and, 16–18; Zwarte Piet controversy and, 151–152

smug ignorance, Essed and Hoving's concept of, 18

social movements, history in Netherlands of, 111–112

Society of Suriname, 42–43

Somerville, Siobhan, 101–102

Sophiedela (Afro-European women's organization), 13–15

South Africa, history of racism in, 39–45, 73–74, 79

Spijkerman, Jack, 178n20

Spivak, Gayatri, 115

Srebrenica massacre (1995), 5

Stärcke, August, 85

Stedman, John Gabriel, 43–45, 112–113

Stelder, Mikki, 178n22

St. Eustacius, as Dutch municipality, 176n6

St. Martin, as autonomous territory, 176n6

Stoler, Ann Laura, 25, 83–84

Stratz, Carl Heinrich, 102

Stroeken, Harry, 90–91, 185n4

Suriname: Dutch immigrants from, 8–10, 38–39, 176n6; historical research on, 26; history and sexualized racism in, 39–45; independence movement in, 94; interracial mixing in, 36; lesbians from, 118; sexualized racism in, 132–138; Surinamese Jews from, 45–48, 177n13; in World War II, 175n3

De Swaan, Abram, 14

De Swaan, Bram, 171

Sylvester, Joseph (Menthol), 97

Tan, Humberto, 178n20

Thai women: mixed-race family narratives in Netherlands and, 35–36; sexualized images in Netherlands of, 32–33

Third World women: academic programs and research on, 67–70; government policies concerning, 61–64, 114–120

Thistlewood, Thomas, 130–138

token appointments, racism in Netherlands and, 73–76

Tonkens, E. H., 116

"Toothpaste Negro," 97

Tosch, Jennifer, 169

Tracing Slavery (Balkenhol), 94

Trots op Nederland (TON, Proud of the Netherlands), 149

Turkish migrants: Circum-Mediterranean migration patterns and, 176n7; government policies concerning, 60–65, 183n20; in women's/gender studies, 71–73

12 Years a Slave (film), 170

United Kingdom: gender studies in, 72–73; racism in, 79; scientific development in, 99–103

United States: cultural archive in, 3–5; Dutch displacement of racism to, 79; Dutch relations with, 178n19; gender studies in, 72–73; memory of Holocaust in, 163–164; mixed-race family narratives and, 35–36; racist discourse on black women in, 31; scientific development in, 99–103

University of Amsterdam: IMES program in, 67, 184n26; sexuality issues at, 109

Utrecht University, ERCOMER program at, 67, 184n26

Van Abbemuseum, 28–29, 143–144, 147–148, 152–153

Verborgen Verleden (Hidden past) (television program), 7

Verdonk, Rita, 10, 149, 154, 159, 177n12

Vereeniging voor Vrouwenkiesrecht (Association for the Women's Vote), 91

Volkskrant, De, 109, 126

voting rights for women, history in Netherlands of, 91

Vrolik, Willem, 102

Vuijsje, Robert, 11, 180n4

VVD (People's Party for Freedom and Democracy), 10–11, 14, 126, 177n10; ethnic minority policies of, 55–56

Walton, Jean, 83

Well-Being, Health and Culture, Ministry of, 52–56

Wereld Draait Door, De (television show), 33–35, 180n5

Western culture, imperialism and archive of, 2–5

white male rescue fantasy, Dutch immigration policies and, 11

whiteness: in Dutch self-representation, 2–5, 20–21; in Dutch terminology, 24; of gay movement, 110–111, 115–120; government policies towards minorities and role of, 59–65; Hottentot nymphae case study and role of, 81–84, 103–107; migrant ancestry in Netherlands and, 6–7; paradoxes in Dutch concepts of, 5–16; psychoanalytic ethnography in Netherlands of, 31–33; sexualized racism and, 40–45; in women's studies, 66–76; Zwarte Piet controversy and role of, 150–167

Wijdenbosch, Robert, 119

Wilders, Geert, 14, 28, 78, 109–111, 126, 149, 154, 159, 187n2, 187n4

Williams, Patricia, 180n7

Williams, Rhonda, 35–36

Wit over Zwart (White about Black) (1989 exhibition), 97

Witteman, Paul, 170

Women Inc., 59

women's issues in Netherlands: axes of signification in studies of, 70–73; black and Islamic women, differences in racism for, 179n3; BMR women and, 118–120; Dutch cultural archive concerning, 31–49; ethnic studies programs and, 67–70, 74–76; gay politics and, 127; government policies concerning, 58–65, 112–120; historical context for, 91–98; Hottentot nymphae case study and, 81–107; mixed-race family narratives and, 35–36; psychoanalytic

theory and, 86–91; racial divisions over, 27, 177n10; radical agenda of 1960–70s and, 113–120; sexuality and, 117–120; terminology of race/ethnicity women's studies and, 77–78; women's movement history and, 111–112; women's studies and black critique and, 65–70

women's liberation movement, gay men's movement and, 110–111

women's studies. *See* gender; women's issues in Netherlands

Working Group of Experts of People of African Descent, 144–146

World War II: Dutch colonial empire during, 12–13, 173n3, 177n13; Dutch self-representation concerning, 12–13; migrant population in Netherlands during, 175n3, 176n6

youth population, gay politics in Netherlands and, 120–126

Zwagerman, Joost, 180n40

Zwarte Piet (Black Pete), 18, 139–167: academic controversy concerning, 146–147; childhood innocence paradigm and, 150–152; commercial retail and controversy over, 188n3; foreign other and controversy over, 152; gender issues in controversy over, 156–158; history of protests against, 144–146, 158–159; Muslims in Netherlands and, 155–156; in Netherlands popular culture, 28–29, 34, 180n7; origins of, 154–155, 165–167; politics and, 145–154; popularity with ethnic minorities of, 156–157; postcolonial melancholia and, 29, 143–144, 149, 159–166; racism in Netherlands and, 34; as symbol of cultural tradition, 148–150